CALLED BY STORIES

Milner S. Ball

CALLED

BY STORIES

Biblical Sagas and Their

Challenge for Law

Duke University Press   Durham & London

2000

© 2000 Duke University Press

All rights reserved

Printed in the United States of America

on acid-free paper ♾

Designed by C. H. Westmoreland

Typeset in Monotype Fournier

by Tseng Information Systems, Inc.

Library of Congress Cataloging-in-Publication

Data appear on the last printed page

of this book.

For June once more

And now for Connell, Katie, Hannah,

and Marika too

Contents

Prologue

These pages offer both a reading of biblical stories, primarily the Moses saga and the Gospel of John, and an exploration of their critical intersections with law and the practice of law. The texts are exotic and often provocative, and their story-worlds compose a challenge to the power structures of other worlds, including the world of law in which I earn my living.[1]

As I read Moses, he is God's mouth. The fact that God tries to kill him is a measure of the difficulty both of the story and of representing God. Sometimes Moses also represents the people to or against God. He thus speaks for both sides, a form of advocacy generally forbidden to American lawyers, who are instructed to represent only one side and to do so zealously. Moses' double voice raises questions about both his office and the modern, ambiguous practice of lawyering to a situation.

The saga artfully associates Moses with a pair of Hebrew midwives in Egypt. They are defiant and deeply engaged in the lives of their clients. Their story calls attention to the role of women and leads to an exploration of the nature of midwifery as it may be translated into modern law—into the challenge of midwific teaching and practice.

Another richly complex story, that of Rachel, takes me to tears before the law. Rachel's weeping for her children surpasses the advocacy of Moses and raises questions about the law's capacity to accommodate things too deep for words. I follow these questions into a lawyer's labor among women in east Tennessee and Mexico, to the work of a tribunal among Hawaiians, and to powerful tears of supplication.

The last story I take up is The Gospel According to John. Remarkably, John makes extensive use of the language of litigation and, more remarkably, puts law on trial. The outcome of its simultaneously talking law and trying law yields the possibility that lawyers are most justly captivated by law when they are most free to be in but not of it. This possibility and its promise for the independence of lawyers is radically different from the bar's promotion of professionalism and of full devotion to the legal system.

I did not write this book to engage in provocation and controversy with either lawyers or biblical scholars, but I accept the fact that dispute with both may be an unavoidable consequence of my work. And although I cannot predestine the direction of disagreement, I can help focus it by giving brief accounts of the guiding images of the book, of the narrative mode of reflection I pose, and of how these stories came to have authority for me.

As I realized in retrospect, the stories themselves provided an image that was my primary guide in writing. The image is familiar in the biblical texts, and Isaiah gives it particular, poetic expression: "For as the rain and the snow come down from heaven, and return not there but water the earth, / making it bring forth and sprout, giving seed to the sower and bread to the eater, / so shall my word be that goes forth from my mouth; it shall not return to me empty, / but it shall accomplish that which I purpose, and prosper in the thing for which I sent it" (Isa. 55:10–11).

This image of the word going forth and fruitfully returning takes narrative form in other biblical texts: God sends out a person or a people with the promise of a productive return. Abraham, for example, is sent from Haran with the promise that he shall be made "a great nation" in which "all the families of the earth shall be blessed" (Gen. 12:2–3). In the stories that figure in these pages, Moses is sent to Egypt with the words that will return him to Mt. Sinai with the liberated Israelites; Israel is then sent from Sinai with the words of the law to prosper in the promised land; and John the Baptist is "sent from God" with words of testimony so that, in return, "all might believe through him" (John 1:6–7).

One image entailed another. A person who is sent—messenger, representative, ambassador, outlaw—will be an outsider along the way, always passing through. The people in these stories, caught up in the going forth and returning of the word, are sojourners. They are distinctive because they do not travel alone. They are at the same time alien and embraced as they make their journeys through first one wilderness and then another. They are distinctive, too, because, although they pass through, they do not pass by. As they wander, they remain deeply engaged in the life that lies close at hand. The image of this company of the word—apart together, in transit and involved—also proved to be for me a guide in writing.

In addition to supplying these images, the stories also suggested an approach: Let the narrative carry the argument.

To make the most of storytelling, as I try to do, is a common, useful habit of mind and is companion to the work of others.[2] Even so, although lawyers tell stories all the time, we have been unable to recover fully from thinking that law is a science. We are still hobbled by a reluctance to make full use of stories as a mode of critical reflection.

System and theory are important and necessary, but narrative has the advantage of apperception. In one of his typically intricate sentences, my teacher Paul Lehmann described apperception as "the uniquely human capacity to know something without knowing how one has come to know it, and to bring what one knows in this way to what one knows in other ways, and in so doing, to discern what is humanly true or false."[3] His description works best as a performance of its subject. He wagered that readers would have had some experience of apperception and would therefore be able to catch his meaning without knowing exactly how or what.

My concern just now is with the knowing-without-knowing-how that, together with other ways of knowing, issues in true discernment. In my own experience, this knowing-without-knowing-how is nurtured by love, ritual, theater, art, music, poetry, and not least by stories.

Arthur Danto notes that one cannot become, for example, a temperate person by doing things from a list of things temperate people do. "Having the list is inconsistent with being that sort of person."[4] He says that what it takes instead is intuition and the ability to judge and act appropriately in situations not encountered before.[5] Rather than self-help lists — say something like the seven habits of seven successful people — Danto concludes that we require examples "to direct the development of judgment, which is to carry its possessor through unstructured moral and legal spaces. 'Examples are thus the go-cart of the understanding' " (quoting Kant).[6]

I put the matter somewhat differently. In place of "intuition" and "examples," I would say that "apperception" is what it takes and that "stories" are the go-carts. But the aspiration is the same. I, too, would have understanding, the development of judgment, and the enlivening of imagination — the things that carry us through the unstructured places of the world and the heart.

That is why this book is driven by narrative and why, in consequence, it could not assume the form of systematic treatise or social-scientific analysis. I have depended upon stories. And their image of the word in circulation — sent and flourishing in return — led me on a recursive course that sometimes critically intersected paths of the law and the teaching and practice of law.

As the book proceeds, when the "real" world of the stories intersects the "real" world of law, I interrupt the narrative to explore the intersection. Legitimate objections can certainly be raised to the fruits of these interrupting performances. The fruits are important to me, but my greater investment is in the underlying mode of reflection that produces them.

What cuts against the grain of established ways of thinking about what lawyers do is my attempt to give priority to the biblical stories in particular. I have tried not to bring questions to them in search of answers. I have tried instead to allow them to discover to me what the questions and needs are. What I most hope to engage readers in conversation about is our attending these and other stories and the stories' inhabiting our thinking, writing, and acting.

Why these stories? The biblical sagas are not the only fundamental, constituting stories that have worked their way into my life, but I have been particularly seized by them. I am no systematic theologian or apologist, but I am an ordained minister of the Presbyterian Church as well as a lawyer and teacher of law. For almost three decades, I have made my living exclusively from secular law because, although my ordination has never been revoked, compensated labor in the denominational institutions has not been an option for me.

Under sponsorship of the denomination, I became the Presbyterian campus minister at the University of Georgia in Athens in 1966. Athens was caught up in the turbulence of the '60s: racism, Vietnam, misogyny, confusion of mind. By the time I arrived, the chaplaincy had already suffered a high incidence of vocational mortality, as was to be expected in any position in which people attempted to make responsible sense of the biblical tradition, for themselves as well as others, in the midst of social and political upheaval.

The turning point in my own demise was 1968, that generally fateful year. The Presbyterian Student Center, as had been true since the integration of the university in the early '60s, welcomed black students, and it became a regular gathering place for all kinds of students, including but by no means restricted to some who were thought to be leftist radicals because of their youthful commitment to justice. I was thought to be harboring enemies of the people. And then, too, I had taken part in some local demonstrations and had attended the 1968 Democratic

National Convention in Chicago as part of the delegation that success-fully challenged the seating of the regulars elected by the state party. Some of the regulars were wealthy, prominent Presbyterians.

The center's local board courageously supported my work, and I drew strength from them. Elsewhere around the state, some of the "fathers and brethren" of the denomination grew unhappy, bitterly so in some cases. They did not read the biblical stories in the same way that I and my board did. My days were numbered. The chair of the local board was Lindsey Cowen, dean of the law school. He encouraged me to audit some law courses, and I did so. The board and I held on for about a year, but then the synod, the statewide governing body, fired me. I could find no work in the denomination (generally known then as the Southern Presbyterian Church before its merger with the larger national denomi-nation). My wife was in graduate school. We had three small children and no money. Thanks to family and substantial loans, I was able to take up the study and practice of law officially and full time. (I continue to perform the formal offices of a minister as occasion allows.)

I made no decision to abandon the biblical texts. I had never confused them with the denominational power structure and had no reason to be alienated from the former. Even so, my interest in them dissipated com-pletely for a number of years. I was too delightfully enthralled by the law.

Nor did I make a decision to return to the stories. Gradually and in-creasingly, however, I found that the more I engaged in and thought about law the more necessary it became to have recourse to their ca-pacity for generating understanding and critique. Then — and this is where I am now — I discovered that I had to start with the stories. They impressed themselves upon me as compelling and normative. They seized me. I have no better way to say it. The experience was not mysti-cal. It was and is ordinary living, acting, thinking, writing, and reading.

In this, I speak only for myself. To say that the stories must have the authority for others that they have for me would constitute a betrayal of the texts and my experience of them. They do not authorize such an assertion.[7]

The biblical sagas are meant to be read and heard. Their first audience is their first communities: Jews and Christians. But they have never been limited to these communities and were not meant to be.[8] Like the texts, I seek without presumption to be read by the other audiences as well as by the first ones.

Readers will have their own approaches to these stories and others like them found to be fundamental and freeing. There is a common enterprise here. Paul Lehmann taught me long ago that such stories have always been the way "one generation tells another how the future shapes the present out of the past." [9]

I

Moses

1. Law and the "Mouth" for God

When Turner Network Television produced its version of the story of Moses and the Ten Commandments, it had to contend "not only with what the text says but also with what modern audiences believe the text says—impressions now as likely to be based on past films as on children's Bible stories or regular reading of the Bible." [1] Cecil B. DeMille's *The Ten Commandments* is one film—*the* film—that influences belief about what the text says. It is a wonderfully bad movie and a send-up of the text, but I find it hard to think about Moses without thinking about Charlton Heston. The same was true for critics of Ben Kingsley's uncharismatic, self-doubting Moses in the TNT production; they inevitably saw him as "anti-Heston." [2] This is a kind of curse.

So I come to the text with Charlton Heston and now Ben Kingsley and a collection of other images and information gathered from childhood recollection, religious education, scholarship, and my own prior reading. I come to the text thinking I know what it says. And I am surprised, the more surprised the more deeply engaging the stories become.

The broad outline of the Moses saga is familiar enough and unchallenging. It is basically what many of us remember:

In order to save her infant son, an Israelite mother places him in a basket among reeds. An Egyptian princess finds him there and will later adopt him as her son. After the child grows up, he kills an Egyptian and must flee to the land of Midian, where he marries Zipporah, daughter of a Midian priest. For the time being, he becomes a shepherd. When he leads his flock into the Sinai wilderness by a sacred mountain, God speaks to him from a burning bush and tells him to return to Egypt to deliver the Israelites from slavery. Moses confronts Pharaoh with the demand to let the people go, and he calls down a series of plagues upon the Egyptians. At last he guides the Israelites in an escape through the sea to the sacred mountain where he receives the law from God. From there Moses leads the people on their long journey north through the desert to the land of Canaan, the promised land that he is allowed to see but not enter.

This is the general, familiar outline. It is the details of the story that make it strange, not what I, like many others, thought I knew.

Early in the text come bits and pieces—intimations—of the strikingly unfamiliar. It is strange that God chooses as the leader of Israel an inarticulate, fugitive prince of Egypt. No less strangely, the book of Exodus announces that "Amram married Jochebed his father's sister and she bore him Aaron and Moses" (6:20). This brief, matter-of-fact identification contains two violations of biblical rules of legitimacy: Aaron and Moses are sons of a forbidden, incestuous union (Lev. 18:12);[3] and, although firstborn sons are the ones to be consecrated and to inherit the father's wealth (Exod. 13:1–16), God prefers Moses, who is second born.

And then there is the incredible moment near the beginning. Moses had yielded to God's commission and was returning to Egypt when "the Lord met him and tried to kill him" (Exod. 4:24).[4] The text offers no mitigating explanation and instead deepens the mystery. God let him alone, it says, after Zipporah hastily circumcised their son and "touched Moses' feet" with the foreskin (Exod. 4:25). Moses is remarkably saved, and not for the first time, by a woman.

These details charge the story, upset expectations, and invite the reader to a closer look. They challenge beliefs about what the text says and what it should say, and the challenge brings with it much difficulty but also the promise of a journey.

The Moses of the biblical saga is a complex figure of many parts, but he is foremost a person of the law.[5] The text does not say that he is a lawyer. It says that he is "mouth" (*peh*) for God, and the story furnishes the notion with meaning.[6] Moses as mouth for God is the figure I follow to the episodes at Sinai and to intersections with rules of common law and lawyering to a situation.

When God calls to Moses from the burning bush, Moses is first humble: "Who am I that I should go to Pharaoh?" (Exod. 3:11). Then he is uncertainly inquiring: When the people of Israel ask who sent him, he wants to know: "What shall I say to them?" (3:13). He is next shrewdly wary: "Suppose they do not believe me or listen to my voice?" (4:1). Then he is modest: "I am slow of speech and of tongue" (4:10). Finally, he is simply reluctant: "O my Lord, please send someone else" (4:13).

God introduces the image of the mouth in response to Moses' argument that he speaks poorly. God says: "I will be with your mouth and teach you what to speak" (Exod. 4:12). The image returns at the conclusion of the exchange when Moses' truculent self-effacement at last makes God angry. Enough humility is enough. To Moses' "send someone else," God answers that He will send Aaron as a companion: "You shall speak to [Aaron] and put the words in his mouth; and I will be with your mouth and with his mouth. . . . he shall serve as a mouth for you and you shall serve as God for him" (4:15–16).[7] Moses is to God as Aaron is to Moses: "a mouth for."[8]

Not out of weakness or incapacity does God call Moses to be His mouth. God speaks when, to whom, and through whom He wishes, including, wonderfully, Balaam and Balaam's ass (Num. 22–24). He does not require empowerment by Moses. God summons a mouth for Himself because of who He is and how He acts and not because of some external necessity.

God's awful presence is consuming. There is danger in it for humans. Come too close to God or in the wrong manner and you die.[9] For this reason, in giving Himself to His people, God provides Israel with the media, forms, being, and history that serve as the locus of His presence. Insofar as Israel's life is constituted by these gifts, they are not consumed when He is near.

But Israel must be exact in observance. In preparation for their meeting with God at Mt. Sinai, the people must consecrate and wash themselves, and in the event keep the proper distance with great care (Exod. 19:10–15). God warns and twice repeats: "You shall set limits for the people all around, saying 'Be careful not to go up the mountain or touch the edge of it. Any who touch the mountain shall be put to death'" (Exod. 19:12, 21, 24).[10]

The ranking, ritual, purification, structure, detail of tabernacle construction—and law—must be precisely observed, for only so does Israel move forward with the presence of God. The violent, destructive potential continues. Unsurprisingly, Moses "did everything just as the Lord had commanded him" (Exod. 40:16).[11] And when he instructs the people, he is careful to employ a kind of careful, practical teaching.[12] He wants to make sure the people get it.

The first nine chapters of Leviticus portray the careful unfolding and flawless observance of the commanded ritual. But then comes the formal inauguration of the priesthood when Aaron's two eldest sons interrupt the flow. In an excess of zeal they make an offering of fire, an added offering not prescribed by God. It is a terrible mistake. "The fire came out from the presence of the Lord and consumed them" (Lev. 10:2).

To live with God's presence Israel must keep to the order without subtraction or addition. Precisely observed, it makes them a people apart but allows them to be animated by God. "You must therefore be careful to do as the Lord your God has commanded you; you shall not turn to the right or to the left. You must follow exactly the path that the Lord your God has commanded you, so that you may live, and that it may go well with you, and that you may live long in the land that you are to possess" (Deut. 5:32–33).[13]

That God provides a mouth for Himself is the cardinal gift of enablement to His people. He is characteristically present to them as word. God talks. In the texts, He calls to Moses from the bush and later speaks to him all the words of the law. His voice is to be obeyed (Exod. 19:5). He creates by word. He speaks the world into being: "God said, 'Let there be light'; and there was light" (Gen. 1:3). The word of God can be destructive and terrifying. When the people hear the sound of His speaking at Sinai, they are afraid and tremble and stand at a distance. They cannot withstand His words spoken directly to them.

God's commission of Moses to be His mouth is an expression of His courteous power. Through Moses He speaks, and the people do not die. Through this mouth He is present to His people and does not consume them.[14] God speaks through Moses, and the people are able to bear the word that will in turn sustain them in their journey to the promised land. God's distinctive power is expressed not so much in great and terrifying noise as in His speech through this person to this people.

When Moses acts as mouth for God to Pharaoh, he speaks for the people as well as God, and at least initially they accept his office and the words he brings: "Aaron spoke all the words that the Lord had spoken to Moses, and performed the signs in the sight of the people. The people believed; and when they heard that the Lord had given heed to the Israelites and that he had seen their misery, they bowed down and worshiped" (Exod. 4:30–31).

This popular belief in God and its attendant support for Moses prove to be fleeting. Moses' first confrontation with Pharaoh ends in failure, and afterward God does not visit a plague upon the Egyptians as He will do later on similar occasions. This time it is Pharaoh rather than God who speaks and acts. He demands more brick from the enslaved and already overburdened people. In response, the people turn away from Moses: "You have brought us into bad odor with Pharaoh and his officials, and have put a sword in their hand to kill us" (Exod. 5:21).[15] They "would not listen to Moses, because of their broken spirit and their cruel slavery" (Exod. 6:9).

The people then drop out of the story as active participants until the last of Moses' confrontations with Pharaoh, when they receive God's instruction in the Passover. At that time they once again bow down and worship and do "just as the Lord had commanded Moses and Aaron" (Exod. 12:28–29).[16]

Even so, the Israelites do not solicit Moses to act as their spokesman. When they arrive at Mt. Sinai to complete the first stage of their long sojourn in the desert, they at last approach Moses to plead for his help, but they do not propose that he speak for them. They ask that he speak *to* them: "You speak to us, and we will listen; but do not let God speak to us, or we will die" (Exod. 20:18–21).[17] Moses is God's mouth and not theirs.

Sometimes, however, especially in the events surrounding the giving of the law at Mt. Sinai, Moses does represent the people before God, and he appears then to act as *their* mouth.

The particulars of the writing of the law may constitute such an occasion. I think they do not, but the possibility rewards exploration.

According to both Exodus and Deuteronomy, God summons Moses to the mountain, writes the commandments on two stone tablets, and gives them to him. That the law is written is worthy of note. The act of writing is first mentioned in the Bible in association with other impressive events in Exodus 17. That chapter opens with an episode in which Moses draws water from a rock by striking it with his staff. A clash of arms with the Amalekites follows. On the day of battle, Moses surveys the action from the top of a hill. Whenever he "held up his hand, Israel prevailed; and whenever he lowered his hand, Amalek prevailed. But Moses' hands grew weary; so they took a stone and put it under him, and he sat on it. Aaron and Hur held up his hands . . . until the sun set. And Joshua defeated Amalek" (Exod. 17:11–13).

At the conclusion of that long day, God commands Moses to write. The command is brief: "Write this as a reminder in a book and recite it in the hearing of Joshua: I will utterly blot out the remembrance of Amalek from under heaven" (Exod. 17:14). It is a striking conundrum. God directs Moses to memorialize in writing the erasure of Amalek. But because Amalek is inscribed in the book, he whose remembrance is utterly blotted out is nonetheless still with us millennia later. Thus does the Bible's first mention of writing perform its power.

The references to writing that follow in the story of the long journey are associated almost exclusively with writing law: the book of the covenant, the tablets of stone at Mt. Sinai, the law written on plastered stones set up at Mt. Ebal, and the written law deposited in the ark. Moses does most of this writing.[18]

Moses erases what God writes. When he descends the mountain bearing the two stone tablets and approaches the encampment, he sees the people engaged in the idolatrous worship of a golden calf, and he smashes the tablets. They will be replaced later by a second set of stone tablets on which the commandments have been rewritten. Arthur Jacobson focuses on this erasure and rewriting of the commandments in an argument about the authenticity of law.[19] He reads the Sinai events as a kind of negotiation with God carried forward by Moses on behalf of the people. This negotiation or participation, he believes, is what makes the law legitimate and effective among the people. I think Jacobson is wrong, but helpfully so.[20]

The first time that God hands down the law, He speaks it with frightening power and then gives Moses the two stones on which He has written it. Clearly God does the writing. The scene is interrupted by the people's calf worship and Moses' erasure of God's handiwork. After the people offer an atonement, a measure of peace is restored, and God has Moses cut two more stone tablets and return with them to the mountain. God restates the covenant, and then "the Lord said to Moses: 'Write these words; in accordance with these words I have made a covenant with you and with Israel.' He was there with the Lord forty days and forty nights; he neither ate bread nor drank water. And he wrote on the tablets the words of the covenant, the ten commandments" (Exod. 34:27–28).

Jacobson believes that the text is ambiguous and that it is not clear whether the "he" who wrote the second edition is God or Moses.[21] I think it is clear in the Exodus account that Moses did the writing, but I accept Jacobson's point about ambiguity on other grounds.[22]

Jacobson reads the ambiguity as signaling something about law: If law is rules and God unilaterally hands them down, people have no creative role to play. The law written by God on the stones will appear not as propositions for conversation but as rules that are a graven image to be bowed down to like the golden calf. Moses must destroy the first tablets to teach the people that these writings are not idols but propositions that lead to further creative conversation with God. Moses must then be included in writing the second set of tablets to demonstrate the possibility of collaboration. Moses "will let the people read the propositions only once they are written for a second time. . . . The people will not regard the second writing, the rewriting of a writing they saw Moses smash, as an idol. They will read the propositions, rewrite them in deeds, use them as further propositions in conversation with Yahweh." [23]

I read the writing at Sinai differently. It is not negotiation but God's gift. God wrote the law the first time. Moses erased the writing because he was furious with the people just as God was. Moses thereby deprived the people of the writing that would have placed the gift of law literally in their midst. Without law, God cannot be present to them. When God orders the people to set out from Sinai, He says He will not go with them: "If for a single moment I should go up among you, I would consume you" (Exod. 33:5).

It is when God eventually relents and agrees to go with the people that He also agrees to a rewriting of the law to be placed in the ark. The words of the law, the ark, God, and the people set out together for the promised land. The law is the gift whereby God is present without destroying the people.

Uncertainty about who did the writing on the second set of stones has two functions. It serves first to certify and particularize Moses' role. God speaks, then writes the law. To be His mouth means doing both. Moses is commissioned to write as well as speak for God. When he utters God's word, Moses' speaking and writing are the same as God's.

The other function of the uncertainty is to indicate how the gift is to be received. That there is a second edition of the law exhibits the inexhaustibility of God's commitment to his people, their defection notwithstanding. That the law this time was or could have been written by Moses shows what the people are to do with it. God gives His law into the hands of Moses. Moses in turn delivers it to the people. And then the people are themselves at last bidden to write, like Moses. They are to be saturated with the words: "Keep these words that I am commanding you today in your heart. . . . Bind them as a sign on your hand, fix them as an emblem on your forehead, and write them on the doorposts of your house and on your gates" (Deut. 6:6–9). Israel carries the law about in the ark, on their doorposts, on their bodies, in their hearts, in their lives. So does God's law become the people's law, and so is reception of the gift completed.

The engraved words cannot be mistaken for idols, not because they are smashed by Moses, but because words are exactly what an idol does not offer.[24] Idols do not speak or write. An idol cannot be the words or the source of the words that allow God to be close to His people to lead and not destroy them.

The words of the law are the people's to do. They are to be engaged and animated by them. The law is very much their law and their responsibility. This engagement of the people in the law is testimony to the God who is a collaborator with His people. His law — written by the people on their doorposts, on themselves, and in their lives — is the word of God that will bring Israel home.

Jacobson draws another interesting conclusion from his reflection on writing the law. He finds in the writing a useful warning to modern practitioners of law: It is wrong to hold that rules of law are complete prior to any application of them. He says that Mosaic law and now common law hold that rules are not complete in this way. From the Mosaic perspective, as Jacobson reads Exodus, complete rules would be idols, and to apply them to cases as if the rules were already formed would be idolatry. According to what Jacobson proposes as the dynamic jurisprudence of Mosaic and common law, "rules rule" correctly "only when persons struggle at every moment with them, use them in deeds to create a record." [25] What counts is the creation and re-creation of the rules that is "at once the striving of persons . . . and a spur to action." [26] The struggle, he says, is as difficult today as it was "for those first legal persons in the wilderness, struggling to free themselves, body and soul, from slavery." [27]

I think that Jacobson is exactly right in this: Rules can be idols. They become idols when they become a substitute for responsibility. A judge or bureaucrat or lawyer who claims that he must obey a rule and that he is powerless to do otherwise than to simply apply it thereby refuses to take responsibility for the interpretation and judgment that are his. He makes an idol of the rule. I do not disagree with Jacobson on the point. I am uncertain, however, that it can be grounded in this text in the way he has sought to do.

As I read the Sinai episode, it leads in a somewhat different direction. Those persons in the wilderness were struggling to free themselves, body and soul, from slavery, and they continued to do so. But in order to begin and to continue the struggle to free themselves, they had first to *be* freed. As a matter of narrative sequence and as a matter of being, they could only arrive at that point in their desert life after they had been liberated from Egypt.[28] The priority of God's gift of freedom is embodied in the text when God's gift of law begins with His statement: "I am the Lord your God, who brought you out of the land of Egypt, out of the house of slavery" (Exod. 20:2). Israel is freed for law.

Moreover, neither Moses nor the people create or re-create the Ten Commandments. God gives the commandments as spoken words, then as written words, then again as written words. They are not rules, complete or incomplete, and they are not to be applied. The people are to rewrite the law in their lives rather than apply it to cases. And they are to do so because otherwise *the people* rather than the rules are incomplete. Absent the law and their doing it, absent their rewriting it all the way down, absent their investment in it, absent their responsibility for its lived interpretation and embodiment, they are not God's people, and He is not present in their midst. The law is the imperative transcription of who this people is and is to become.[29] Such law is not to be applied but lived, embodied, abided in, made one's own. Israel struggled to become what it had been freed by God to be. It is God, rather than rules, who rules.

2. Intercession

The rewriting of the law at Mt. Sinai is not a negotiation in which Moses, representing the people, wins for them a collaborative role. Moses simply acts as scribe, just as he is mouth for the God who has given the people a collaborative role with the beginning of the story.

On occasion, however, especially in the Mt. Sinai episodes, Moses does speak *for the people*. Openly and explicitly in the text he intercedes with God on their behalf.[1] He does so movingly and effectively. He persuades God to change His mind, and he saves the people from mighty acts of divine retribution. These intercessions appear to be spontaneous and to lack express authorization by either the people or God. They raise the question: For whom does Moses then speak? The question admits of no easy answer.

I do not number among the singular moments when Moses truly intercedes for the people those instances of alarm, peevishness, and self-pity — both personal and collective — when Moses simply reiterates his and the people's complaints. There are more than a few of these whining times. They start in Egypt prior to the exodus, when Moses remonstrates with God: "O Lord, why have you mistreated this people? Why did you ever send me? Since I first came to Pharaoh to speak in your name, he has mistreated this people, and you have done nothing at all to deliver your people" (Exod. 5:22–23).

Similar instances occur later in the pre-Sinai wilderness[2] and then with some frequency after the giving of the law. One grievance arises from the bland, daily repetition of manna and nothing but manna in the wilderness that revives thoughts of food in Egypt now remembered as varied, abundant, and savory: "If only we had meat to eat! We remember the fish we used to eat in Egypt for nothing, the cucumbers, the melons, the leeks, the onions, and the garlic; but now our strength is dried up, and there is nothing at all but this manna to look at" (Num. 11:4–6). (The narrator slips in a remonstrative dissenting opinion: "the taste of [manna] was like the taste of cakes baked with oil" [11:8] [But, oh, the garlic].) Moses relays such grievances to God and adds his own.[3] I reckon these episodes as registrations of fright, of grumbling, or of self-pity rather than as intercession.

The tapestry of exchanges at Mt. Sinai presents three very different, acute cases of genuine, affecting intercession.[4] I take these up now and will return to them several times.

The first occurs just after God gives Moses the tablets of stone on which He has inscribed the Ten Commandments. The narrative of events taking place atop Mt. Sinai is interrupted by the story of the idolatry taking place below. In Moses' absence, the people have lapsed into the worship of a golden calf. God tells Moses to go down at once. God wishes to be left alone so that His "wrath may burn hot against them" without intrusion (Exod. 32:10). Moses, disobedient, delays. In that critical circumstance, before he will leave, he will first pause to argue. We now would see him as a lawyer appearing before a judge and refusing to be overpowered by him:

> "O Lord, why does your wrath burn hot against your people, whom you brought out of the land of Egypt with great power and with a mighty hand? Why should the Egyptians say, 'It was with evil intent that he brought them out to kill them in the mountains, and to consume them from the face of the earth'? Turn from your fierce wrath; change your mind and do not bring disaster on your people. Remember Abraham, Isaac, and Israel, your servants, how you swore to them by your own self, saying to them, 'I will multiply your descendants like the stars of heaven, and all this land that I have promised I will give to your descendants, and they shall inherit it forever' " (Exod. 32:11–13).[5]

In response to these arguments that Moses makes from reputation and covenant, "the Lord changed his mind about the disaster that he planned to bring on his people" (Exod. 32:14).[6] Only then does Moses descend the mountain to contend with the idolators.

The second intercessory moment in the Sinai sequence soon follows. As Moses approaches the encampment and sees Israel enthralled by the golden calf, he smashes the two tablets of stone bearing the Ten Commandments. He then destroys the golden calf and conducts a purge of the sinners. He still fears what God will do to the people who remain. He returns to the mountain to "make atonement" for them (Exod. 32:30). Instead of offering arguments this time, he employs a different tactic of a type employed by modern lawyers: He confesses the people's guilt and enters a plea for mercy. He is partially successful. God agrees to let the people continue on their journey to the promised land, but He also vows to punish the guilty "when the day comes." In the meantime He sends a plague upon them. When the day does come, all the pioneers must die in the desert short of the promised land (Exod. 32:31–35).[7] Only the next generation will be allowed to enter.

The third of Moses' Sinai intercessions occurs when God orders the people to set out for the promised land but, apparently still nursing His fury, says He will send an angel before them but will not Himself go with them. His absence would clearly be a catastrophe. Without Him, Israel would be defenseless against her enemies in the desert. Moses appeals to God. The place of encounter has shifted from the mountain top to a special tent, the tent of meeting, pitched outside the base camp. A pillar of cloud there has replaced the thunderstorms on the mountain, and the turbulence of Israel's idolatry has given way to calm: "When Moses entered the tent, the pillar of cloud would descend . . . and the Lord would speak with Moses. . . . Thus the Lord used to speak to Moses face to face, as one speaks to a friend" (Exod. 33:9, 11). In this setting Moses now addresses to God a quietly personal, yet cunning argument that touches on his relationship to God, on God's prior statements, and again on God's reputation:

> See, you have said to me, "Bring up this people"; but you have not let me know whom you will send with me. Yet you have said, "I know you by name, and you have also found favor in my sight." Now if I have found favor in your sight, show me your ways, so that I may know you and find favor in your sight. Consider too that this nation is your people." (Exod. 33:12–13)

God is persuaded and interrupts to say so. He says that His presence will be in attendance on the journey after all.[8] But Moses, like a lawyer who would rather argue than succeed, seems not to hear and continues: "How shall it be known that I have found favor in your sight, I and your people, unless you go with us? In this way, we shall be distinct, I and your people, from every people on the face of the earth" (Exod. 33:16). God consents once more.[9]

Moses will represent Israel before God on later occasions, but these three, decisive instances more than justify Jeremiah's memory of Moses as one of Israel's greatest intercessors.[10] At Sinai a great divide opens between God and the people. Moses is in the middle, and three times this mouth for God must speak for the people to God.[11]

When Moses stands there in the middle, representing God to the people and the people to God, he acts as what modern lawyers call "counsel for the situation." Here the story intersects a legal-professional subject, and I pause to explore it. In order to do so, I must give a brief account of the history and significance of the relevant professional terms, and this means momentarily shifting focus from the strange story to the differently strange discourse of lawyers.

Along the way so far I have said first that Moses could be seen as a lawyer before a judge and then that he employed lawyerly tactics. These casual remarks were simple associations of modern law with the story. Subsequently, the discussion of Arthur Jacobson's views on writing and rewriting the law at Sinai constituted a more complex exchange between the story and modern law. Jacobson read the story very carefully and attentively and found that it spoke to him about how to regard rules of law. What he found advanced his understanding not only of Moses but also of himself and his work.

The intersection that I am now set to explore holds promise for enriching understanding of both Moses and a controversial practice of modern lawyers.[12]

At Sinai Moses is fully immersed in a situation at the same time that he remains distinct. The saga will later give us women — Hebrew midwives, Miriam, Rachel — who are also, in their own way, both fully engaged and other. Still later The Gospel According to John will return us to yet another, qualitatively different encounter with what it means to be in but not of a world, including the world of law.

The Sinai episode raises the question of Moses' relation to God and the people and of lawyers' relation to the clients they represent. It raises for the first time the recurring question of a person's independence from and identity with those for whom she speaks. What is entailed in speaking for God? What is entailed in lawyers' speaking for people? I shall return to these issues several times over. But in order to do so, I must first turn from Moses and the story to Louis Brandeis and lawyers' discourse.

3. Counsel for the Situation

The notion of "counsel for the situation" is important in the practice of American law because it runs counter to the dominant idea that a lawyer in our adversarial system must always perform as a zealous advocate for an individual client's interests against all others. This dominant approach is well justified. A person needs a lawyer whose competence, diligence, confidence, enthusiasm, and undivided loyalty she can rely on.

Nevertheless, a lawyer's scorched-earth advancement of an individual client's interest is not always the need. For example, a family may want a single attorney to represent them as a whole for various reasons. (John Frank said that nothing requires "each of the relatives of the deceased to take different counsel to the funeral: if a half-dozen heirs were required to pay a half-dozen counsel, they would indeed have additional grounds for grief."[1]) Or a group of business people may seek a lawyer to represent their joint interests as they undertake a common enterprise. Or clients with a present or potential dispute may be determined to resolve their differences amicably and may turn to their attorney for her professional service.

"Counsel for the situation" is a way of thinking about such instances. In alliance with the idea that lawyers ought to serve the interests of the people and not the interests of large corporations only, it is also a way of introducing into a discussion of lawyers' responsibility a possible obligation to communities, to relationships, to the public good, to something in addition to an individual client's interests.[2]

Louis Brandeis invented the term "counsel for the situation" to describe some of his work.[3] He also advocated the role of people's lawyer and was known for sometimes playing that role himself.[4] His heroic image continues to inspire public interest lawyering.[5]

Brandeis became an associate justice of the Supreme Court after surviving opposition at contentious hearings on his nomination in 1916.[6] Although the opposition to him by leaders of the bar may actually have been prompted by the fact that he was "an intellectually powerful liberal and a Jew," its ostensible subject was his professional conduct.[7]

The term "counsel for the situation" was introduced publicly during the 1916 hearings, but the story of it begins with an episode that took place in 1907.[8] A tannery had accumulated large debts and could not meet the payments when they fell due. An owner of the business, James Lennox, together with one of his creditors and the creditor's attorney, sought Brandeis's advice. (Brandeis's firm represented one of the other creditors.) In the course of the conference, Brandeis determined that the tannery was insolvent and suggested that the assets be assigned to his law partner as trustee for the benefit of creditors, in the hope of saving the business from bankruptcy. Lennox adopted Brandeis's suggestion but did not understand that he was thereby gaining a trustee for the firm's property rather than a lawyer for himself. In the complexities that followed, bankruptcy became necessary, and Brandeis's firm represented the petitioning creditors in those proceedings. Lennox felt betrayed and retained another Boston lawyer, Sherman Whipple, to investigate.

Whipple met with Brandeis and later recounted the meeting at the 1916 hearings. He remembered Brandeis saying, among other things:

> "When a man is bankrupt and cannot pay his debts, . . . he finds himself with a trust, imposed upon him by law, to see that all his property is distributed honestly and fairly and equitably among all his creditors, and he has no further interest in the matter. Such was Mr. Lennox's situation when he came to me, and he consulted me merely as the trustee for his creditors, as to how best to discharge that trust, and I advised him in that way. I did not intend to act personally for Mr. Lennox, nor did I agree to." "Yes," I said, "but you advised him to make the assignment. For whom were you counsel when you advised him to do that, if not for the Lennoxes?" He said, "I should say that I was counsel for the situation. . . . I was looking after the interests of everyone."[9]

In 1965 John Frank revisited the nomination hearings and Brandeis's action. He concluded that Brandeis had violated no standard of professional ethics, but he agreed with Whipple's criticism that Brandeis should have made clearer to Lennox what he was proposing.[10] Frank also thought that counsel for the situation was a "misty phrase" and "one of the most unfortunate . . . [Brandeis] ever casually uttered."[11]

Despite its colorable, inauspicious origin, the notion has survived doggedly and honorably. Reputable lawyers who were contemporaries of Brandeis had done the same thing, and lawyers still do.[12] In 1978, Geoffrey Hazard commended the practice as "perhaps the best service a lawyer can render to anyone."[13] Hazard argued that lawyering for the situation could be officially defined and should be officially recognized. At the time Hazard wrote, the American Bar Association offered little guidance on the subject.

The ABA adopted its first set of standards, the Canons of Professional Ethics, at just about the time of Brandeis's involvement with Lennox and the tannery. Of these thirty-two aspirational canons, one held that it was "unprofessional to represent conflicting interests, except by express consent of all concerned given after a full disclosure of the facts." [14] Beyond this, the canons did not address what Brandeis and others were doing in situational representation.

In 1969 the ABA adopted a Model Code of Professional Responsibility that offered something more. According to one of its "disciplinary rules," lawyers may represent multiple clients if they provide full disclosure and "can adequately represent the interests of each." [15] One of the accompanying "ethical considerations" also provided that lawyers may serve as arbitrators or mediators for clients. [16] This is more than what the earlier canons had offered, but it was not much clearer or more helpful. [17] Hazard said that it allowed "only a fragment of [lawyering for the situation], and with some reluctance at that." [18]

Hazard became the reporter for the next installment, the 1983 Model Rules of Professional Conduct produced by an ABA commission. His influence is to be detected in Rule 2.2, which allows a lawyer to "act as intermediary between clients." [19] Thomas Shaffer believes that the rule is stingy and not as generous as Brandeis would have wanted, but useful nonetheless. In his judgment it bears possibilities for understanding that lawyers may represent families and other communities and in doing so represent the harmonies of the relationships. [20]

Meanwhile, a committee of the American Law Institute, which Hazard now directs, has been at work on a Restatement of the Law Governing Lawyers. The 1996 final draft of the Restatement abandons the modest effort of Rule 2.2 on the grounds that the rule did not mean what it seemed to say and that, in any event, the term "intermediation" had not entered the professional vocabulary. [21] And a commission appointed by the ABA to review the Model Rules agrees: It proposes eliminating Rule 2.2, replacing "intermediation" with "joint representation," and viewing the latter as a problem to be dealt with under the rules governing conflict of interest. [22]

At present, lawyering for the situation stands just about where the 1969 Model Code left it: without much positive guidance. [23] It remains what Hazard described as "marginally illicit professional conduct," [24] much as it was when Brandeis engaged in it at the beginning of the century.

Lawyers do serve as counsel for the situation and will continue to do so, even though the practice is probably destined to remain marginally illicit.[25] This is as it should be. A rule legitimating the practice, if the bar were to achieve a consensus, would nonetheless be a rule, and no rule can carry a lawyer through the unstructured spaces of the situations at issue.[26]

Brandeis intended no evil. He sought only to maintain his own autonomy,[27] but that desire may have compromised his representation. In a careful reassessment of Brandeis's practice, Clyde Spillenger finds that autonomy and high-mindedness were specifically characteristic of Brandeis's lawyering for a situation. Brandeis typically sought to be fair to all and to harmonize competing interests. Also typically, however, the fairness and harmony he sought were not what a sensitive inquiry into the goals and needs of the parties revealed. Rather, he "saw a 'situation' that he could solve, in the manner of a good Progressive problem-solver—a 'one-man New Deal'—and he sought to impose a solution that made reference less to the expressed desires of the parties involved than to a vision nurtured by and known only to himself."[28]

Lawyering for the situation is a tricky business, trickiest of all, perhaps, for those who, like the heroic Brandeis, intend to do good by engaging in it.[29] Because he represented a detached vision of his own, Brandeis was above the situation and not in it. His vision could be a good vision with good intentions and good results. It was nonetheless his own.

The ABA's 1983 Model Rule 2.2 that allows attorneys to act as intermediaries—the official version of lawyering to a situation—supports such Brandeisian detachment. It expresses some concern for the extra risks to which clients are exposed in these circumstances. The interpretive comments that follow the rule thus direct the lawyer to be mindful of additional costs, embarrassment, and recrimination that failure could produce for clients.[30] But the lawyer is not thought of as having anything at stake. The rules say nothing about her venturing herself. Or her fee. Were the attorney to take the job and in the process foresee trouble, she would simply withdraw, apparently with her fee and her reputation for independence intact. The implied ideal is that of an attorney, like Brandeis, above the situation, detached from the clients and the joint enterprise.[31]

Back in 1978, Geoffrey Hazard had a view that conflicts with the ABA's notion of a lawyer detached from the situation. An attorney may be entrusted with the role of intermediary, Hazard said, "only if he knows that in the event of miscarriage he will have no protection from the law" and only if success prevents his performance from being questioned afterward.[32] I read Hazard's admonition to mean that an attorney may be entrusted with the role only if he is fully, vulnerably invested in the situation—like Moses.

4. The Word in Moses' Situation

Moses never surrenders his office as mouth for God. He is as aligned with God as a mortal can be. And yet he is also aligned with the people and speaks for them.[1] When he stands at the outermost reaches—the text gives a geographical location on the mountaintop surrounded by a cloud—he is physically separated from the people but not humanly detached from them. His identification with them takes poignant form in the narrative.

Just when God finishes speaking the law to Moses and gives him the stone tablets, the people's idolatry interrupts. In His fury, God would be let alone "so that my wrath may burn hot against them and I may consume them." But that is not all that God says. He has a last comment. He will consume the people, "and of you," He adds, speaking to Moses, "I will make a great nation" (Exod. 32:10).

Moses lingers. His response is to say nothing about the offer of a kingdom of his own. He pleads instead for the people, for the nation that is his now, such as it is. This is the first of his great intercessions on the people's behalf, and it changes God's mind. Arthur Jacobson notes about the moment that "the highest political drama . . . is whether Moses will become a new Pharaoh."[2] He does not.[3]

When Moses returns to the mountain to make atonement for the people's sin and to intercede powerfully for them the second time, he says: "Alas, this people has sinned a great sin; they have made for themselves gods of gold. But now, if you will only forgive their sin—but if not, blot me out of the book that you have written" (Exod. 32:31–32).[4]

This is not simply to resist the offer to become a new pharaoh. Moses now places himself fully with the people. God has written a book. If God is to destroy the people, Moses asks to be erased from the book. Earlier God had determined to erase the memory of Amalek, but, since Moses wrote down God's intention in his book, Amalek is still remembered. Now Moses would have himself erased from God's book. No longer to be written in God's book is more than to have resisted the pharaonic temptation and worse than to be unremembered. It is not to have existed at all. Moses risks all that he has and is. He is as fully the mouth for the people as he is mouth for God.

Moses' advocacy in this situation poses a difficulty of interpretation. Is he to be read as both mouth for God and voice of the people? If so, does he slip from one role into another? Is he duplicitous?

The problem can be resolved by saying simply that Moses speaks for the situation. Along this line it can be noted that he identifies with and pleads for "this" people, not "these" people, and therefore for the collective, for the enterprise, for both God and people together. Or it can be argued that acting as an intermediary sometimes requires representing one party to another or changing roles within a developing situation.

This reading solves the problem of double voice, but only by raising it to a higher level. Moses still acts as God's mouth, but now God is two: God Forgiving and God Angry. Moses speaks for the people and God Forgiving to God Angry.[5] In the stories, God certainly acts as first the one and then the other. And Moses' intercessions succeed in convincing God to change from one to the other. God does respond to intercession on the people's behalf.

This is a valid reading. I take a somewhat different approach. I think that Moses' intercessions at Sinai are genuinely intercessory, are prayers to God for the people, because they arise out of the word of God: Moses is mouth for the people exactly because he is mouth for God.

There is in the saga no ear for God. The people need an intermediary to be able to hear God's voice. God hears theirs unaided.[6] This is how he comes to send Moses. "The Israelites groaned under their slavery, and cried out. Out of the slavery their cry for help rose up to God" (Exod. 2:23). He hears and responds because of what he had earlier said,[7] the promises he made in electing Israel as his people: "God heard their groaning, and God remembered his covenant with Abraham, Isaac, and Jacob" (Exod. 2:24). Because He hears, He sends Moses to speak: "I have heard their cry . . . , and I have come down to deliver them. . . . So come, I will send you to Pharaoh to bring my people, the Israelites, out of Egypt" (Exod. 3:7–10).

Entailed in God's speaking is a return hearing and in the hearing a return speaking. In Isaiah's figure of the ongoing hydrologic cycle, the rain and the snow come down and do not return empty.

At the beginning, at the burning bush, Moses objects: "I have never been eloquent," and God answers: "Who gives speech to mortals? . . . Go and I will be with your mouth and teach you what you are to speak" (Exod. 4:10–12). God supplies Moses with the words he speaks to Pharaoh and to the people. He also supplies Moses with the words Moses speaks to God. God's word returns to Him as intercession.

Moses' first intercession at Sinai is a precise example. He has made several round-trips to the mountain summit. As chapter 32 opens, the reader assumes that Moses has returned to the top for the last time. There is the expectation that the vertical movement of ascending and descending will now translate into horizontal progress across the desert plain and that the energy of exchanges between summit and base will now fuel the long march forward to Canaan.

Already from prior exchanges, law has come down the mountain in oral form and been agreed to and set out in writing (Exod. 19:3–8, 24:1–8). Already there has been promise that, with this law in their midst and with the doing it, the people will be led by an angel and that terror, confusion, and pestilence will precede them to cut a path of destruction through their enemies (23:23–33).

It remains only for Moses to descend with the two tablets of stone and to deposit them in the mobile ark. Then, with the production of the required equipment completed, Israel will be set in motion once more. At the end of chapter 31 Moses has the law stones in hand and is ready to descend. That is just about where chapter 34 later picks up the story, with God parading his glory before Moses on the mountaintop in rehearsal of the passage God will make in company with the people below (Exod. 33:17–23, 34:6–7).[8] Then the two stones make their final descent safely, all the way down. And when at last they are placed in the ark (40:20), the people embark, charged by their law and the presence of God.

The story has moved from the revolt in Egypt, to the liberation of the people in the exodus, to the founding of the nation's freedom at Sinai. And it is in process of turning north to complete the trajectory when chapter 32 intervenes.[9] The forward movement is brought to a sharp and unanticipated halt, and its continuation is thrown into radical doubt.

The story precipitously takes us to the edge of the abyss. Just as the sin of Adam and Eve interrupts the idyll of Eden, so here the idolatry of Israel halts the turn toward home and calls everything into question. The people have abandoned their being. How could Israel do this thing? How could Aaron conduct this act? How could he declare it to be "a festival to the Lord" (Exod. 32:5)? This cannot be. It is impossible. But it is done. And what must follow but that the people and the journey must end? Have already ended in an impossible act of self-destruction? And the story, if it, too, is not to end, will surely have to take up with some other people.

God's speaking in chapter 31 concludes in the two stone texts. Moses stands there, clutching them, when, in chapter 32, God's fury breaks out. Facing God, Moses intercedes for Israel. And his final, intercessory argument in this scene, the one that changes God's mind, is the express return of words God had sent earlier: "Remember Abraham, Isaac, and Israel . . . how you swore to them by your own self, saying to them, 'I will multiply your descendants like the stars of heaven. . . .' And then the Lord changed his mind. . . . Then Moses turned and went down from the mountain, carrying the two tablets of stone" (Exod. 32:13–15).[10]

God's word sends Moses to Egypt and returns him fruitfully to Sinai with the gathered Israel. It brings him to the mountain summit, where he will receive more words and where he may now intercede for the people. And as he speaks, the word assembles around itself the various arguments he offers. And then — simply, decisively — it emerges expressly: Moses quotes God to God to produce a reversal in judgment.[11] And the quoted words provide, as well, an interval for further intercessions. And the further intercessions allow the law stones to reach the people. And these words, too, will have issue.

God is the origin and end of speech. The word goes forth in many seminal forms: creation, promise, judgment, prophecy, and law. And it returns in many fruitful forms of production and delivery: creation, childbearing, a people, exodus, journey, conquest, exile, return from exile, poetry, and intercession.

As mouth for God, Moses speaks the word that does not return empty but accomplishes its purpose and prospers in the thing for which it is sent.[12] Law and intercession are moments in this cycle.

Participation in this cycle of the word leaves all parties vulnerable, in unresolved complexities and tensions. Moses and Israel are not inert conduits of the word, and God's presence never loses its capacity to destroy. God, Moses, and Israel are mutually imperiled.

God is vulnerable in His commitment to Israel, in His word in their midst. The recent writings of the systematic theologian Robert Jenson and the biblical theologian Walter Brueggemann provide a helpful point of departure for exploring the subject.

The Greeks, Jenson notes, assumed that gods to be gods must be immune "to time's contingencies and particularly to death."[1] The Olympian gods are immortal. In the biblical sagas, Israel begins with no such assumption. Unlike the gods of Olympus, the God of the biblical sagas is vulnerable to time. He is said to be eternal, Jenson argues, not "because he lacks time, but because he takes time," not because "he secures himself from time," but because "he is faithful to his commitments within time."[2] In the stories, He is personally engaged: He changes His mind, reacts to events, makes threats, and repents of them. That He listens and responds to His people, "far from being a condescension, is the very way he is faithful to himself."[3]

Brueggemann points out that the people start with no generic assumption about God at all.[4] From the beginning, what they know of God is what God reveals to them about Himself in relation to them and their history, along the way. "Even where God is said to be 'elsewhere,' " Brueggemann notes, "this 'elsewhere' is most often in response to Israel's life, either negatively or positively."[5] God is the God of Israel. He is not detached. He is not "above the fray"; indeed, He is "at risk in the ongoing life of Israel."[6]

Moses' intercessions for Israel may then be understood to speak for God because they are occasioned by and are occasion for God's performance of His faithfulness to Israel and therefore of His faithfulness to Himself. Jenson draws on the rabbinic tradition:

> The old rabbis, looking back on the whole of Israel's Bible, could state the matter in drastic fashion: "Israel [can even say] to God: 'You have redeemed *yourself*. . . .' Wherever Israel was exiled, the Sheki-

nah—if one may speak so—went with them into exile. . . . And when at the end of days they return, the Shekinah will return with them." What the Lord does to Israel, he does to himself, in that the Shekinah shares Israel's *lot* and the Lord's *being*. . . . With the phrase "the Shekinah" the rabbis gathered a whole range of biblical discourse that speaks of God as "settled" to and within Israel.[7]

God and Israel share identity. In speaking for the one, Moses cannot but speak for the other.

When Moses addresses God at Sinai—the word returning to its speaker—his three intercessions are versions of a single theme: He appeals to God to be God. This is also to ask that Israel be allowed to be Israel. The one is linked to the other.

In the first scene, God sees Israel's idolatry. Their worship of the calf is an act of self-annihilation. God directs Moses to leave; He wishes to be left alone so that He may consume the people and make another nation of Moses. But this God, because He is God, cannot be left alone. Moses' argument is a reminder that Israel is the nation God has committed himself to (Exod. 32:7–14). Israel has done the impossible in its sin. God must overcome the impossible with the possibility of a future, for He, no less than Moses, cannot be Himself without Israel. He is the one who is faithful over and against Israel's faithlessness. He cannot be left alone, and He cannot be left not alone but with another nation.

In the second scene, Moses acknowledges Israel's sin and then says: "If you will only forgive their sin—but if not, blot me out of the book that you have written" (Exod. 32:32). Moses places himself fully at risk with Israel. His doing so reminds God that God, too, is at risk with Israel. What book would there be without Moses? What God would there be without the book with Moses? God is the God of this nation in this book.

The third intercession is offered in the tent of meeting. In the course of it, Moses reminds God "that this nation is your people." If God is not present with them as they move out for Canaan, Moses asks, "how shall it be known that I have found favor in your sight, I and your people, unless you go with us? In this way, we shall be distinct, I and your people, from every people on the face of the earth" (Exod. 33:13–16). Without God, Israel could not be known as God's people. Without this distinction, with only the mass of humanity, God could not be known as the God of Israel. What would distinguish Him?

God shares identity with Israel. But, as Jenson says, God is identified with Israel without ceasing to stand over against her.[8] God is both settled in Israel and other than Israel.[9]

Like God for whom he speaks, Moses is fully invested in the people, prepared to be erased with them, and yet, like God, he, too, is other than they. He is Israel's leader, but he is nonetheless a fugitive Egyptian prince. He bears God's word of judgment upon the people. And in the course of the journey through the desert, his brother and sister lead a revolt against him.[10]

Like Israel, for whom he also speaks, Moses is fully identified with God and is yet other than God. God chooses the second born Moses to be primary among His firstborn, instructs him in what he is to say to Pharaoh, and then tries to kill him. Thanks to Zipporah, God lets him alone. But what about the future? Where will Zipporah be?

The tension remains to the end, to the story about the conclusion of Moses' life on the verge of Israel's entry into the promised land. Moses begs God: "Let me cross over to see the good land beyond the Jordan, that good hill country and the Lebanon" (Deut. 3:25). God rejects his plea. At the end of the long journey from Egypt, God will not allow Moses to enter. This is a painful lack of fulfillment for the conclusion of a remarkable, deserving life. The confoundment of it lives on in the stories and minds of the people. Moses' exclusion is a punishment. He committed an offense in the process of drawing water from a rock.

After the people leave Sinai, they arrive at Meribah (Quarrel). The desert is bone dry. The people and their animals suffer. They have a desperate thirst. The people gather against Moses and Aaron and quarrel with them about their predicament and no prospect of relief. The story continues:

> The Lord spoke to Moses, saying: "Take the staff, and assemble the congregation . . . and command the rock before their eyes to yield its water. Thus you shall bring water out of the rock for them." . . .
>
> So Moses took the staff from before the Lord, as he had commanded him. Moses . . . gathered the assembly together before the rock, and he said to them, "Listen, you rebels, shall we bring water for you out of this rock?" Then Moses lifted up his hand and struck the rock twice with his staff; water came out abundantly, and the congregation and their livestock drank. But the Lord said to Moses . . . , "Because you did not trust

in me, to show my holiness before the eyes of the Israelites, therefore you shall not bring this assembly into the land that I have given them." (Num. 20:2–13)

There are various possibilities for identifying Moses' offense.[11] For example: He was told to speak to the rock, but he struck it instead or struck it too many times or too hard and thus evinced lack of trust in the word. Or, when he asked the people "shall *we* bring forth water," he was taking credit for the miracle and thus succumbed to self-glorification, perhaps a version of playing God. Or there is no precise explanation of the details in the text. In any event, the text says he failed to show God's holiness.[12] Like the rest of the first generation except Caleb and Joshua, the generation of the pioneers, he, too, must die without crossing the Jordan.

When the end comes, the text delivers it simply. Moses climbs to the top of a mountain opposite Jericho,

> and the Lord showed him the whole land: . . . "This is the land of which I swore to Abraham, to Isaac, and to Jacob, saying, 'I will give it to your descendants'; I have let you see it with your eyes, but you shall not cross over there." Then Moses, the servant of the Lord, died there in the land of Moab, at the Lord's command. He was buried in a valley in the land of Moab, opposite Beth-peor, but no one knows his burial place to this day. Moses was one hundred twenty years old when he died; his sight was unimpaired and his vigor had not abated. (Deut. 34:1–7)

Moses is left outside in an unknown grave. He was mouth for God, but he was not God.

Israel is both bound to God and independent. "The Israelites wept for Moses in the plains of Moab thirty days; then the period of mourning for Moses was ended" (Deut. 34:8). After Moses dies, the people mourn. And then they cease their mourning. They continue the journey. They, God, the story, and the writer move on. The terms are the same: There is assurance, but also the tension present from the start.[13]

In their identity with God, they are a people apart from other people. For Israel to bear the word through the desert and in the promised land, they must be holy, and, as David Damrosch says, "to be holy, *gadosh*, is to be set apart; the root means 'separation, withdrawal, dedication.' . . . God himself repeatedly makes the point that the people's separateness is to mirror his own: 'Ye shall be holy, for I the Lord your God am holy'

(Lev. 19:2)."[14] Their separation requires certain political connections to others: "You shall love the alien as yourself, for you were aliens in the land of Egypt: I am the Lord your God" (Lev. 19:34). But these are connections with other aliens formed in transit along the way. This people are resident aliens in Egypt and then wandering aliens in the desert.

The closer to God Israel is, the more separate she is from other nations and the closer to herself, to her true nature. God's commands express who Israel is, and obedience to them—her nearness to God—does not then infringe on Israel's autonomy but instead enables it.[15] And especially as she approaches God in prayerful dependence—we see this with Moses' intercessions—the more independent she is. As Jenson says: "Unabashed petitionary prayer is the one decisively appropriate creaturely act over against the true God."[16]

Israel can always act over against God inappropriately and abandon her identity. So when wandering in the desert concludes in occupation of Canaan, her presence in that promised land "expresses not a sense of possession but a permanence of exile."[17] The land was possessed by others when Israel conquered it, and Israel, too, can be dispossessed in turn. If the people are to continue in the land, they must obey the law. "The ideology that contributes to a theology of the gift of the land," Patrick Miller observes, "can also be used against the people and made the basis for their removal. . . . Deuteronomy, which builds upon the promise of land to the ancestors, recognizes and affirms the tenuousness of Israel's life there."[18]

God's settlement in Israel is unsettling and remains so. It unsettles Israel in the story, and it unsettles interpretation of the story. In the biblical saga, there will be no "after all is said and done." There will be, as Brueggemann puts it, "another speech, another challenge, another invitation, another petition, another argument, which will re-open the matter."[19] God is both incommensurate with Israel and mutually engaged with her. In Israel's speech about God, the irresolution remains. "For after Israel has given witness to the relatedness of [this God], one who hears the testimony still wonders: What in fact is the nature of this relationship?"[20]

A lawyer who finds herself having to decide whether to act as counsel for a situation will certainly want to make a careful, contextual analysis of the particular components of the situation and their implications.[21] She will want, too, to think carefully about what the rules of law and the rules of professional conduct require. But she may also want to keep in mind, along with other stories, the story of Moses at Sinai and what was required of him.

Rigorous analysis of a situation's texts and facts is necessary but will only sometimes issue in an obvious course of action. A greater or lesser leap of faith is necessary to a great many decisions that professionals and nonprofessionals alike must make. Remembered stories do not offer, as a substitute for the responsibility of judgment, a mechanical literalism of one-to-one correlations between story and present action.[22] Stories nurture apperception and the discernment of guiding presences between the lines of legal texts and between the facts of situations.

In the instance of whether to act as counsel for a situation, the story of Moses at Sinai raises the possibility that the lawyer's decision and the situation have a larger context: "When your son asks you in time to come, 'What is the meaning of the testimonies and statutes and the ordinances which the Lord our God has commanded you?' then you shall say to your son: 'We were Pharaoh's slaves in Egypt and the Lord brought us out of Egypt with a mighty hand' " (Deut. 6:20–21).

Paul Lehmann taught that it is "the *environment* of decision, not the *rules* of decision" that gives our acts their significance.[23] In the terms of Moses' saga, the environment is God's active presence in the midst of life in the delivery of Israel. No specific act of a lawyer (or any other) can realize a principle or rule of liberation in a literal way, but it can be a participatory sign of the environment of liberation in which it takes place.

Remembering the story of Moses and how he was free to put himself at risk, an attorney may choose to act as counsel for a situation. She will remember to expect not that she will remain invulnerably safe or certain but that she will be carried through this like other unstructured moral and legal spaces.

A lawyer who acts as counsel in this way and discovers herself in trouble with the bar or the law will also remember that both the bar and the law are constructed and not given worlds. Walter Brueggemann observes that the biblical world is spoken into availability and that there is, absent speech, no objectively given world that stands as a measure of the reality of the biblical one.[24] There are many other spoken worlds. Those among them that are regarded as something other than spoken, regarded as perhaps necessary or natural, have only been "spoken so long, so authoritatively, and so credibly that they appear to be given." [25]

The biblical texts debunk false appearances and false claims. They do so not by counterclaiming that their world is more truly given or that their story is *The* Story of Everything. They do so by engendering critique and liberation as it is the nature of the word of God in the biblical story-world to do. That world serves "as a subversive protest and as an alternative act of vision."[26]

The Moses saga is thoroughly and patently a world of words. Beyond its intersection with lawyering for a situation, it advances a more general, curing challenge. The American legal system and its subsidiary institutions like the American Bar Association are worlds that have been long, authoritatively, and credibly spoken. Against their settling into the self-destructive attitudes and establishments of givenness, the Moses saga projects an unsettling God, an unsettled people, and a chosen, ravaged man of law.

6. The Promise of Succession

I have dwelt upon complexities, risks, and threats in the saga. There is also great promise in it.

The death of Moses, like the attempt to kill him, is unfair to Moses. It is also risky for God. God cannot be God without words and Israel, and He cannot talk to Israel without a mouth. Therein lies promise for the joint future of God and Israel: There will be successors to Moses. In fact, a succession has already begun. In the story, it is set in motion in the beginning in the person of Aaron.

I have looked through Aaron as though he were not in the text. But he is there, importantly present. Moses suffers a speech impairment. In order to speak for God, he must have another. God appoints Aaron. Aaron is the first to share in the office of mouth for God. Moses' limitation makes the participation of another necessary and possible.

In quoting the story of Moses striking the rock at Meribah, I omitted Aaron's name. In fact, it is not Moses but his mouth Aaron who does the talking at Meribah, as he usually does. ("Moses and Aaron gathered the assembly together before the rock, and he said . . .") Perhaps Aaron fatefully includes himself in the overreaching. If he implies that he is a mover as well as a mouth, he, too, is playing God, and Moses' offense is his as well. He had been, moreover, a leader of the idolatry at Sinai. Whatever the explanation, he joins in Moses' transgression.[1] He will not cross the Jordan because, God says, he "rebelled against my commandment at the waters of Meribah" (Num. 20:24).[2]

Aaron climbs Mount Hor to die as God tells him to do. He is accompanied by his son Eleazar and Moses. At God's command Moses strips Aaron of his vestments and places them on Eleazar. After Aaron dies, "Moses and Eleazar came down from the mountain" (Num. 20:28). Moses' office is first shared with Aaron and then devolves upon Eleazar. The priesthood will continue.

And so will political-military leadership. At the end, Moses prays for the appointment of "someone over the congregation who shall go out before them and come in before them, who shall lead them out and bring them in," and Joshua is the answer (Num. 27:16–22, Deut. 34:9). Moses lays his hands on Joshua, and, after Moses dies, Joshua leads the people of Israel into the promised land (Joshua 1:1–11).

And not only will there be priests and commanders; prophets, too, will be sent. Moses promises: "God will raise up for you a prophet like me" (Deut. 18:15).[3] Moses' death makes room for others and gives hope for the future.

There is another, more delicately accomplished succession, that of the writer. It can be detected in process at several points in Deuteronomy, including a critical instance near the conclusion: "On that very day the Lord addressed Moses as follows: 'Ascend this mountain of the Abarim, Mount Nebo, which is in the land of Moab . . . ; you shall die there . . . ; because . . . you broke faith with me among the Israelites at the waters of Meribah-kadesh . . . , by failing to maintain my holiness among the Israelites'" (Deut. 32:48–52).[4]

These are words of God, and Moses does not report them. The writer offers them directly to the reader. At work here is what Robert Polzin describes as "a subtle but effective strategy on the part of the Deuteronomist gradually to blur or soften the unique status of Moses at the very same time that most of the . . . elements in the book explicitly enhance it."[5]

Deuteronomy is presented as an oration of Moses. In the course of it, Moses quotes words God has spoken to him. However, toward the end of the book, when Moses finishes speaking and writing, the narrator continues on. As Polzin points out, the narrator—not now Moses—five times reports God's words directly.[6] God's account of Moses' default at Meribah is one of these occasions. The narrator quotes God simply, without calling attention to the fact that he is suddenly doing so. With no break in the narrative flow, he writes as one who, like Moses, has been present, has heard God speak, and can now relate what God said. He writes as though he is "a privileged observer and reporter of God's words, just as he describes Moses describing himself to be."[7]

Both by leading us to question the exceptional status of Moses and by himself unobtrusively quoting God directly,[8] the narrator assumes some of Moses' role and little by little becomes, like his hero Moses, a mouth for God. We are thereby readied to accept the legitimacy of the writings that follow, when this narrator and others and compilers of their work begin to set forth the Deuteronomic history from Joshua through 2 Kings. The distinction between narrators' words and those of Moses becomes practically irrelevant.[9]

This is an enactment on the page not of rebellion or self-aggrandizement or disparagement but of the gift of succession. There will be priests, prophets, and political leaders—and tellers of their stories and of the stories of others after them. In the continuation of the story, there is assurance that God will have a people and that He will be present with them in His word.[10]

7. The Promise of Justice

The Moses saga seldom speaks expressly of justice. Its concern is with holiness. Justice is to be understood as an expression of holiness. Justice is a precise, practical, active form of regard for those who are types of fellow exiles and strangers along the way: "For the Lord your God is God of gods and Lord of lords, the great God, mighty and awesome, who is not partial and takes no bribe, who executes justice for the orphan and the widow, and who loves the strangers, providing them food and clothing. You shall also love the stranger, for you were strangers in the land of Egypt" (Deut. 10:17–19).[1]

God is and acts otherwise. He unaccountably chooses Israel as His people. For Israel to be holy as He is holy, its politics must be constituted by the justice that is love of fellow strangers, what Damrosch refers to as "a fellowship of exile."[2]

Israel's practice of this justice is to have future consequences that can only be hinted at in the sagas. In one of the earliest stories, God commands Abraham to leave his home and kin in Mesopotamia and head south where He promises to make of him "a great nation" (Gen. 12:1–2). God adds: "By you all the families of the earth shall bless themselves" (Gen. 12:2–3). Abraham's separation is to lead not only to the nation his descendants will become but also to all nations "blessing themselves" by him. From the start, Israel is set apart en route to a gathering blessing for all.[3]

Moses particularly embodies Israel's holiness. The story leaves him in an unknown grave outside the outsiders. He could not be left further from a pharaonic kingdom. But neither could he be left closer to others who find themselves aliens in a strange land. Or closer to the God whose word draws them into a fellowship of exile. It is a just conclusion.

The Moses saga gives narrative expression to the image of the word going forth and returning. But that image is also poetically elaborated in texts within the saga and in texts related to it. Psalm 114 is a related poem. I give it an extended, close reading in this last chapter of part 1.

The psalm is a poetic gem that uniquely illuminates the image of the word in circulation. My reading of it is consistent with the way that I read the stories and that I presumptuously, aspirationally align with the work of interpreters like Phyllis Trible. In patiently exposing a biblical text's details — the density that warns against "easy historicism or . . . facile theological extraction" — Trible allows it to yield "hints of its own advocacy, even if it does so with reticence and delicacy." [1]

I try to follow her good example. In doing so, I also bear in mind Walter Brueggemann's admonishment that an interpreter should "not be so protective of the text as to shrink from" its capacity to generate theological extrapolation. [2] I therefore undertake some of the same modest extrapolation here that I have been venturing already in connection with the stories.

The textual details of the poem matter and are helpful. Even so, readers may elect to proceed directly to part 2, where I return to Moses. Moses also figures in the psalm.

The Psalms are often the poetic, meditative representation of the heart of biblical narratives. So is it with Psalm 114. Its corresponding stories are from the exodus, the desert sojourn on the way north, and the entry into the promised land:

1 When Israel went out from Egypt,
    the house of Jacob from a people of strange language,
2 Judah became God's sanctuary,
    Israel his dominion.

3 The sea looked and fled;
    Jordan turned back.
4 The mountains skipped like rams,
    the hills like lambs.

5 Why is it, O sea, that you flee?
    O Jordan, that you turn back?
6 O mountains, that you skip like rams?
    O hills, like lambs?

7 Tremble, O earth, at the presence of the Lord,
    at the presence of the God of Jacob,
8 who turns the rock into a pool of water,
    the flint into a spring of water.

In these brief lines and with a few lyric strokes, Psalm 114 first brings to the mind's eye a sweeping view from the exodus across the parted waters of the sea to the entry into the promised land, when the Jordan River halted to let the people cross,[3] and then it renders the events as forms of praise. The fleeing sea and leaping mountains in the poem are the earth's trembling recognition, its worship, of God present in His people.

The poem gives pleasure and nourishment taken to heart just as it is. But then, too, it yields fruitful meaning to those who come to it from different interpretive approaches and who explore its possibilities at different levels of complexity. Biblical poetry is generally rewarding and welcoming in this generous, unprejudiced way. But there is added promise in the details and in the working at them.

Psalm 114 exhibits what Robert Alter refers to as "the focussing dynamic of biblical poetry."[4] Biblical poetry, he observes, tends "to move from large to small, container to contained, outer to inner," achieving a heightened concentration,[5] and that is what happens in Psalm 114. It moves from cataclysmic political-natural events to a spring, from earth-shaking to an immediate, inner moment. It glides down to a quiet pool of water that invites meditation. The God before whom the earth trembles is also the God who redeems his people and who preserves them with a flowing spring in their hour of need.[6]

The chief dynamic of Hebrew poetry — well illustrated by Psalm 114 — is parallelism.[7] One part of a verse is repeated in some form in the next. No repetition is simply a repetition. *No* repetition is *simply* a repetition. Repetition may serve multiple purposes; it may specify, elaborate, intensify, or complicate and enrich.

In this poem's first verse, "Israel" in one line is repeated or paralleled as "the house of Jacob" in the next, and "Egypt" in the first line returns as "a people of strange language" in the second. In verse 2, the parallel to "Judah" is "Israel," and "God's sanctuary" becomes "his dominion."

The parallelism performs significant work. Although house of Jacob is a familiar way of saying Israel, a people of strange language is an unusual substitution for Egypt.[8] The parallel is meant to excite reflection, and I shall return to it. Also intriguing is verse 2's use of dominion as the parallel for sanctuary. It makes clear that God's holy presence occupies a political entity.

All the remaining verses are also parallels. The sea in verse 3 is answered by the Jordan River, and the mountains/rams in verse 4 become hills/lambs.

The structure of Psalm 114 is another conventional device of Hebrew poetry. It is a kind of structuring parallelism or mirroring (a reversing or crossing) called chiasm. An example of a single line following the chiastic pattern *abba* is Ecclesiastes 7:1, translated as "A good name is better than precious ointment." In Hebrew it reads *tov shem mi-shemen tov*.[9] The whole of Psalm 114 forms an *abba* chiasm in which the first four verses are mirrored in the last four. The movement can be seen in this way:

1. When Israel went out from Egypt,
   the house of Jacob from a
      people of strange language,
2. Judah became God's sanctuary,
   Israel his dominion.
3. The sea looked and fled;
   Jordan turned back.
4. The mountains skipped like rams,
   the hills like lambs.

7. Tremble, O earth, at the presence
      of the Lord,
   at the presence of the God of Jacob,
8. who turns the rock into a pool of water,
   the flint into a spring of water.
5. Why is it, O sea, that you flee?
   O Jordan, that you turn back?
6. O mountains, that you skip like rams?
   O hills, like lambs?

As the reader makes the turn after verse 4 and starts back up the page, the tense changes from past to present,[10] and the stanza formed by verses 3 and 4 is mirrored in the stanza formed by verses 5 and 6: the sea and Jordan of verse 3 are repeated in verse 5, and the mountains/rams of verse 4 are repeated in verse 6.

Verse 7 then gathers the sea and the Jordan River together with the mountains and hills to become "the earth." It also ties verses 1 and 2 to verses 3 to 6. Its emphasis on the presence of God completes understanding of the great political and natural events of Israel's beginning as functions of His power. Israel went out from Egypt and Judah became God's sanctuary because God was actively present, and the earth trembled at these events because He was present in them. The earth is in movement: the sea flees, the Jordan turns back, and the mountains and hills skip. In the forms available to it—fleeing, turning back, skipping—the earth makes response to God's presence among His people. Israel was brought from Egypt and into Canaan with acts of worship brought from the earth.[11] The historical and the theological, the natural and the political, the poetic and the liturgical, join at God's active presence in this people in this poem.

That brings us to verse 8: "Who turns the rock into a pool of water, / the flint into a spring of water."

Has the chiasm played out? What does verse 8 have to do with either verse 1 or verse 2? Verses 1–7 lead us to understand that the presence of God is politically-naturally-liturgically dynamic. His presence is to be seen in the actions of the exodus and the entry into Canaan. Judah became His sanctuary, and the earth responded astoundingly to His presence. But what has that to do with any parallel to be discovered in verse 8?

Verse 8 is loaded. Its references to rock and water correspond to the sea and mountains of the earlier verses. However, in verses 3–6 the poet speaks first of water and then of solid land, whereas in verse 8, rock precedes water. Verse 8 also reverses the action. In verses 3–6 water parts to provide dry ground for the people to cross, but in verse 8 the dry rock opens to provide water for the people to drink, and this reversal in action turns the emotional focus from natural and political upheaval to nurturing care.[12]

More pointedly, verse 8 concludes the poem with the introduction of a new narrative reference. Verse 7 has been a summary: the miracles at the exodus and conquest were responses to the presence of God. But verse 8, in the poem's only identifying characterization of God, describes Him as the one who turns rock to water. The poem's narrative subject is chiefly the exodus from Egypt but also the entry into Canaan—until the last verse, when the reference shifts to another story.

I have already rehearsed the story of Moses striking the rock to make water flow from it and his offending God in the process. That was the Numbers version, and it is placed in the narrative after the people leave Sinai. There is another version in Exodus placed before they arrive at Sinai. The desert sands have left the people thirsty but yield no water. Moses intercedes. God instructs him to strike a rock with his staff. Moses does so, and water flows from the rock (Exod. 17:1–7). All is well. Moses gives God no offense. The psalm does not mention Moses, but I find it impossible to think of the story without thinking of him. I expect the same was true of the poet and his audience. The allusion to the benign version allows the reader to think well of Moses, free of praise or blame. The shift to the story of the miracle is abrupt but almost unfelt and unseen.

"Within a small compass," Alter notes, "through the use of intricate and closely clustered devices of linkage and repetition, [the Bible's lyric poetry] can create the illusion of simultaneity, offering to the mind's eye a single panorama with multiple elements held nicely together." [13] Psalm 114 achieves such simultaneity. By ending with water from a rock as a structural parallel to the exodus at its beginning, the psalm artfully lays out the exodus, the conquest, and this episode so that the reader then sees and accepts their linkage effortlessly: the presence of God draws a response from the earth.

Alter observes how the license of another biblical poem reproduces in its narrative sweep "a strong and recurrent rhythm of God's action in history." [14] It projects "out of the stunning experience at the Reed Sea [or Red Sea] a larger pattern of God's powerful—one might say 'heroic'—acts in history." [15] The narrative sweep of Psalm 114, too, projects this larger pattern of God's acts. As God brought Israel from Egypt and into Canaan, so did He bring water from a rock in the desert. But Psalm 114 adds a small, quiet touch to its offering of the pattern of God's acts. It allows the reader to contemplate the nurturing provision of water as of a piece with the heroic act of the exodus: The presence of God draws a response from the earth to redeem and sustain His people.

The first verse uses the phrase "a people of strange language" as a parallel to "Egypt" ("When Israel went out from Egypt, the house of Jacob from a people of strange language"). Possibilities for interpreting this parallel are opened by the same chiastic association of the first and last verses that poetically connects water from a rock to the exodus.

The exodus is the template of God's actions in the story. When Psalm 114 gently associates the miraculous provision of water in the desert with the exodus pattern, it links turning the sea into dry ground with turning rock to water: God redeems His people from Egypt in the exodus / He redeems them from thirst in the desert; He brings Israel freedom from a people of strange language / He brings them water from a rock. The relation is poetic. It is poetry.

Blues is often about singing the blues, country music is often about singing country music, and the Psalms are often about psalmody. Psalm 114 is by inference, I think, such a psalm. The implied, mirrored connection is that from a people of strange language went out a people with language for psalms. And the narrative series becomes: Israel was brought from Egypt; water was brought from rock; poetry is brought from the prosaic. The suggestion is that God's word not only moves the sea to divide and the rock to open with water. It also moves the Psalmist to sing. The reader is invited to receive the poem as a gift belonging to the pattern of God's acts. God frees His people. He also nourishes and delights them — with poetry as well as with water. Psalm 114 celebrates the presence of God in His word accomplishing freedom, sustenance, and poetry. The earth trembles; the poet writes. The poet's art is turned to praise.

There is another element in the series. If you read the poem well and it works, you cannot but understand that your interpretation is a gift. It has happened not because you are such a smart and clever reader ("see what a fine interpretation I have made"). It has happened because, just as Israel was led from Egypt and just as water was drawn from a rock and just as the poem was made to flow from the poet, so is interpretation a miracle brought from the reader by the hand of God. The gift makes the reader participant in the freeing, sustaining subject of the poem.[16]

The connection between the three events — Israel going out from a people of strange language, flint turning to a spring of water, and the writer producing Psalms — highlights God's mighty acts as natural and political wonders performed on behalf of His people. He has been powerfully present in His word, both freeing and sustaining His people.

The word does not come to a stop among the people. The dynamic includes a return. Moses is mouth for God. The people, insofar as they conform to the law, are a medium for His presence. They receive the word, and they return it. Earlier, I noted that there is not an ear for God equivalent to the mouth for God, and, following Isaiah's image of the hydrologic cycle, I suggested that the word's fruitful return is implicit in its utterance. When it is spoken, the word of God, the *davar*, animates His people, gives them voice, accomplishes its purpose, and returns to — is heard by — Him.

The law drops like rain not to return empty but to accomplish its purpose and return in the form of ascription of greatness to God.[17] One form of return is the obedience of the people. Another is their praise. The song of Moses in Exodus 15 after the victorious crossing of the Reed Sea begins:

> I will sing to the Lord, for he has triumphed gloriously;
>   horse and rider he has thrown into the sea.
> The Lord is my strength and my might,
>   he has become my salvation;
> this is my God, and I will praise him,
>   my father's God, and I will exalt him.

God accomplishes the exodus, and his mighty act is forthwith turned into art and returned to Him as praise. Psalm 114 brings to the mind's eye a sweeping view from the exodus to the conquest, and in doing so it, too, renders the events as artful forms of praise.

Alter says: "Again and again in Psalms, man's divine gift of articulateness, his ability to confirm God's majesty in song, is the culmination of the poem and of the whole order of creation. . . . God speaks the world and man into being, and man answers by speaking songs unto the Lord." [18]

II

The Encompassing Women

Moses is not the only one who lies in a lonely grave outside. In this he has the company of Rachel. She, too, was buried along the way. Her story will return me to the subject of intercession and exclusion. But not yet. Rachel does not figure directly in the Moses saga. Other women do, and they have their own contributions to make. They take me back to the beginning of the saga.

Moses is the leading human figure in the exodus story, but narratively and substantively, he follows women, including two midwives. The text invites the reader to construe Moses in their image and therewith provides an additional way to think of him: Moses as midwife at the delivery of Israel.

The Book of Exodus opens in the comfortable, received manner with no clue of the decisive role women will play: "These are the names of the *sons* of *Israel* who came to Egypt with *Jacob*" (1:1). And it lists the sons. No mothers. No daughters. And next it says: "The total number of people *born to Jacob* was seventy" (1:5). And when the story then turns to the Egyptians, this scene, too, opens with an all-male cast. Pharaoh warns his people that the enslaved Israelites pose a threat to Egypt because they "are more numerous and powerful than we" (1:9).[1] He imagines the possibility of war and of Hebrew defection to the enemy. To lower the Israelites' birthrate and to reduce the threat of revolt, Pharaoh's people "set taskmasters over them to oppress them with forced labor" (1:11). The slaves are made to build cities and to do "hard service in mortar and brick and in every kind of field labor" (1:14). But the more they are oppressed, the more they multiply and spread, "so that the Egyptians came to dread the Israelites" (1:12).

Riding this Egyptian anxiety, women enter the text and set in motion a politics of resistance.[2] When Pharaoh's first policy fails to control the growth of the Israelite population, he is driven to enlist the aid of midwives, and abruptly the text produces two of them, Shiphrah and Puah: "When you act as midwives to the Hebrew women, and see them on the birthstool," Pharaoh directs them, "if it is a boy, kill him; but if it is a girl, she shall live" (1:16).[3]

The midwives—they "feared God"—defy the order and lie when Pharaoh confronts them. They say: "The Hebrew women are not like the Egyptian women; for they are vigorous and give birth before the midwife comes to them" (1:19). (The word for "vigorous" can be read as "like wild beasts.")

The slave mothers bear more babies, God rewards the midwives with families of their own,[4] and the proliferation of children presses more heavily upon Pharaoh. He must venture a new policy. He revises his command to the midwives and broadcasts it to "all his people, 'Every boy that is born to the Hebrews you shall throw into the Nile, but you shall let every girl live' " (1:22).

This concise story of rebellious midwives, fecund mothers, and fearful Egyptians swells with satire, irony, and suggestion. Driven to exhaustion, the Israelites nonetheless continue to copulate and to reproduce in the fertile valley of the Nile. The alien labor source that drives Egyptian development achieves a critical mass that cannot be controlled, so that Pharaoh's fearful imagination propels him to ever more extreme measures. The climactic madness is fixed in his order that the Nile, the nation's source of life, become the means for mass infanticide.

The story then shifts momentarily to a domestic scene and then to quiet transactions among women. A Levite man marries a Levite woman. She conceives and, presumably aided by the midwives, bears a son. Against the fury of Pharaoh's command, she hides her baby as long as she can and, when she must, sets him in a basket among reeds at the spot on the riverbank where Pharaoh's daughter habitually bathes. The baby's elder sister keeps watch nearby.

Pharaoh's daughter arrives, and the text works her seamlessly into the female conspiracy. She takes pity on the crying infant, and, in defiance of her father but in narrative alliance with the other women, she delivers the baby from the river. Pharaoh's daughter — even she — joins the resistance of midwives and mothers. Naturally. How could she have done otherwise? Would she wash herself in the river as the little corpses of babies float by? Would she throw another in? What could Pharaoh have been thinking? How ignorant could he be of women? What confusions does he express by killing boys but letting girls go free?

Before God enters the story to harden Pharaoh's heart, Pharaoh has proved himself mad. His madness is not personal but political and systemic, and it passes as a rational policy that proceeds in responsive, proportional stages: First oppress the slaves, then enlist their midwives, then, as necessary, make a posse comitatus of the whole. It is impossible now to read the story without seeing in Pharaoh a prototype of the modern politics of nationalism: enemies without, aliens within perceived as enemies who must be destroyed, a rational construction of national interest that is both destructive and self-destructive, and a final spasm of powerlessness realized as a wholesale surrender to the use of force.

Within the terms of the story, Pharaoh aligns himself and his nation with oppression and death. The women align themselves with each other, delivery, and life. The reader scarcely notices that the women occupy the sane, steady center of the story by committing acts of rebellion and deceit.

And when the story continues, it is generous with irony. At the suggestion of the baby's sister, the Egyptian princess pays the Hebrew mother to nurse her own Hebrew son. After the child is reared into young manhood, the princess adopts him into the royal house. Pharaoh, even in his most manic dreams, could not have envisioned a Hebrew son clasped to the bosom of his family.

The rich narrative play is not a virtuosic extravagance. It adorns the women to highlight their shaping, sustaining presence. The story is in the process of producing Moses. First it gives us midwives, a mother, a sister, and a princess — women woven into a verbal womb around the child.

There is some textual as well as nontextual evidence for supposing that, like the princess, the midwives, too, are Egyptian.[5] The possibility is sufficient. That they could be either Egyptian or Hebrew is testimony to a sympathetic company undeterred by ethnic, political, or religious boundaries. There is loyalty within this company, but it is not loyalty to the reigning power. None of the women acts deliberately to become an outlaw. Each simply acts humanly. The text forms them protectively around a male child to give him life and prominence in a male-dominated world that would otherwise kill him.

Among these women, at this point in the story, the midwives draw attention. The text cultivates an interpretive connection between them and Moses by its deployment of names. After the opening list of Israelites in Egypt, there is a considerable interval in the story when the only names to appear are those of Shiphrah, Puah, and Moses. The text speaks of Moses' father, mother, and sister, but it does not identify them until much later. All it says about his adoptive mother is that she is Pharaoh's daughter. Such silence is pregnant in a book that begins: "These are the names . . ." And it brings to the fore the names that do appear. Shiphrah and Puah are linked by emphasis with Moses. The reader wonders why, and the word "Moses" helps supply an answer.

That name is a play on words. The Egyptian word *mose* means variously "to beget a child," "to be born," or "child," and was employed as an element in names, as in Thut-mose: "Thut is born" or "son Thut." Pharaoh's daughter could easily have used *mose* in naming her adopted son, but she does not. Instead she chooses a Hebrew word. It is as close in sound to the Egyptian as moses is to mose, but it has a very different meaning. The Hebrew *moshe* means "to draw out." "She named him He Who Draws Out, 'because,' she said, 'I drew him out of the water'" (Exod. 2:10).[6]

This is a play on grammar as well as on words. The text gives us an Egyptian princess who apparently speaks Hebrew, and the reader expects her to employ the passive voice to match her meaning. She should name her adopted son "He Who Was Drawn Out" because she drew him out of the water. Instead she uses the active voice and calls him "He Who Draws Out."

In this way the text invites the reader to understand that Moses' defining performance in the exodus will replicate his adoptive mother's action. He will do for others what she did for him. The Egyptian princess draws a Hebrew slave child from the river. That child, become an Egyptian prince, will draw other Hebrew slaves through the sea to freedom. Gender and circumstance change, but the action remains the same. Thus does the text by artful association lead the reader from Shiphrah and Puah to the Egyptian princess to Moses.

Drorah O'Donnell Setel notes that the exodus event is "a dramatic image of birth: the parting of the waters of the sea. As if to underline this connection, the Hebrew word for Egypt . . . is also associated with labor pains."[7] Moses is on hand for the exodus, but Shiphrah and Puah are the first to deliver children of Israel in defiance of Pharaoh. They are the archetype, and they imprint the story. The origin of Israel is a delivery, and Moses is the midwife.

When the Book of Exodus encourages the reader to associate Moses with midwifery, it does so without devaluing the labor of women. This is a creditable achievement, and its elements warrant notice.

At least as much as midwives now, the midwives of Egypt would have been steeped in the reality of blood — the blood of life and the blood of death. And they would have known from their own hands the lingering, strong smell of it, and the joy and celebration as well as the suffering and agony that accompanies it.

The text does not idly appropriate the images of mothers' labor and midwives' work. The exodus event with which the text associates childbirth is at the same time horrifically destructive and miraculously life-giving. It is preceded by the terrible physical suffering of the Egyptians, and in its accomplishment many die. Israel, too, suffers great trauma before and as it emerges. When Moses successfully delivers Israel to the far side of the sea, women sing with their first breath of freedom and go out "with tambourines and with dancing" (15:20). The pain of birth is done, and joy takes over. The frenzy of the celebration is left to the reader's imagination: powerful women in the desert, released from the constraints of Egypt, smacking tambourines, an unearthly timbre in their voices, their feet whirling sand into a storm.

Implicit in all this presentation of the exodus as parturition is the text's unsentimental respect for women and their labor. Such appreciative valuing of childbirth is not altogether singular. Other biblical texts regard the obstetric metaphor as necessary to the poetic imagery for God. Psalm 22:10–11, for example, addresses God as both midwife and mother: "For you brought me forth from the womb, / made me safe upon the breasts of my mother. / Upon you was I cast from the womb, / from the womb of my mother, my God are you." [8]

Moses as midwife is a reflection of God as midwife, and in the story of the exodus, women's work is placed at the center of imagery for God's action. A male sense of inside status is not restored when the story later reserves it to priests to draw much animal blood in sacrifice and to splash it on altars. The bellowing of the animals and the stench of their blood on hot stones produces no life and is no compensatory substitute for motherhood and midwifery.

The order of the sexes is not thereby reversed — a prejudice against men substituted for a prejudice against women. The differentiation of the sexes is transvalued.

I want to be as clear as Phyllis Trible in noting that the biblical employment of human sexuality in talking about God and His action in history is not a description of God in sexual terms but a statement of His transcendence and, I would add, His politics, for the emancipating conspiracy that Shiphrah and Puah set in motion has its origin in the transcendence of God ("They feared God"). Trible begins where the Bible begins, with the first chapter of Genesis and the creation of humans who, as male and female, are made in the image of God: "And created God humankind in his image; / in the image of God created he him, / male and female created he them" (Gen. 1:27). [9] In this metaphor "male and female" is the vehicle and "the image of God" is its tenor. [10]

With respect to God, the metaphor points toward His otherness.

Trible notes that His image is "neither male nor female, nor a combination of the two." [11] The metaphor is a medium for speaking about a transcendent God with clues from the human language and experience that He transcends. Because it is a speaking beyond itself, such biblical "metaphor allows no resting place in the image of God female—nor in the image of God male." [12] One image is countered by another. At one time or another God is mother, midwife, and father. [13] The language of the Bible thus "preserves with exceeding care the otherness of God." [14]

With respect to male and female, the metaphor points toward their difference and similarity, their separation and unity. [15] In the biblical poem, male and female are created simultaneously and presented to the reader as a verbal unit, differentiated but united. In the sentence and its context in the first chapter of Genesis, male and female are lexically and grammatically equal terms. The relation will shortly be overtaken by hierarchy as the story proceeds, but insofar as the image of God is concerned, humankind is male-and-female.

So do womanly metaphors continue in the vocabulary of the biblical writers undiminished and undiminishing in their speech about God. Unsurprisingly, when the writer needs a powerful image for the powerful act of God in the exodus, the obstetric metaphor presents itself.

At times—strikingly, unforgettably, terribly—the biblical texts enact abuse of women. Phyllis Trible identifies them as texts of terror. The story of Hagar is an example (Gen. 16, 21). Hagar is a lone Egyptian woman in bondage to the Hebrews in Canaan. She flees, making her own exodus. But an angel arrests her and forces her to return to be abused further. "Inexplicably," Trible writes, "the God who later, seeing . . . the suffering . . . of a slave people, comes down to deliver them *out of the hand* of the Egyptians . . . here identifies with the oppressor and orders a servant to return not only to bondage but also to affliction." [16] There are other examples: like the nameless concubine in Judges 19, who is tortured, gang-raped, and cut in pieces.

However, in the beginning of the exodus story, women and their labor are valued and placed at the center. The image of the midwife is thereby made available for just labor of its own, and Moses may justly be counted among the company of Shiphrah and Puah.

"Show us a hulking woman with scales, blindfold, and sword," write Dennis Curtis and Judith Resnik, "and the association is immediate: Justice." [17] She is the accepted image, usually stationed in an exalted location atop a pedestal or public building, gripping her sword and scales.

Were there to be an image of the holiness that the Moses saga counts as justice, it would be a midwife, on the ground, her eyes wide open, and her hands fully employed in the work of delivery.

Modern teachers, including teachers of law, say that they employ the midwife method. They identify it as maieutic from the Greek rather than as meyaledethic from the Hebrew. They do not have Shiphrah, Puah, or Moses in mind. They are affiliating themselves instead with Socrates, the hero of Plato's dialogues, who says he is a midwife. Midwifery in the biblical stories provokes reassessment of the claim.[1]

Socrates introduces himself as a midwife in Plato's dialogue *Theaetetus*. He says that his mother was "a midwife, brave and burly," and that he is one, too, because he aids in delivering the thoughts brought forth by young men.[2] He claims that his art is in most respects like that of midwives, "but differs, in that I attend men and not women, and I look after their souls when they are in labour, and not after their bodies."[3]

In the course of a long argument in the *Theaetetus*, however—and on this point I depend upon Gregory Vlastos's interpretation—he does not deliver the brainchild of another. Instead he attributes to the docile interlocutor an imaginative construct of his own making.[4] Socrates is the productive party. Either not much of midwifery is involved (Socrates draws little of the subject from Theaetetus) or something other than midwifery is performed (Socrates provides the theses with their real interest).

Moreover, Socrates refers to "pangs of labor" induced by his art and says that they are of such "perplexity and travail" as to be "even worse" than the labor pains of women.[5] He adds that, although the work women do as midwives is very important, it is not so important as his own.[6] And, he says further, when pregnant men give birth to ideas, the product, too, is worthier. According to Socrates' statements in the *Symposium*, the souls of creative men "conceive that which is proper for the soul to conceive," and they give birth to children "fairer and more immortal" than the babies born to mothers.[7] In Socratic midwifery males *displace* the mother, the midwife, and the blessed event.[8]

In a thoughtful essay on Socratic midwifery, M. F. Burnyeat refers to the "compelling naturalness" of the metaphor of the mind giving birth to ideas, and he believes that it corresponds to felt experience.[9] I wonder whether what he feels is felt as compellingly natural by others and whether the feeling devalues the pain and significance of labor. Do women who have given birth to babies feel that they also give birth to ideas? Those whom I have recently consulted say no.

Modern practitioners of the question-and-answer method of teaching —as exemplified by Professor Kingsfield of *The Paper Chase*[10]—routinely identify their method as maieutic or Socratic. Although the method is better identified as catechetical, eristic, or simply question-and-answer, it can be sensibly called Socratic to the extent that Professor Kingsfield stars in a rerun of the *Theaetetus*.

Philip Areeda of the Harvard Law School was a distinguished practitioner of the question-and-answer method. He identified it as Socratic and commended it to others. He said that it immerses students in the methodology of the lawyer's work: deciphering texts, reconciling textual inconsistencies, grappling with principles, making arguments by analogy, etc.[11] In class, the teacher frames a series of questions in such a way that students are cleverly led to answers that they think they have discovered for themselves.[12] The method succeeds when the student internalizes the process and develops the ability to ask the kinds of questions that the teacher raises in class.[13] The teacher could offer lectures on legal method, but "methodologies are better absorbed when actually practiced by the student and when made concrete by actually being used to solve a legal problem."[14]

The method can work well in the hands of teachers as skilled as Areeda, especially in the early weeks of such classes as Property Law and Contracts, but no more than Socrates in the *Theaetetus* do teachers in law school classes perform deliveries.[15] The very thing that commends the method—the higher degree of absorption—discloses its underlying image to be that of osmosis. The dense mind and experience of the teacher flow to the less concentrated student. This is not the movement of childbirth. The midwife does not come to her work with a fetus tucked away out of view that she inserts into the womb and then extracts so skillfully that the mother has the impression that the labor and the baby are her own.[16]

Perhaps, too, negative effects of the law school method's aggressive practice may have greater specific impacts on women.[17] Some critics suggest, for example, that the method is an authoritarian, competitive form of interaction that may tend to exclude and silence women in particular.[18]

In biblical usage God and Moses deliver Israel, and the association of their performances with midwifery pays respect to women's labor. When Socrates draws no beliefs from another or performs a delivery of sorts but regards it as impressively superior to childbirth, and when teachers of law induce students to absorb a methodology or beleaguer them until they succumb, they do not act as midwives, certainly not in keeping with the biblical example. The metaphor of midwifery is either unjustly employed or works only for those with an impoverished and impoverishing sense of what is involved in childbirth.[19] Socrates and Professor Kingsfield are not Shiphrah and Puah.

11. Socratic Midwifery That Is

The image of the midwife fails in the *Theaetetus,* but the hero of that dialogue is not the same Socrates that he is in the other dialogues. There is another Socrates with a better claim to be a midwife. This is the Socrates who appears in dialogues that Vlastos identifies as falling in Plato's early period of writing. (The sequence of the dialogues is debated. I make limited use of Vlastos's approach because I find it the most presently useful of the valid interpretations.)[1]

In Vlastos's reckoning, the *Theaetetus* comes from Plato's middle period of writing.[2] The Socrates of these materials lays "to rest the demon of contentiousness within him" and becomes the character who supplies his own subject matter; he refutes theses that he has himself proposed.[3] In other dialogues he will become a didact who expounds truth to consenting listeners.[4]

The Socrates of the early dialogues is complex and pugnacious: "Show that what I say is false," he challenges an interlocutor in the *Gorgias.* "If not, stand up to questioning."[5] This Socrates never claims that he is a midwife, but I think that his action traces the movement of one. He draws statements of belief from interlocutors and then draws from them others that are inconsistent with the first. The proponent produces both the theses and the material for their refutation.[6]

The demonstration of inconsistency is not precious work. It often humiliates the interlocutor and leaves onlookers and readers alike in perplexity. I. F. Stone says that Socrates does not so much bring thoughts to birth as "stifle them one by one as they emerge from the dialectical womb. The midwife seems to be an expert abortionist."[7] Stone's is a credible view. Another is possible, and I pursue it: Socrates' destructive exercises are the delivery of a certain kind of life.[8]

Men are not so wise as they think. They can be freed from their pretense through robust, testing dialogue that provides no relieving certainty but does fuel the ongoing quest for moral truth that constitutes the worthy life.[9] The mandatory, frequently stated prerequisite for participation is to say only what one truly believes about how best to live.[10] Socrates' exposure of these beliefs' inconsistency *is* destructive and shaming and in this sense painful, but it is necessary to the beginning and continuation of an examined life and is more delivery than abortion. He delivers a new life.

The Hebrew midwives deliver Israelites into a hard life in Egypt, and Moses delivers them into a long trial in the desert. Socrates liberates young men of Athens for a lifelong, periodically humiliating struggle. He is as loyal and vulnerable in the work as Shiphrah and Puah are. To Critias he says: "You come to me as though I professed to know about the questions which I ask, and as though I could, if I only would, agree with you. Whereas the fact is that I enquire with you into the truth of that which is advanced from time to time, just because I do not know." [11]

Socrates employs irony, but he does not engage in put-ons. He is fundamentally invested in what he does. "I should like to examine further," he says at one point, "for no light matter is at stake, nothing less than the rule of human life." [12] His trial and death realize the truth that all along he has risked his own life in his labor.[13] After his trial and under sentence of death, he explores with Crito the proposal of escape to a neighboring city. He cannot do it. What would he say to the citizens of another city? Who could he be? How could he live "eating and drinking . . . , having gone abroad in order that I may get a dinner"? [14] As James Boyd White says, "he cannot leave without abandoning himself." [15] He cannot be more fully committed.[16]

This Socrates is more the midwife, but not if he is equally dismissive of women. At his trial he remarks that certain men are "no better than women." [17] The statement is made in the context of Socrates' refusal to bring his family into court, as others have done, for the doleful purpose of tearfully petitioning for his acquittal. He will not discredit himself, the court, and the state in this manner, for, he says, men of reputation ought not demean themselves. And then he adds:

> I have seen men of reputation, when they have been condemned, behaving in the strangest manner: they seemed to fancy that they were going to suffer something dreadful if they died, and that they could be immortal if you only allowed them to live; and I think that such are a dishonour to the state, and that any stranger coming in would have said of them that the most eminent men of Athens, to whom the Athenians themselves give honour and command, are no better than women.[18]

The comment about women is what a "stranger coming in" would say. This may be the strange Socrates' way of expressing what he had himself spent a life concluding: The most eminent men of Athens are no better than women — or than other men. Athens was built around proud men, Thomas Brickhouse and Nicholas Smith observe, and Socrates' "mission had the effect of showing young people how little their fathers really knew about how to live, and how ill-supported their values and traditions were."[19]

Socrates' critique proceeds within the shared morality and is directed at received conduct sustained and limited by the received institutions.[20] Nevertheless, he challenges the most fundamental understanding and practice of justice.[21] What he expresses variously in the dialogues and finds unrefuted to the end is that "we ought not to retaliate or render evil for evil to any one, whatever evil we may have suffered from him."[22] This is not an assault on patriarchy; it is a trial of the masculine, heroic tradition.[23] And although it is no express valuation of women, it does confront the source of their devaluation.

Socrates did not practice his strange vocation with women. As Martha Nussbaum points out, however, he could not really do so, since women were not commonly to be found outdoors.[24] And then, in the life after death he anticipates, when, he says, he will "be able to examine the leader of the great Trojan expedition; or Odysseus or Sisyphus," he will be able to examine numberless other men as well—and at last, he adds, "women too! What infinite delight would there be in conversing with them and asking them questions!"[25]

There is then a Socrates, or the possibility of a Socrates, who practices a type of midwifery. In his life after death, released from the constraints of Athenian life, he would continue his work in company with the valued, original practitioners of the art.

It is textually sufficient to say that the Hebrew midwives delivered babies, feared God, and defied Pharaoh. But it is rewarding to find their example unfolding more fully in poetic association with Moses: his delivery of Israel is like theirs, his complete devotion to the subject and the community is like theirs, his guidance from the higher politics of God is like theirs, and his resistance to the established order of Egypt is like theirs. The associations enhance understanding of both Moses and the midwives.

The Socrates of the early dialogues, in obedience to his own god, gives himself to delivering the worthy life. The leading men of Athens perceive his practice to be capitally subversive. I read this Socrates as a midwife after the fashion of Shiphrah, Puah, and Moses.

I detect no embarrassment when modern practitioners of the question-and-answer method of teaching casually refer to it as maieutic or Socratic. There is attraction in the figure of the midwife, and I, too, am drawn to it. I should like to imagine myself as a midwife: The teacher of law who delivers the lawyers that students have conceived the notion to become; the lawyer delivering clients' thoughts, plans, hopes, and aspirations in forms nurtured by law. (A group of committed women in Athens, Georgia, conceived the idea for a day care center for the children of homeless families, and lawyers helped give it birth as a nonprofit corporation.) I could then say that there is correspondence between the teaching and the practice of law: the teacher performs for students a type of the exemplary maieutic service that they are expected to perform for others.

I should like to press the idea that the teaching and practice of law can be maieutic or, better, meyaledethic. I should especially like to do so against arguments that the image is sentimental. But I hesitate. The justness of the metaphor requires testing.

The early, maieutic Socrates comes to his encounters without notes in hand or a carefully planned series of hypotheticals and follow-up questions in mind. He makes no assignments. He has no lesson to be absorbed by students. He has neither information nor methodology.[26] He brings himself, and he takes his material from the interlocutors. He engages them in dialogic trial not because questions and answers are more effective than lecturing but because only so do the participants have something to examine. He draws from them one at a time what they truly believe about life, and his life as well as theirs is at issue.

That the law school method is not Socratic has been well argued.[27] That we nonetheless continue to say that it is may be a statement of aspiration: We would be more like Socrates. If so, the claim may serve as a critical encouragement to do better, and some legal scholars have taken it just this way to good effect.[28] But the broad challenge of the Hebrew midwives, Moses, and Socrates is not to be exhausted in the reformation of teaching methods and classroom dynamics. More than a method, maieutics is a way of being and acting, a way of living in delivering the lives of others.[29]

What would it really mean for a lawyer or a teacher of law to be a midwife as Shiphrah and Puah, Moses and Socrates were midwives? Answers will likely be several and open-ended, and they will depend upon experiments followed by curing, critical examination in the community of practitioners. I offer a venture of my own for scrutiny.

This report of my experiment is an act of hope rather than a statement of accomplishment. I feel obliged to offer it for testing because I imagine a reader asking: "What do you mean by midwifery in the legal profession? How can a lawyer or teacher be a midwife? Can you not give a specific example?" I feel bound to draw the example from my own experience in response to the imagined reader asking: "How do *you* act? What are *you* actually doing as a lawyer and teacher of law? Have you made no attempt to practice what you talk about and believe?"

In what follows, I am not Socrates. I am the interlocutor who speaks in anticipation of critical dialogue that will prove as unexpectedly humiliating as curing.

For many years I taught a course in jurisprudence, and for a long time in teaching it I pressed students to ask two questions: "Who am I as a lawyer?" and "What am I doing when I do law?"[1] It became increasingly necessary to take our readings less from standard jurisprudence and more from such sources as the Moses saga and Plato — and Greek tragedy, Icelandic sagas, and modern works like *Black Elk Speaks,* Bessie Head's *Maru,* and Toni Morrison's *Beloved.*[2]

To read such texts in context meant that my students and I had to read them consciously in *our* context as well as in what we could construct of theirs. And that in turn meant that we had to take our law school context more seriously. We needed to explore how my life as a lawyer in a nexus of responsibilities and theirs as law students could be part of the material to which we would bring our imagination and critical scrutiny.

All of us had extracurricular responsibilities that had acquainted us with the streets of Athens, and we knew people there who led hard lives. It seemed natural that we should add to the discipline of reading texts together the discipline of responding together to the school's neighbors, those who inhabit the streets, shelters, and jails.

Encouraged by the example of others at other schools, I set in motion the Public Interest Practicum, a two-semester course with a summer component.[3] Participants began in the second year of law school, and most continued through their third year to help conduct the class.

Other teachers of law have noted that there is a connection between Socrates and clinical education.[4] Philip Areeda unintentionally made a case for clinics when, in endorsing the Socratic method, he noted that students are more likely to stay awake and to learn better when they actually practice thinking like lawyers and use the peculiar logic of law to solve real problems. In clinics, students really do have to employ legal materials like lawyers, and classroom stupefaction is rarely a problem.[5] Clinics have a substantial history, and my experiment, which was in part clinic-like, was coincident with a renewed interest in them and in theories of lawyering.[6] I was a latecomer on the fringes.

When the class ventured out of the law school and into Athens, some of our early stops were at sites in the legal system. One was an early morning bail hearing at the local jail in a room set aside for the purpose. Among the assembled prisoners was a young man who wouldn't bend to the metal folding chair provided. He remained nearly straight, his body in contact with only the top of the chairback and the front edge of the seat. His eyelids were heavy, as though he had been waked too soon from sleep. Or hadn't been to sleep. Whenever his heels lost purchase on the floor, he slid down and out of the chair. The presiding magistrate court judge was upset by his attitude and his extensive record and set a bail so high there was no chance of an early release. When the judge announced the amount, the prisoner's only perceptible response was the silent flexing of his jaw muscles. He was not very old. I thought he was fighting back tears. Later, the judge told me he thought I was wrong.

That visit had two consequences. Our class subsequently worked with the public defender/legal aid clinic in providing a range of services to clients in addition to criminal defense, and I agreed to serve as a magistrate from time to time as the need arose.

Another early stop was juvenile court. The first hearing centered on a fourteen-year-old girl. Early in September, not long after school began, she had been cited for truancy. No one tried to get her back in school. Instead, a hearing was set for mid-January. She lost the fall semester. At the January hearing, the judge gave her a severe lecture and depicted the bleak future waiting for her if she failed to get her life in order. She was forlorn. She found it hard to sit still. She shuffled her feet. When the judge threatened to have her detained in what is known as the Youth Development Center and when he put hard questions to her that she did not want to answer, she looked down at the table and the fingers of her right hand went to the back of her head for the reassurance of a quick, light caress of her ponytail curl. She was overweight. A scar angled across her face. She hadn't much to say for herself. But the ponytail had been so carefully done. And there was a gold ring in one ear and another in her nose and a gold chain around her neck. These may have been the adornments of a brutal sex trade that young girls are forced into, but I hoped that they were emblems of an embryonic core of self-esteem, some small, stubborn sense of self-worth that could yet be delivered.

From that first encounter in juvenile court, some of the law students went on to become court-appointed special advocates, others developed an educational program for children on the verge of involvement with the juvenile justice system, and others began to work with young people doing time in the county's alternative school. As was generally true in the course, these efforts were the product of the law students' initiative and inventiveness.

Some individuals we worked with came to us through the legal system, others were sent by community service organizations that also became clients of ours. (The students began to identify and fill gaps in law-related community services and so founded, for example, a protective order project for abused women.) The source for most of our contacts was regular visitation to places like Project Safe for threatened women, the Salvation Army, and Our Daily Bread, a local soup kitchen.

The soup kitchen occupies the basement of a red brick Methodist church. Volunteers cook and serve lunch each weekday to people who unpredictably number from 50 to 150. Our Daily Bread sometimes receives food to distribute. Clothes may also be available and, in the winter, blankets. Alcohol and drugs are not permitted on the premises, but people enslaved to their use are welcome. Once a hungry but sober man came with a circular wound to the middle of his forehead. He told one of my students that he had taken a fall. Later the Methodist minister explained to her that the man could not afford alcohol or drugs and had attempted instead to knock himself unconscious against a tree.

Not everyone comes to the soup kitchen for food. There is a core of repeat guests who come for the company. In the winter some people come to get warm. In the summer an elderly couple, whom I have never seen eat, bring a pickup load of neighborhood kids, many of whom still have light and fun in their eyes and leave with food all over themselves. Evangelists from other denominations sometimes come to work the crowd. The Methodists feed everyone and make no demands.

When we first started our visits there, we did not eat. We would be introduced at the beginning of mealtime, and then dutifully wait in Sunday school rooms in an adjacent building. Clients sought us out, but the numbers and the dynamics improved dramatically when we learned to sit at the table and eat with everyone else. A lot of business was done that way, at the tables. Only when privacy demanded was it necessary to retire to the other rooms or to chairs under the oak tree outside.

The work included an abundant variety of issues. Employment disputes were a frequent subject, and the students were generally successful in resolving them. One dispute involved three women who had quit working at a direct dial business when they became suspicious about the legality of the operation. The owner had refused to pay the wages he owed them when they left. They were afraid to return and demand payment. They asked one of my students what to do. My student made a simple but very effective move. She sent the three back to their former place of business after telephoning the police to meet them there in order to ensure the public peace. Confronted by the women and the police escort, the owner ponied up on the spot — in cash.

That was a handy bit of lawyering, but I had trouble helping the student, and the class when we talked about it afterward, acknowledge the obvious use of force. The police dress in paramilitary gear and carry sidearms. They are members of "the force." My student's employment of them was understandable and effective, but she had employed force against another person nonetheless. I think it is difficult generally for lawyers, especially lawyers who represent poor people, to acknowledge that their work involves the use of force. The subject of violence in law is not easily taught.

Easier to learn at the soup kitchen is how to deal with questions about social security, health, mental health, housing, birth certificates, IDs, landlord-tenant disputes, child support payments, and clothes left at a laundry for washing and no money to redeem them. Sometimes the most difficult part is the follow-up. Clients typically have no telephones and no certain addresses, and they may return to the soup kitchen only rarely or not at all.

In all of this, I was learning along with my students, and they often came to know more and better than I did. One advantage of my serving the joint novitiate was that my office as a teacher did not derive from knowing more than the students about the particulars of the work. Another was that the students had to take more than the usual responsibility for themselves, the course, and our service. When, in serving a client, students confronted a problem they did not know how to solve, they would ask me what to do. Often I would say: "I don't know," and we would try to figure out together how to proceed.

It took students several weeks at the beginning of each year to understand that I really didn't know and a good many more weeks to recover from that realization. They were at first disconcerted ("What kind of teacher is this?"). So was I ("I don't know"). But the long-term effect for the majority was the release of their responsive creativity and a renewed commitment. They now had an immediate reason to learn about property law, employment law, procedure, and the like. And they began to look upon their other teachers, including the Professors Kingsfield, as welcome aids to self-education in time of need. I was not a failure as a supervisor of the street work, but I was rather more lucky than successful.

Some recent literature on lawyering correctly criticizes how lawyers with their expertise, language, and peculiar manner may abuse clients by disempowering them.[7] Lawyers who engage in public interest and pro bono work are especially susceptible to what William Stringfellow described as the "peril of tyrannizing the one of whom it is said he is being helped," because the reason for doing good to the other is the justification of the doer.[8] We were also liable to measure our success by the regrettable standard he warned about: "How far the one who is being helped becomes like the one who is helping him."[9]

The students and I suffered the temptation to do-gooding and its attendant attitude of self-righteousness. Sometimes clients were a cure. Some were wily, strong, knowledgeable, and impressively skilled in the art of survival, and they wouldn't tolerate our self-righteousness. Less productively, others simply skipped appointments. It also helped when other faculty members and lawyers attended class meetings at our invitation and offered criticism.

We continued to be troubled about disempowering our clients—about our not acting as midwives to the extent that we could—but sometimes talk about empowerment and disempowerment was an irrelevant luxury. Some of our clients were worn out by life, by alcohol and other drugs, by their spouses, by their parents, by their children, by the system, by the clock. Anything other than survival was not a present option. We learned simply to offer help in those cases and not to make much of it when the offer was accepted.

We also learned that there were circumstances in which nothing could be done. In Emily Fowler Hartigan's description, we could only "dwell with" the person.[10] And if the person disappeared, we could not do even that much.

Those exceptional occasions prevented our becoming lost in technique and kept before us fundamental questions about our work. Such questions were also regularly raised by our reading. Our work with people was demanding and often compelling, and its growth made it difficult to continue reading literary and jurisprudential texts together each week. But I insisted on the practice, and the students persisted. A few of the discussions were failures, but the students, in spite of some grumbling, grew grateful for the reading and even depended on it. They were capable of impressive care and creativity in their interpretations and of inspired connections between the texts and their work.[11]

The nature of what we did was another continuing source of questioning. Sometimes the students and more often their colleagues and mine asked whether our labors were not social work, or business, or organizing, or whatever, instead of law.[12] Their questions were another, useful type of those provoked by the texts: "Who am I as a lawyer?" and "What am I doing when I do law?" [13]

Much of our work did not require specific legal training, but that can be true of the practice of law as well. Nevertheless, acquiring the skills and knowledge of lawyers and thinking like lawyers, as my students were quickly learning to do, counted for them. And it counted for our clients, too. They attached special significance to our association with law even when we performed work for them that could have been done by people with no legal training at all.[14]

As we made our regular rounds and attended people in their own venues—we had no office for them to visit—conversations repeatedly began with the question: "Are you the lawyers?" It was a straightforward, practical question, but it also bore larger meaning when the students and I tried to sort out its connotations.

Our questioners were undeterred by students' careful explanations that they were law students, not lawyers, and many things could follow. One soup kitchen client had been born at home in rural Georgia in 1942, an event given fleeting attention by custodians of official records who had written the mother's name on the birth certificate in the space where the son's was required. Our client was officially his mother. He asked if we could do something about it so he could qualify for disability benefits. (We could.) Another client said that a Brooklyn jury had awarded him $150,000 after he had been falsely arrested and jailed for a year: Could we do something to get the money for him? (We could not. What he said proved to be true, but the award had been overturned on appeal.) He had a record showing only the arrest and imprisonment, and he could not find work without clearing it. Could we do something about that? (We could.)

We never knew what would follow after the question: "Are you the lawyers?" Usually it would be a story. So we did a lot of listening, and our capacity for listening was improved. Sometimes listening was enough, but typically we were expected to shape the stories into words that produced action.[15] To that end we made telephone calls and personal contacts for our clients, frequently in their company, and we wrote letters and drafted documents on their behalf. Along with their stories people often brought texts for us to assess: bills, dunning letters, form letters from governmental agencies, notices from courts, old deeds, contracts. And we generated more texts in response.

This speaking and writing for others had a certain scribal character. The image of the scribe was made freshly vivid for me by a National Public Radio interview with Jimmy Santiago Baca that aired in the early stages of the course. Baca is a poet, essayist, screenwriter, and sometime prisoner. He taught himself to write while he was in prison because, he said, "I wanted to make an epitaph for myself. I wanted to tell the world I had been here."[16] He wrote for himself, but his literacy caught the notice of his illiterate fellow inmates:

> So they were coming up to me. . . . Could you write my mother a letter? . . . so I'd write him a letter . . . and this man who was the most feared in society would start to weep. And I'm standing there . . . seeing the power of language for the first time in my life. And then another man came by and said, hey man, I've got this girl in Georgia, man, could you write her a letter 'cause I want her to come visit me but I don't know how to tell her. . . .
>
> So I became a scribe, it's no big deal. . . . It was like you give me a box of pencils, I'll write the poem for your girlfriend. . . . And what happened to me was the people that wanted to beat me up were then coming to me saying, hey you know what man? You're alright . . . and ultimately, I became the spokesman.[17]

When people came up to us and asked, "Are you the lawyers?" I think they were asking for someone like a scribe in Baca's sense. They associated us with the power of language. They were asking something like:

"Could you write the system a letter for me in the effective language of lawyers?"

Scribes like Baca are not scriveners.[18] They do not merely copy. They combine heart with mastery of technique to deliver the voices of others. If there were midwifery with words, this would be it.

In the biblical story, God rewards the midwives. He gives them families (Exod. 1:21). My students received a similar gift in kind. In serving our clients, they learned substantive law and techniques of lawyering, but more than that, in giving voice to others, they began to find their own voices. They grew in confidence, creativity, responsibility, skill, and a sense of their vocation. I frequently had to urge restraint. Because the work was at once so captivating and freeing, students could become totally immersed in it, and I would have to ensure that they did not neglect their other classes whether or not the subjects bore directly upon our work.

There was reciprocity for me as well. The students had multiple teachers in the course: clients, the work, each other, and me. I supplied them with support, some guidance, and a place to bloom. It was and it wasn't a big deal. In return I received the compelling need to write this book. The last book I wrote helped generate the course, and the course helped generate what I am doing now. I am still unpacking the question: "Are you the lawyers?" If you are the lawyer, who may you be said to be? And how? What are legitimate guiding images for a person who is a lawyer? What are the sources for these images, and where do they lead? The answers are my present occupation.

What the students learned to do for others and the way they learned to do it exhibited some maieutic characteristics. Although our clients' concerns might have been seen by others as trivial, they did not seem trivial to either the clients or us. Their stories were critical to their lives and well-being, and they warranted delivery in the forms of lawyers' language and in the unspecialized forms that have added effect when law students and lawyers use them. In investing themselves in the work, the students absorbed knowledge and skill, but they could also find that their inherent potential was liberated, enlivened, and confronted with ongoing, fundamental questions.

Some important signs of midwifery were missing. There was no central figure like Shiphrah, Puah, Moses, or Socrates. We precipitated little or no systemic change in the school or the community. We posed little or no threat to the establishment. And for not disturbing the fathers — or for not disturbing them too much or for only seeming to disturb them — I continue to enjoy tenure and a comfortable salary. But am I wrong to think that, on balance, we made a start in the right direction?

Moses is midwife, but he is also not midwife. At Sinai, after he descends the mountain, sees the Israelites at their celebration of the golden calf, and smashes the two tablets of stone, he presides over a murderous slaughter:

> When Moses saw that the people were running wild (for Aaron had let them run wild, to the derision of their enemies), then Moses stood in the gate of the camp, and said, "Who is on the Lord's side? Come to me!" And all the sons of Levi gathered around him. He said to them, "Thus says the Lord, the God of Israel, 'Put your sword on your side, each of you! Go back and forth from gate to gate throughout the camp, and each of you kill your neighbor.' " The sons of Levi did as Moses commanded, and about three thousand of the people fell on that day. (Exod. 32:25–28)

By shedding the blood of their own, the Levites consecrate themselves as priests: "Moses said, 'Today you have ordained yourselves for the service of the Lord, each one at the cost of a son or a brother, and so have brought a blessing on yourselves this day' " (Exod. 32:29). It is an astonishing reversal of the art of midwifery and an alarming introduction to the nature of priesthood.

Moses is midwife and not midwife, and in this he reflects God. Biblical texts employ the image of the midwife in talking about God. As Phyllis Trible notes, however, there is no resting place in such an image in a text that would speak of the transcendent God.[1] In calling for the slaughter of his neighbors, Moses utters the words of God, and the text thus bears witness to His otherness. The Deliverer and Nurturer receives the death of three thousand of the delivered and nurtured.

This episode is prefigured early in Moses' story when God first sends Moses to Egypt and on the way inexplicably attempts to kill him. The difference in that circumstance is the presence of a woman. Zipporah thwarts God's murderous intent with a bloody foreskin. Women shelter Moses in his early years, and a woman saves him in his maturity. The text provides no woman to save the three thousand killed at Sinai. In fact, after Zipporah, women no longer figure as prominent actors in the story — except for Miriam.

Miriam is introduced as Moses' sister at the beginning on the banks of the Nile, but she is not identified by name until she returns to the story immediately after the exodus on the far side of the sea. At the conclusion of its prose account of that crossing over, Exodus appends a song of Moses that rehearses and celebrates the triumph. And then it adds a repeated, shorter section of the poem, the Song of Miriam: "Sing to the Lord, for he has triumphed gloriously; Horse and rider he has thrown into the sea" (15:21).[2] Miriam is a prophet, capable of ecstatic rousing, and it is she who provokes the women's victory festival with tambourines and dancing in the desert. The song she composes for the occasion celebrates God's triumph in Israel's liberation. To the women there is satisfying symmetry in the deed. The Egyptians would have thrown their babies into the river; God has now thrown the Egyptians into the sea. Revenge in the biblical stories is neither repressed nor casual. To the Hebrew women it is sweet and heady, and they do not spare their unbridled rejoicing.

Miriam, releasing praise, moves at the center of Israel's defining moment.[3] It therefore comes as no surprise when Micah remembers Miriam as one of the leading actors in the exodus. He reports the words of God: "For I brought you up from the land of Egypt, and redeemed you from the house of slavery; and I sent before you Moses, Aaron, and Miriam" (Micah 6:4).

Later, during Israel's journey through the wilderness, Miriam's continuing political power emerges a last time in the text. She and Aaron challenge Moses' exclusive authority as mouth for God: "Has the Lord spoken only through Moses? Has he not spoken through us also?" (Num. 12:2). God descends in a pillar of cloud and puts down the rebellion. He punishes Miriam with a skin disease and temporary excommunication.

The punishment is discriminatory. Only Miriam suffers, although the text plainly states that "Miriam and Aaron spoke against Moses" (Num. 12:1). After she is struck with disease, Aaron pleads with Moses on her behalf, and Moses in turn appeals to God for her healing. God commands: "Let her be shut out of the camp for seven days, and after that she may be brought in again" (Num. 12:14). She is, if only for a week, shut out and shut out by God, who leaves her male coconspirator untouched. In response to this text, Katherine Doob Sakenfeld suggests that Miriam belongs to a line of women who are "rejected or humiliated for doing exactly the same thing as their male counterparts."[4] She reads the incident as testimony to a God who is unfair. That is a viable reading of the incident, but it may also be read as testimony to Miriam's leadership: She was the prime mover in the rebellion.

Miriam is the last of the strong, strong-minded women in the exodus story. Other biblical stories present other women differently, and even the Moses saga, in addition to omitting women from much of the action, contains dismissive passages such as Moses' instruction at Mt. Sinai: "And he said to the people, 'Prepare for the third day; do not go near a woman' " (Exod. 19:15).[5] However, Miriam is another of the women who encompass Moses and establish the tenor of the text.

She also prefigures his end. The text places her death and burial immediately before the story of Moses' and Aaron's offense to God in the miracle at Meribah (Num. 20:1).[6] At the end of the story, when Moses dies alone and is left to the lonely abandonment of a grave outside the promised land, he follows a woman to the last.

I shall return briefly to Moses and Miriam after taking note of Rachel, a third person buried along the way.

Rachel belongs to the Genesis treasury of stories and plays no role in the Moses saga. But the later poetry of Jeremiah suggests an association between her and Moses: Both are left outside, and both intercede for the children of Israel. But Rachel's weeping for her children is a form of advocacy that surpasses Moses' arguments.

In the Genesis story, Jacob, by sharp dealing and deception, obtains the birthright of his elder brother Esau as well as his father's blessing, and then he flees north to the family's ancient home in the region of Paddan-aram, where he takes refuge with his uncle Laban. He straightway falls in love with Rachel, deeply enough to agree to serve seven years of labor to earn her hand. On the wedding night, Laban surreptitiously brings to him instead the veiled Leah, his eldest daughter, and she becomes Jacob's first wife. Jacob has to labor seven years more for the right to take Rachel as his second wife.

Because of her father's treachery, Rachel must share her husband with her sister and then must suffer her sister's fecundity in the face of her own infertility. Jacob loves Rachel, but Leah bears his children. Leah, too, suffers. She is not only the instrument of her father's trickery but also, in consequence, the object of Jacob's hate (Gen. 29:30–33). Rachel yearns for children — "or I shall die" (Gen. 30:1) — but none is forthcoming until Leah has already given birth to six sons and a daughter.[1] At last God "remembers" Rachel, and she bears Joseph.

After prospering in Paddan-aram at the expense of his uncle/father-in-law, Jacob leaves to return with his household and wealth to Canaan, to Esau, and to his father's land. Rachel is pregnant. She enters a difficult labor, and she dies as her second child, Benjamin, is born. It is bitterly ironic. She would die if she did not have children and dies having one.[2] She is buried along the way.

The text returns to Rachel when Jacob nears his own end. In a death-bed conference with Joseph, he sorrowfully recounts what happened to Rachel: "For when I came from Paddan[-aram], Rachel, alas, died in the land of Canaan on the way, while there was still some distance to go to [Bethlehem]; and I buried her there on the way to [Bethlehem]" (Gen. 48:7).[3]

Rachel's grave has narrative moment. Explicit in the text are the facts that Jacob buried her "there on the way," that Jacob attaches burdening but unexplained significance to the circumstance of her burial, and that her grave is separate. (Her sister Leah was later buried with Jacob in the family burial site at Machpelah, the location of Abraham's grave.) [4]

The rabbinic literature offers an explanation for the siting and circumstance of her burial: Rachel was consigned to a wayside grave so that she would be strategically placed. She was buried by the road her descendants would travel centuries later when they were driven into exile. She could then evoke God's mercy with her tears as the nation — Ephraim, her descendants, her children — passed by in captivity.[5] This elaboration of the text creates an interpretative link between the Genesis story about her burial and a poem in Jeremiah. The Jeremiah passage strikes the dominant, remembered image of Rachel: "A voice is heard in Ramah, lamentation and bitter weeping. Rachel is weeping for her children; she refuses to be comforted for her children, because they are no more" (31:15). In the poem God hears and takes pity. Her children will return (31:21).[6]

Rachel is left along the way, outside. In Jeremiah's poem, her tomb is inhabited by her weeping. She is another of the abandoned women, left out to intercede. She is an alien pleading for other aliens.

The opulence of the Rachel story schools readers in complexity, contradiction, and paradox and prepares them for more — for otherness — yet to come. Consider what I have either not dwelt upon or not mentioned in the story. Jacob tricks his elder brother, Esau, and deceives their father, Isaac. God honors the result and undercuts the rule of primogeniture. Jacob is subsequently duped by his uncle, Laban, whom he later swindles in return (Gen. 32:20). Rachel — the text commits no gender discrimination in its portrayal of craftiness and treachery — steals her father's household gods as the mass of Jacob's family and possessions move out for Canaan. Laban discovers the theft and chases after them. When he catches the caravan, Rachel hides the gods in her camel's saddlebags and sits on them. After Laban has searched through the possessions of all the others, he approaches Rachel on her camel. She says that she is menstruating. The claim keeps Laban's hands out of the bags beneath her (and serves as a comment on the gods stuffed into them) (Gen. 31:33–35). All of this transpires between brothers, father and son, nephew and uncle, and father and daughter, all in a single family, the one specially chosen by God to be His people.

The reader is made ready for the contradictions, paradoxes, and dialectics necessary to human speech about the God who is other.[7]

15. Jeremiah's Rachel Poem

Jeremiah's verses on Rachel weeping belong to a longer poem located in that part of the Jeremiah text known as the Book of Consolation, a collection of oracles written mostly in verse. Jeremiah was a prophet in the southern kingdom of Judah, from about 627 B.C.E. until the destruction of Jerusalem in 587, when he was carried into Egypt and soon died. Much of his prophecy is directed to Judah and the doom that awaits it.

But the Book of Consolation sounds a note of hope. The oracles convey a sense of promise that God will one day return His people to their land. The poem about Rachel is addressed to the northern kingdom, known as Israel, or Ephraim. The original kingdom of David had split, with Israel and its capital eventually at Samaria to the north and Judah with its capital in Jerusalem to the south. The two together covered an area about the size of Wales. Small kingdoms were not viable in the volatile politics that prevailed in that part of the world. The northern kingdom had departed from the law and had turned from God. It fell, and its people had been deported about a hundred years before Jeremiah became a prophet. The southern kingdom, too, had sinned against God, and it, too, would be destroyed and its people sent into captivity during Jeremiah's lifetime. The poem about Rachel offers hope to the scattered remnants of Ephraim, and perhaps it will offer hope as well to the people of Judah when they are forced into exile.

Rachel weeping for her children constitutes the first of the poem's five strophes. I follow for the most part Phyllis Trible's translation:

I

15. Thus says the Lord:
> A voice on a height!
> > Lamentation can be heard,
> > > Weeping most bitter.
> Rachel is weeping for her sons,
> > Refusing to be consoled for her sons
> > > "Oh, not one here!"

II

16. Thus says the Lord:
> Keep your voice from weeping

and your eyes from tears.
    For there is a reward for your work—
        oracle of Yahweh—
    They shall return from the land of the enemy.
17. And there is a hope for your future—
        oracle of Yahweh—
    Sons shall return to their borders.

III

18. Truly I have heard Ephraim rocking in grief:
        You whipped me, and I took the whipping
            like an untrained calf;
        bring me back that I may come back,
            for you are Yahweh my God.
19. For after I turned away, I repented;
        and after I came to my senses, I slapped my thigh.
        I was ashamed, and I was confounded,
            because I bore the disgrace of my youth.

IV

20. Is Ephraim my dear son? my darling child?
        For the more I speak of him,
            the more I do remember him.
        Therefore, my womb trembles for him;
        I will truly show motherly-compassion upon him.
                        Oracle of Yahweh.

V

21. Set up waymarks for yourself;
        make yourself guideposts;
    consider well the highway,
        the road by which you went.
    Return, O virgin Israel,
        return to these your cities.
22. How long will you dillydally,
        O Turnabout daughter?
    For Yahweh has created a new thing in the land:
        female surrounds man. (Jer. 31:11–22)[1]

The traditional translation of verse 15 is "a voice heard in Ramah." Ramah is the location of Rachel's tomb, but its literal meaning is "on high." Trible's translation gives a sense of Rachel's lamentation carried to the precincts of heaven.[2] Trible also employs "my womb trembles for him" in verse 20 rather than "I am deeply moved for him" (NSRV), or "I am filled with yearning for him" (Bright), or "my bowels are troubled for him" (KJV).[3] Trible's translation is consonant with the motherly voice of God. The last line, "female surrounds man" or "a woman encompasses a man" (NSRV), is so obscure that John Bright, in his translation, places it in brackets and suggests that it might have been better to leave the line blank: "Quite possibly we have here a proverbial saying indicating something that is surprising and difficult to believe, the force of which escapes us."[4]

In Trible's account, Rachel's weeping dominates the first strophe, and she is the object of God's consolation in the second. The third shifts focus from Rachel to Ephraim. And in strophe 4 the motherly voice of God, lovingly concerned for Ephraim, moves the poem "from the desolate lamentation of Rachel to the redemptive compassion of God."[5] The final strophe, which Trible construes as the poet speaking, delivers the welcome command to return home.[6] The child addressed has changed sex: son has become daughter.

The last line Trible says, "moves between mystery and meaning."[7] It is Rachel embracing her sons, God consoling Rachel and declaring compassion for Ephraim, the daughter superseding the son, and God creating a new thing in the land. And, Trible concludes, it is also the poem itself, for in the poem's chiasmic form women surround Ephraim.[8] The male child Ephraim speaks in the middle of the poem. The first strophe is words of a woman (Rachel's lamentations), and the second is words to a woman (God's response to Rachel). Then comes Ephraim's strophe followed by words of a woman in strophe 4 (God as mother) and words to a woman in strophe 5 (Jeremiah or God addressing virgin Israel).[9] In Trible's interpretation, the form and content of the poem embody a womb containing Ephraim.[10]

Trible's interpretation is creatively helpful, and I draw upon it to arrive at a somewhat different reading. To me the mystery is more evident and manifold than the meaning.

Rachel weeps for Ephraim, but the depths of a more universal grief sound through hers. In The Gospel According to Matthew, Herod is frightened by reports that the Messiah has been born, and he destroys the children of Bethlehem. The text adds: "Then was fulfilled what had been spoken through the prophet Jeremiah: 'A voice was heard in Ramah, wailing and loud lamentation, Rachel weeping for her children' " (Matt. 2:17–18).

The lamentation of Rachel for Ephraim in exile extends in time from one horror to another and gathers grief for all the slaughtered children of Israel. The profound, enduring, more universally enveloping quality of that mother's grief is still felt, still heard.[11] It is one mystery of "female surrounds man."

Another is the character and effect of her grief as intercession. Trible notes that to surround or encompass is also to surpass.[12] Rachel's tears may be read as surpassing. In her grave Rachel is inconsolable. Worse than her death is the erasure of her children, and more powerful than her death is the anguish she suffers for them.

In response, God promises to recall Ephraim from nowhere. Thereby does Jeremiah invite a comparison in which Rachel's tears surpass Moses' appeals. In an earlier passage Jeremiah remembers Moses, like Samuel, as one of Israel's greatest intercessors. Moses had successfully appealed to God on behalf of the people when He would have destroyed them at Mt. Sinai. But Moses could not prevent God from sending the people into exile now: "Then the Lord said to me: Though Moses and Samuel stood before me, yet my heart would not turn toward this people. Send them out of my sight, and let them go!" (Jeremiah 15:1).[13] The punishment that Moses and Samuel together could not prevent, Rachel's tears will bring to an end. To this extent her tears surpass the appeals of the two great male intercessors. To surround is to surpass. This is another mystery of "female surrounds man."[14]

Socrates would have no tears at his trial. He thought that weeping would demean him and dishonor the state. To appeal with tears would be to ask a favor of the judge, "thus procuring an acquittal instead of inform-ing and convincing him." [1] He opposed low-level, bribing supplication: If you have only a losing argument, cry.

Rachel's powerful tears, however, do not register as less worthy than argument. They do not demean either her or God and His response. They outlive her death and gather sorrow too deep for words. Rachel's suffering is at once her own and that of Ephraim, at once passionate and compassionate. And its expression moves God and surpasses rather than sinks below Moses' arguments.

In American courts, on a rudimentary level, the expression of emo-tions like those contained in tears that touch the heart simply cannot be excluded and should not be. But when a New Jersey judge ruled in 1845 that the state constitution did not outlaw slavery, he observed that the "arguments and remarks and the pathetic appeals" addressed to the court "seemed rather addressed to the feelings than to the legal intelli-gence of the court." [2] He thought that what counts for reason in law had not been satisfied.

I do not know how this judge dressed for court or in what kind of room he presided; probably, though, if modern judges and courtrooms are a guide, he was costumed in a robe, situated in a dramatic space, and taking part in civic theater. Some years ago, arguing the obvious, I pointed out that courts are theaters and that it is good they are. [3]

Fortunately, not all law is litigation, but courtroom decision making is the core image of the way "legal intelligence" proceeds in our society. Courts are not laboratories or study halls. Nor are lawyers, judges, and jurors assemblies of scientists or logicians. Trials are theater and, like all theater, appeal to the heart and the heart's reasons as well as to the mind. The New Jersey judge reported that he had "listened with great pleasure and deep interest" to the proceedings before him. Doubtless he had, for trial performances are almost always fascinating. The wonder is that he saw no connection between "legal intelligence" and the medium essential to his work as a judge, between the way lawyers are supposed to think and the emotional, artful representation and metaphor making central to the enterprise.

The performances that courts produce are as important as their judgments. They represent what we imagine a legitimate society to be and so mirror our nature as a people, our better selves. That is their chief function as theater but not their only one. They also reconfigure aggression, encourage impartiality, engender creativity in judgment, and certainly serve as a medium for communication of nonverbal information. Feeling is very much of the essence, and tears, ordinary tears, are part of the order.

To maintain that law has no room for tears runs counter to their patent, deliberate presence. The New Jersey judge's inability to embrace the obvious is connected to a worldview in which law is peculiarly rational and unprejudiced and feeling is both vulnerable to prejudice and opposed to reason. Or—and it has been thought to say the same thing—feeling is feminine, and the feminine has no place in what is essentially men's work.

These two strands of assumptions join and become explicit in a scene in Herman Melville's *Billy Budd*. Captain Vere has summoned a drumhead court on his ship *Bellipotent* to try the much loved sailor Billy for killing the master-at-arms. In a kind of charge to the court, the captain says that the officer-judges are not responsible for the rigor of martial law but only for its administration. He adds that the exceptional case of Billy Budd will move their hearts:

> "But let not warm hearts betray heads that should be cool. Ashore in a criminal case, will an upright judge allow himself off the bench to be waylaid by some tender kinswoman of the accused seeking to touch him with her tearful plea? Well, the heart here, sometimes the feminine in man, is as that piteous woman, and hard though it be, she must here be ruled out." [4]

This association of the feminine with tears and of tears with the seduction of uprightness in law echoes an ancient habit. However, one caution of that past, which includes Captain Vere and Creon, is the terrible cost of disobedience to the heart and of the exclusion of the feminine. [5]

Socrates opposed the introduction of doleful tears on his behalf at trial because he believed that judges should be convinced to give judgment and not be asked to give favors. But there is no natural, necessary reason to exclude feeling as a medium for informing and convincing judges. And there is every reason to include it in what Jeremy Bentham referred to as "the theatre of justice." [6] In fact, feeling is already, undeniably included.

There is a larger issue here: Tears like Rachel's that express suffering too deep for words do not demean the law, but law may be thought inadequate to them or an inappropriate medium for them. Hannah Arendt held the view that law occupies a middle ground between "goodness beyond virtue and evil beyond vice." [7] Her argument does not run to so simple a matter as weeping in court.

In a reflection on Dostoyevsky's "Grand Inquisitor" from *The Brothers Karamazov* and Melville's *Billy Budd*, Arendt proposed that law lies within the limits of the political realm where argument, pity, and the eloquence of virtue count, but passion and compassion do not. The latter, she said, are antipolitical and cannot be accommodated in law. If compassion attempts to remedy the causes of suffering, "it will shun the drawn-out wearisome processes of persuasion, negotiation, and compromise, which are the processes of law and politics, and lend its voice to the suffering itself, which must claim for swift and direct action, that is, for action with the means for violence." [8]

Arendt makes a good argument. Rachel nonetheless leads me to reconsider it, at least to the extent of reconsidering the relation of law to the kind of suffering and fellow suffering her tears express.

Like theater, which also requires distance, law occupies ground delineated by convention and commitment. The limits change with time and so does what occurs within them—the subject matter, discourse, styles of performing, and what counts as performance. There are nonetheless limits and discipline, however contextual, and they serve useful purposes. They allow lawyers to reduce agreements and hopes to reliable legal terms that enable enterprises to proceed. They allow lawyers to reduce ordinary controversies and sometimes great social conflicts to judicially cognizable, resolvable terms. And they also aid judgment and the process of judgment by helping eliminate prejudice and by excluding from criminal trials certain kinds of evidence because it is inappropriate to the immediate performance and the larger representation we would have of ourselves as a people. [9]

So the limits and the discipline are appropriate, useful, and necessary, although they are not fixed in permanent form. It is wrong, however, to make too much of them, as though they set off a neutral zone, extending only from vice to virtue, that is safe from surrounding, antipolitical goodness and evil. It is wrong because it grants to law an odd, destructive, and unwarranted combination of necessity and immunity: Law is a bulwark holding chaos at bay — *après moi le déluge*.[10]

Neither the making nor the maintaining of the bulwark are free of force. They claim for "action with the means of violence" no less than does compassion. Their violence is legitimated violence, but it is violence nonetheless. American recognition of this fact began at least as early as John Marshall's observation that even ordinary tax law involves the power to destroy.[11] And it has been extensively elaborated in recent years by William Stringfellow, Robert Cover, and others, myself included. Law does not exclude violence. It orders violence.

Nor is the ordered territory it occupies between extremes necessarily free of anarchy. Madison understood that "in a society under the forms of which the stronger faction can readily unite and oppress the weaker, anarchy may as truly be said to reign, as in a state of nature."[12] This anarchy of law and order takes on a settled, invulnerable appearance, and it is hard to penetrate, as cases both old and new demonstrate.

In a case involving the slave ship *The Antelope*, Chief Justice John Marshall agreed that the "unnatural traffic" in slavery was "contrary to the law of nature" but not contrary to the law of the Supreme Court.[13] "Slavery . . . has its origin in force; but as the world has agreed, that it is a legitimate result of force, the state of things thus produced by general consent, cannot be pronounced unlawful."[14] He pronounced much the same thing about American law enforced against Native Americans. It was unnatural and uncivilized, "yet, if it be indispensable to that system under which the country has been settled, and be adapted to the actual condition of the two people, it may, perhaps, be supported by reason, and certainly cannot be rejected by courts of justice."[15] That which is unnatural (read "unjust") settles into reason, law, and the not altogether ironically titled system of justice.

Although such acknowledgments of unjust but lawful force are exceptional, its use is not. In *Walker v. City of Birmingham*,[16] civil rights marchers had been jailed for demonstrating against racism in defiance of an injunction. The injunction enforced a city ordinance that the Court suspected was unconstitutional and later held to be unconstitutional.[17] The Court nonetheless upheld the defendants' conviction: An illegal court order may not be tested by disobedience. The final sentence of the opinion proclaimed that "respect for judicial process is a small price to pay for the civilizing hand of law, which alone can give abiding meaning to constitutional freedom."[18] The civilizing hand of law in this instance compounded chaos within by exacting from its victims the price for holding at bay a supposed threat of chaos from without.

In *McCleskey v. Kemp*, a black man convicted of murder was sentenced to die. His attorney challenged Georgia's capital sentencing scheme as racially discriminatory.[19] In the process of rejecting the argument, the Court said that "taken to its logical conclusion, [his claim] throws into serious question the principles that underlie our entire criminal justice system."[20] The very possibility that unjust force had become systemic placed it beyond examination.

This is to be stupefied by force and to be used by rather than to master it. The Court presents the organization and entrenchment of anarchic force as either respectable or regrettably necessary and therefore irremediable. In doing so it creates two false, irresponsible attitudes. One is that law occupies a space of decency momentarily safe from the violent extremes of goodness and evil. The other is that systemic evil within that realm is not subject to remedy. These may be formulated as the inconsistent claims: "There is no evil" and "We can't cure it."

The claims are un-American. Alexander Hamilton opened *The Federalist* by saying that the question before the citizenry was whether they could govern their affairs through "reflection and choice, or whether they are forever destined to depend for their political constitutions on accident and force."[21] At the time he wrote, Americans had already given good demonstration of their active determination to govern by deliberation, to rule force rather than to be ruled by it. To this end they had overthrown an imported legal regime and were in the process of discarding one homemade charter, the Articles of Confederation, in favor of another, the Constitution. They would soon produce a very different Constitution with the civil war and at least one other between the 1920s and 1960s. We have understood in our past that law is an artifact, that we are responsible for it, and that, when law does not work or injustice is deeply entrenched in it, we can make fundamental changes, by force of arms in civil war if necessary.

Arendt said that "law, moving between crime and virtue, cannot recognize what is beyond it."[22] But I think that it must do so if the citizenry is to recognize law and the legal system as no more than tools to be deployed responsibly. Arendt argued that "compassion abolishes the distance, the worldly space between men where political matters, the whole realm of human affairs, are located."[23] But it was law in the absence of compassion that abolished distance in the instances of slavery and the Birmingham demonstrators and that continues to diminish it in the instances of Indian nations and Georgia's practice of capital punishment. When law's only appeal is to itself and its power, its last resort is always terminal force and not argument. And then it is self-destructive because it destroys the process that is its essence and the space that is its habitation.

H. L. A. Hart noted that wicked men will always use the forms of law as one of their instruments. And in his view what is most needed to make citizens "clear sighted in confronting the official abuse of power, is that they should preserve the sense that the certification of something as legally valid is not conclusive of the question[s] of obedience [and submission], and that, however great the aura of majesty or authority which the official system may have, its demands must in the end be submitted to moral scrutiny." [24]

I would clarify or extend Hart's assessment in three particulars. First, not only extraordinary confrontation of official abuse of power or extreme crises of obedience are at issue but also ordinary participation in law. Daily tending and assurance and therefore regular clarity are required.

Second, not only *abuse* of legitimacy but also legitimacy in its common functioning requires us to see through the aura of the official system. The continuing relation between the United States and the Indian Nations provides an extensive illustration of the need and difficulty of discernment. Constitutional supremacy and equal protection of the law are great achievements of a great people, and they have helped us grow much good. But at the same time they constitute an act of aggression against tribes and the life of tribes on our shared continent.[25] Vigilance is especially necessary and especially difficult in those instances where good people employ good law but with nonetheless injurious effects on others who are without fault. In such circumstances we are far more likely to blame the victims than to see ourselves and our law clearly.

Third, although it is certainly to be hoped that the demands of the official system will always be subjected to moral scrutiny, morals, too, require subjection to scrutiny. The point is quickly, memorably fixed in the critical moment of *The Adventures of Huck Finn*. A raft bearing Huck and the fugitive slave Jim floats down the Mississippi. A skiff with two white men approaches. Huck detaches a canoe from the raft and paddles out to meet them. He is thrown into a crisis of conscience. Law and morality urge him to turn Jim in. Now is the time. But he resists. Instead, he lies to the boatmen. He leads them to think that his companion on the raft is his pox-ridden father. They retreat quickly. Jim, undiscovered, continues his escape. Huck says:

> I got aboard the raft feeling bad and low, because I knowed very well I had done wrong. . . . Then I thought a minute, and says to myself, hold on; s'pose you'd a done right and give Jim up, would you feel better than you do now? No, says I, I'd feel bad — I'd feel just the same way I do now. . . . So I reckoned I wouldn't bother no more about it, but after this always do whichever come handiest at the time.[26]

The "handiest" is more reliable than the conscientious, where conscience is instructed by no more than law and morality. Virtue, too, requires critical scrutiny.

Supplication — and that is what God takes Rachel's weeping to be — transcends both law and morality and in doing so provides occasion for their needed testing. A powerless supplicant places the powerful supplicated in the role of recipient and puts him to trial. As Paul Valliere observes, the supplicated speak for themselves and their power. Supplicants, on the other hand, do not speak mainly for themselves and instead invoke a higher reality. In Arendt's terms, compassion gives voice to suffering and invokes goodness beyond virtue. "It is this prophetic power of supplication," Valliere says, "that establishes the dialectic of power and powerlessness, thus putting the whole question of power into a new perspective. Supplication is historical action which bears witness to social and political theonomy."[27] This is not victim politics, not an appeal to pity, generosity, or guilt. Rather, it is the dialectic of power and powerlessness that summons a beyond that can recall power from its self-destruction. It is thus action undertaken on behalf of the powerful as well as the powerless.

Some degree of self-transcendence, of recognizing the beyond and being drawn after it, belongs to law. For example, one purpose of the reductive, theatrical discipline of trials is to evoke from jurors and judges a willing suspension of disbelief in their own civility. It thereby draws them into performing their better parts as citizens who have put aside prejudice and personal interest in making judgments about each other. Such acting beyond themselves that courtroom law encourages among jurors and judges, constitutional law encourages the citizenry as a whole to perform.

Law helps draw us out in this way. It suits such self-transcendence for law to acknowledge its limits and point beyond itself.[28] Law then gives us reason to take responsibility for governing our affairs, including law and force, and hope for guidance in doing so from beyond law.

I would therefore develop forms that allow us to hear in law tears like Rachel's invoking what is beyond law: the potential of silences shaped by the wordiness of law but also the possibilities of what is said, written, and done in law. The bitter sorrow of families sometimes finds expression in divorce proceedings. The suffering of the innocent and the guilty alike is to be heard at times in criminal trials, war crimes tribunals, and the making of peace treaties. And the lamentations of the enslaved and of those who suffered to end their enslavement may still be heard in the post–Civil War amendments, although the sound of them is the more muffled the more the Supreme Court covers the amendments with little rules and with nice arguments about standards of judicial review.

Fran Ansley's work on plant relocations and the International People's Tribunal in Hawai'i in 1993 are extended examples of tears brought to law.

Fran, who has a substantial history as a practitioner, is now a professor at the University of Tennessee's School of Law in Knoxville. As plants close in east Tennessee, jobs are lost, and women are hurt. In an attempt to understand what is happening around her, Fran has become a student of deindustrialization and globalization, of the particulars of temporary employment, the failures of job retraining, the nature of industrial recruitment, sustainable development, environmental impacts, international politics and economics, and transnational investment.[29]

Her journey from law into alien territories of the academy inhabited by experts in the relevant subjects is emblematic of other frontier crossings her effort has required. She crossed social boundaries in order to find the women most affected by the plant closings and to learn from them about the realities of their experience.[30] And then she was led to cross the border between the United States and Mexico.

Plants were closing in east Tennessee not because they were going out of business but because they were going to the maquiladora region of Mexico.[31] Women in the Knoxville area wanted to have a look at the Mexican women now at work in their former jobs — "those people," the enemy, who seemed "so ready to snatch away American jobs on the slightest excuse." [32] Fran helped make the wish become reality in a 1991 exchange of visits between women from the maquiladora zone and from east Tennessee.[33]

The Mexicans made the first trip. Their stories of the maquiladoras where they worked and the colonias where they lived combined with the ritual of sharing family pictures to disarm the audience in Tennessee and inaugurate an appreciative exploration of commonalities and differences between the foreigners from Mexico and the outsiders in America.[34]

When the Tennesseeans made the return visit to Matamoros, across the border from Brownsville, Texas, they were struck by the scale of investment shifted south and the form it had taken in huge, gleaming new factories enclosing "acres of young, quick workers."[35] The factories were surrounded by well-watered, manicured lawns, but what the visitors found when they arrived at the nearby colonias resembled "an aerial bomb site."[36] Some of the American women had known extremely harsh circumstances themselves. They were nonetheless staggered by the shock of the living conditions of the Mexican women who were working full-time for the prosperous corporations: "One-room houses overflowing with people, suffocating summer heat filling the boxes where mothers fanned their sweating babies, stagnant pools of water with scum and garbage right next to where people were living, drainpipes carrying toxic industrial waste into ditches that ran through neighborhoods, bare feet, sick animals, horrible smells, open sores."[37]

The Tennesseans felt a "horrified distance" from what they saw, but they also felt "the possibilities of connection" with the people they met who were struggling to build a life in the colonias and whose intelligence, determination, and dignity moved them.[38] "More than once," Fran reports, "we had to compose ourselves and try to stop crying before we could go on."[39]

They recognized shared circumstances. Both the Mexicans and the Americans wanted the jobs. Both also favored increased trade between the two countries. And both were hurt by a "system that pits workers against each other on the basis of which one can be forced to take the lowest wage."[40] The powers arrayed against the women on both sides of the border appear overwhelming: " 'And you think,' one of the Mexican women said, 'What can I do against something so big and so rich and so powerful as that shiny new plant full of shiny new machines?' "[41]

Near the end of the visit, the Mexican hosts provided a supper on the beach—homemade food and a huge fish purchased from a boat along the way. There was singing, and there were silences, and the sharing of painful tears and memories of painful tears. But tears shed beside the Gulf of Mexico were not enough, one of the hosts said: "We workers here in Mexico in the maquilas, we need the help of people in the United

States to make our voices heard. . . . we must remember what the factory owners forgot: we must remember what we have in common. That we are all children of God."[42]

Fran and her colleagues have tried to give expression to the suffering and compassion of the women on both sides of the border. They have tried personal appearances, news interviews, public broadcasting presentations, organizing efforts, continued exchanges, and a play.[43]

They have also tried law. Fran's legal scholarship identifies and describes the vast forces at work and provides an opportunity to tell portions of the women's stories in law reviews.[44] And she and her colleagues offered testimony in hearings held on the North American Free Trade Agreement (NAFTA).[45]

Workers and communities presently have little legal leverage on plant closings in the United States, on the transfer of production to Mexico, or on working and living conditions there.[46] Although extensive, sophisticated legal arrangements had to be put in place to create and maintain the maquiladora system, law imposes almost no restraints on corporations that reject responsibility for the workers they leave behind or those they will use next.[47] "Large business enterprises are increasingly 'free,' " Fran observes, "while workers and communities are increasingly stuck."[48]

The NAFTA hearings are symbolic of the scant purchase the women's suffering has in law. The women of Tennessee told their stories and those of their Mexican sisters during hearings held at a time and place and under conditions that made it almost impossible for affected workers to participate. When Fran and her colleagues managed to appear, they found that the presiding officials lacked both decision-making authority and knowledge of the subject matter. The chairman said the witnesses' concerns would be passed on to relevant parties, but there was no way to monitor the trade agreement process of negotiation.[49] "For some of us present," Fran writes, "it seemed at times that questions, challenges, protests, and compliments alike were dropping quietly into . . . a hole."[50]

Fran is convinced that the necessary social change does not come "about through skillful engineering, guided from above by intelligent, highly trained policy wonks possessed of savvy, brains, and even heart" but through social struggle in which those without other resources must resort to "mass mobilization and social disruption of various kinds and at various levels."[51] She notes that such actions are "legal" in that they are "mediated . . . by the surrounding legal rules"[52] and constitute attempts to invoke the power of the state. They seek limitation of industries' freedom to withdraw major productive resources, and they seek expansion of worker and community freedom to participate in relevant decisions affecting those resources.

There has been little or no response to these appeals. I surmise that they are tears refusing to be denied expression in law. They are more complex than what Aeschylus called "tears for the rule of wrong," for they are shed also for the rule of the partially right.[53]

The International People's Tribunal was convened in 1993 under the sponsorship of more than one hundred Hawaiian groups and citizens' associations dedicated in one way or another to the sovereignty of the islands' indigenous people, the Kanaka Maoli. Kekuni Blaisdell, a distinguished physician and leader, was the moving spirit behind the tribunal.

The history of such tribunals begins with the war crimes trials that followed World War II, especially the Nuremberg trials but also the trials in Tokyo. The victorious Allies agreed that punishment was necessary, but they had to decide how to administer it. They could have chosen executive or military action but instead chose trials and so gave their exercise of power the cover of law.

The trials set a precedent for expressing and enforcing principles to govern international war crimes, and it was not long before opponents of the Vietnam War invoked the precedent.[54] In 1967, for example, Bertrand Russell convened a tribunal in Stockholm to consider whether U.S. actions against Vietnam constituted violations of international law.[55] Robert Cover observed that "it is an irony of the history of this age that Nuremberg—an act often characterized as a fig leaf for naked power—[engendered] the attempt to empower the fig leaf standing alone."[56]

Lord Russell's fig leaf was not backed by state force and did not pretend that it was, but it, too, had precedential power. It spawned calls for various other tribunals to sit in judgment of states and governmental institutions accused of large-scale abuses of fundamental rights. A number of such tribunals have been convened. Among them were an International Tribunal on the Rights of Indigenous People held in Rotterdam in 1980 and a similar one held in San Francisco in 1992 that focused specifically on such rights under the U.S. government.[57]

The International People's Tribunal in Hawai'i falls within this tradition. It took place August 13–20, 1993, to hear charges that the United

States had committed fundamental wrongs against the Kanaka Maoli. I was asked to sit as a judge alongside eight others. We came from six nations and a variety of backgrounds.

As we construed them, there were five charges: that the United States had interfered in the internal affairs of the sovereign nation of the Kanaka Maoli; that in 1893 the United States had aided and abetted a coup d'état against the nation's legitimate government headed by Queen Lili'uokalani and then wrongfully annexed the territory; that the United States imposed statehood on the territory without the consent of the Kanaka Maoli; that the United States, its corporations, and its citizens have appropriated the Kanaka Maoli's land and resources and imposed economic colonization on them; and that the United States has committed acts of genocide against the Kanaka Maoli.

The tribunal received testimony in sessions that were held at numerous sites around the islands and were attended by great ceremony and generosity. Along the way we accumulated a vast amount of oral, written, and physical evidence. We had videotapes of the testimony that we heard and testimony that time did not allow us to hear. So many people appeared that we could not accommodate everyone, even though we worked from very early in the morning until very late at night, sleeping little or not at all.

We found that the offered evidence supported the claims made. I have included an edited version of the tribunal's findings and recommendations as an appendix to this book. It was not put in final form and distributed until 1995 and has not been published before. (The materials that follow are based upon that document and its underlying sources.)

Testimony repeatedly and movingly referred to the overthrow of the government and the confiscation of the people's land, resources, and life.

Witnesses spoke about Queen Lili'uokalani with deep feeling. Her goodness and the wrong done to her and to the people by the U.S. usurpation of their government are vividly remembered. Subsequent to the tribunal and unrelated to it, the United States admitted the illegality of its action and apologized to the native people.[58] The apology had no binding legal effect and led to no meaningful redress.[59]

The loss of land began before the seizure of the government and has continued. Beginning in the nineteenth century, American citizens, with the direct or indirect support of the U.S. government, destroyed the indigenous land tenure system. They did so primarily through the Western legal concept and practice of property. A few nonnatives then took over the bulk of the land. By the 1960s, seventy-two private owners held 47 percent of the land, and state and federal governments held 49 percent. Since then, land ownership has been more widely dispersed, but without effect on Kanaka Maoli holdings.

One subject of frequent testimony about land was 200,000 acres that the United States placed in trust in 1921 for Kanaka Maoli homesteading throughout the islands. These trust lands constitute a promise abused. The acreage set aside was drawn from some of the worst in the archipelago — "remote, inaccessible, arid, and unsuitable for productive development." A helicopter flight along the coast of Maui provided a clear image. We saw lush plantations in the highlands and lush resorts far below them along the sea. The two were separated by extensive, barren hillsides where sandalwood once grew. The plantations and resorts are mostly owned by large transnational corporations. The land between is Kanaka Maoli homelands.

Plantations produce cash crops alien to Hawai'i: 200,000 acres devoted to sugar cane, 130,000 for pineapple and other crops. The staples of the Kanaka Maoli diet are poi and fish. Poi is made from taro roots. By 1991 only 310 acres of land remained under taro cultivation. Fresh water is limited. Water for taro has been diverted to the agribusiness plantations. Hawai'i grows the only irrigated sugarcane in the world.

Water is also diverted to coastal resorts. In 1992 there were 65 eighteen-hole golf courses among the islands, with state encouragement to build 102 more. Each course occupies 150–200 acres of land and consumes 500,000 to 1,000,000 gallons of water per day. We visited a golf course under construction among the coastal dunes on Maui where bulldozers ravaged a sacred burial site of the Kanaka Maoli.

Run-off from the plantations and golf courses together with development along the coast is devastating the fisheries. Of one hundred fish ponds on O'ahu in 1901, only two remained in 1993.

In addition to their sterility and inaccessibility, the lands set aside for Kanaka Maoli homesteading are available only to people who can prove that they are of at least 50 percent Hawaiian blood. This test of Kanaka Maoli membership was imposed by the U.S. Congress. The people did not define themselves this way. Those who likely qualify under the standard often find it impossible to produce the paper records required. No written records ever existed. Such things were alien to the society. While the Kanaka Maoli presently constitute some two hundred thousand of the islands' population of one million, only five thousand have met the imposed standard. If there are no more than the five thousand qualified so far, their number is likely to dwindle to zero by the middle of the twenty-first century.

Even for those who qualify, distribution of the homelands remains a well-documented scandal. Only 17.5 percent of the land has been placed in the hands of homesteaders, despite a waiting list of twenty thousand applicants, some of whom have been waiting for thirty years and more. Over 62 percent is now used by nonnatives, often for minimal compensation to the trust. The U.S. government pays virtually no compensation for the homelands it occupies. Those Kanaka Maoli who make unauthorized use of their homelands are jailed as squatters, and bulldozers destroy their houses, cultural centers, and gardens.

The pauperization of the Kanaka Maoli and their loss of land and traditional food has subjected them to serious illness. Indigenous people make up 20 percent of the population but account for 44 percent of infant mortality and over 30 percent of deaths from heart disease. Their rate of death from cancer is more than double that of the rest of the population.

Witnesses told of the destruction and attempted destruction of their language, law, culture, religion, dignity, and way of life, as well as the seizure of their government and resources. The evidence they offered included stories, documents, objects, histories, studies by experts, rituals, music, dances, and songs. Testimony was sometimes accompanied by great, rollicking good humor. More often it was punctuated by tears and painful, heaving silences when the burden of speaking terrible things became too great.

Evidence supported the claim that over an extended period the Kanaka Maoli sought in good faith to obtain redress through state and federal courts. Redress was not forthcoming. Despite the nonresponsiveness of the courts, the people continue in the hope that their story can be effectively articulated in legal terms. In this hope they convened the tribunal. I suspect that they were encouraged to do so by the conviction that their cause is just, by the dignity of their suffering, and by pride in their own, subtle law that has been unrecognized as law by the colonizing powers. I think that they were encouraged, too, by the hope that they will one day find a language that will work in the Western world.

A documentary video of the proceedings produced by a native film company captures the tears.[60] I hear them also in the tribunal's opinion — in the fact of it and in what it says and leaves unsaid. But my hearing them may be a function of memory and not of what the pages of the opinion offer to others. The opinion is a considered judgment about the evidence presented. Although the judges included a Japanese novelist, a Korean theologian, a Maori attorney, a Palestinian attorney, a Cree attorney, and a Cherokee rapporteur, our joint product is easily recognizable as cast in legal discourse familiar in the United States.

Because the language of law is a language of careful if protracting use, the tears sound, if they sound at all, in the opinion's details: the structure, the findings of fact, the findings of law, the shaping of precedent, the shaping of silences and blank spaces.

As I stood in an airport line with my wife, June, waiting for a return flight home after the tribunal, both of us exhausted, I thought about the conclusion to *Black Elk Speaks*. Black Elk had witnessed the slaughter of Indians conducted by American troops at Wounded Knee. One U.S. official saw a positive lesson in the massacre: It had taught the Indians that it is dangerous to oppose "the law of the Great Father." [61] Black Elk saw something very different, something he had not seen before: an enemy who would stop at nothing. Late in life Black Elk recounted the episode for John Neihardt and concluded:

> I did not know then how much was ended. When I look back now from this high hill of my old age, I can still see the butchered women and children lying heaped and scattered all along the crooked gulch as plain as when I saw them with eyes still young. And I can see that something else died there in the bloody mud, and was buried in the blizzard. A people's dream died there. It was a beautiful dream. . . . [T]he nation's hoop is broken and scattered. There is no center any longer, and the sacred tree is dead. [62]

Shortly after, in a trip Neihardt recorded, Black Elk returned to Harney Peak in the Black Hills. It had been central in his early vision. There he invoked the Great Spirit:

> "Hear me, not for myself, but for my people; I am old. Hear me that they may once more go back into the sacred hoop and find the good red road, the shielding tree!"
>
> We who listened now noted thin clouds had gathered about us. A scant chill rain began to fall and there was low, muttering thunder without lightning. With tears running down his cheeks, the old man raised his voice to a thin high wail, and chanted: "In sorrow I am sending a feeble voice, O Six Powers of the World. Hear me in my sorrow, for I may never call again. O make my people live!"

For some minutes the old man stood silent, with face uplifted, weeping in the drizzling rain.

In a little while the sky was clear again.[63]

The Kanaka Maoli and Native Americans have similar relations with the United States. Waiting to board the plane, I wondered whether the tribunal would generate anything more than a little sympathetic rain on the islands, if that much. I reckoned that it would not.

Fran Ansley believed that the words she and her colleagues offered at the NAFTA hearings dropped into a quiet hole. Insofar as an audience beyond the Kanaka Maoli is concerned, I have much the same feeling about the tribunal's judgment and the artful video documentary as well. Nevertheless, I am unsure that the NAFTA and tribunal testimony failed.[64]

Fran and the tribunal judges were asked to give voice to suffering and compassion in the language of law. We were asked to employ law as a medium of supplication. However poorly or well we expressed the people's words, tears, and silences, our action places the powerful who are supplicated in the role of recipients. It would put them to trial as a form of service to them as well as the powerless. That the tribunal's work was a nonevent for the United States may itself usefully highlight the limits of American law and point beyond them.

Among the Kanaka Maoli, the tribunal was not without effect. Many who came to our sessions heard each other's stories and the full recounting of their history for the first time, and they understood that they were not alone. One judge, Te Moana Nui A Kiwi Jackson, director of Maori Legal Services in Wellington, New Zealand, pointed out to me that colonialism destroys the ability to make connections of many kinds and that our proceedings had provided occasion not only for restoring connections between the individual stories but also for conceptualizing them. The common stories could be conceived as connected to law, international norms, and broader meaning.

The Kanaka Maoli had found themselves and the validity of their way of life affirmed in some way. I expect that the same was true for the women of east Tennessee.

17. The Womb of God and Tears

What I have said about compassion in law raises a theological question. If supplication invokes a beyond, how can we explain the effect of Rachel's weeping? There is no goodness greater than God to summon. Neither her lamentations nor Moses' Sinai intercessions can be read as animating God to perform the role of greater or better God. They can be read as appealing from a God the just to a God the merciful, but only if justice and mercy are read as opposites in a divine personality that can be switched from one to the other by sufficient human intervention.

I think that there is another possibility indicated by a further mystery of "female surrounds man," the image struck by the last line of Jeremiah's Rachel poem: God surrounds the human as the life-giving womb surrounds the fetus. In John Calvin's terms from the beginning of his *Institutes*, "our existence is nothing but a subsistence in God alone."[1] There is and is not distance between the two, is and is not the immediacy of compassion, is and is not room for politics and persuasion.

Within the womb of God, people live, move, have their being, and speak. Robert Alter refers to the "quintessential biblical notion" of a "nexus of speech that binds man and God."[2] The sense of Jeremiah's poem is that this nexus of speech is umbilical. The word of God supplies voice to Rachel no less than Moses so that her tears, like his intercession, are a return within the uterine circulation of expression. On this reading, a God the just does not switch to a God the merciful in response to what He hears. Rather He is who He is in the mystery of God the mother. I return to the poem:

I

15. Thus says the Lord:
   A voice on a height!
       Lamentation can be heard,
           Weeping most bitter.
   Rachel is weeping for her sons,
       Refusing to be consoled for her sons
           "Oh, not one here!"

II

16. Thus says the Lord:
    Keep your voice from weeping
        and your eyes from tears.
    For there is a reward for your work —
        oracle of Yahweh —
    They shall return from the land of the enemy.
17. And there is a hope for your future —
        oracle of Yahweh —
    Sons shall return to their borders.

III

18. Truly I have heard Ephraim rocking in grief:
    You whipped me, and I took the whipping
        like an untrained calf;
    bring me back that I may come back,
        for you are Yahweh my God.
19. For after I turned away, I repented;
        and after I came to my senses, I slapped my thigh.
    I was ashamed, and I was confounded,
        because I bore the disgrace of my youth.

IV

20. Is Ephraim my dear son? my darling child?
    For the more I speak of him,
        the more I do remember him.
    Therefore, my womb trembles for him;
    I will truly show motherly-compassion upon him.
                      Oracle of Yahweh.

V

21. Set up waymarks for yourself;
        make yourself guideposts;
    consider well the highway,
        the road by which you went.
    Return, O virgin Israel,
        return to these your cities.

22. How long will you dillydally,
　　　O Turnabout daughter?
　　For Yahweh has created a new thing in the land:
　　　female surrounds man.

In the first strophe Rachel weeps, and in the second God responds with the promise of her children's return. In the third, her child groans with repentance, and in the fourth God responds with the promise of mercy. This pattern of human call and divine response is transformed in the last strophe, which may be the voice of the poet, as Trible suggests, or may be the voice of God. The two are not distinguished, just as there is now no distinction between what God commands and what Israel most seeks. The command: "Return to these your cities" is exactly what Israel hopes to do. The command is an answer to their prayers. There remains only Israel's performance: "How long will you dillydally?"

Between God's promising command and its fulfillment lies a time of waiting. (Is it a period of gestation?) Between "Let there be light" and there being light, between the now of the poem and the future of the return, between the uttering of the word and its performance, lies the hard time of history when the turnabout dillydallies.

For this meantime or at its completion or both, there is a new creation. In the old creation "God created humankind in his image, in the image of God he created them; male and female he created them" (Gen. 1:27). In the new creation, too, male and female point to God, but now the Genesis image of God in the parity of the sexes yields to a new one: "female surrounds man." This colon points to God by concentrating the womanly mood, voice, and imagery of the poem as a whole.

Other poems within the Book of Consolation in Jeremiah make use of male identifiers. In one, God is "a father to Israel, and Ephraim is my firstborn" (31:9). In another He is "husband" to both kingdoms (31:32). But a monopoly of male metaphors would be insufficiently expressive, and Jeremiah turns to labor pains as a figure for intense human suffering.[3] The first poem in the Book of Consolation provides a complex example of such usage:

Thus says the Lord:
We have heard a cry of panic,
　　of terror and no peace.

Ask now, and see,
    can a man bear a child?
Why then do I see every man
    with his hands on his loins like a
        woman in labor?
    Why has every face turned pale?
Alas! that day is so great
    there is none like it;
it is a time of distress for Jacob;
    yet he shall be rescued from it.
                (Jer. 30:5–7)

In this poem, to say that men will suffer the pains of a labor known only to women is to express how extraordinary will be the event that lies ahead. In the Rachel poem, to speak of God's trembling womb is to indicate a mystery of God that lies beyond.

When the Rachel poem, following familiar biblical practice, describes God as hearing and remembering, it conveys a close, responsive link between God and the one heard or remembered. (In Exodus, God sends Moses to the enslaved Israelites because He hears them and remembers his covenant with Abraham.) The creative good sense of translating strophe 4 as Trible does is to connect God's remembering Ephraim with God's womb trembling for him. The pregnant woman feels the fetus moving. (Whose movement is it?) Breast-feeding follows delivery. Neither the severing of the umbilical cord nor the weaning of the child ends the singular, life-giving attachment. The mother's feeling for the child emanates from the core of her being, continues throughout her life and, in Rachel's case, after death. The womb and the sympathetic trembling of the womb serve the poem's language about God as no male image can.

Israel has been scattered among other nations but has never been so far removed as to escape the embrace of either Rachel's sorrow or God's compassionate memory. And now the great ingathering will commence. Female surrounds man.

Trible notes, and I call particular attention to, the Hebrew word *suv*, turn or return.[4] It occurs twice in the second strophe ("They shall return"; "Sons shall return"). To return to the land is also to return to God. *Suv* is used three times in the next strophe, twice with the geographical/theological meaning ("bring me back that I may come back"), and once with the connotation of apostasy ("I turned away"). This same sequence of meanings is repeated in the final strophe ("Return, O virgin Israel"; "return to these your cities"; "Turnabout daughter").[5] "Return" becomes — turns into — "surround" in the last line. And the "Turnabout daughter" of the first half of the verse is newly created in the last as "female surrounds man."[6]

The word *suv* highlights and belongs to a cycle. Rachel's tears go up to heaven and do not return empty. They precipitate God's promise that Israel will return to the land. The pattern is then repeated. Ephraim's grief is heard in heaven and returns as God's promise of motherly compassion. In this pattern God is not inactive, for Rachel does not shape her flood of sorrow into a petition. She cannot. It is too deep for words. When God hears her weeping, He actively translates the sound as supplication, and He responds. When He hears Ephraim's words of repentance, He translates them, too, into a plea by Ephraim to be brought back, and He responds. God's active hearing and the general responses He makes to Rachel and Ephraim become specific, active command in the last strophe: "Set up waymarks for yourself. . . . return to these your cities."

God seems to have been roused to action by the calls of Rachel and Ephraim. They appear to be the moving parties. Word goes up and cycles back to earth as a promising command that waits only to be fulfilled. This is the reverse of rain and snow coming down from heaven.[7]

However, the poem is careful to preserve the mystery of the original cycle that begins with the word of God. It does not directly present Rachel weeping and Ephraim pleading. In the poem only God speaks. What he utters is hearsay. The voices of Rachel and Ephraim in the poem are God saying what He has heard from them. The word of God enwraps the poem.[8] The poem begins with the formula: "Thus says the Lord." Rachel's weeping is said by God. Ephraim's words in the third strophe are God's declaration of what He "heard Ephraim pleading." With the possible exception of the last strophe, which may be either the voice of God or the poet, the entire poem is presented as the words of God.

Rachel's weeping is distinctively and genuinely hers. What we and the Gospel of Matthew (2:18) remember is Rachel and her tears, not God's reporting them. Their effect, too, is her achievement. And yet, in the poem, they are the word of God.

Similarly, Ephraim's pleading and repentance are his, and so are their effects. And yet they, too, are the word of God in substance as well as form. Trible notes about Ephraim's plea "bring me back that I may come back" that "theologically the repentance of Ephraim is an act of God," and "geographically, the return of Ephraim is the work of God." [9] Both acts, like the words, are Ephraim's and also God's.

God's word gives voice to Rachel and Ephraim, and He is moved by the voices he hears in return. The uterine figuration of the poem and its colon point to this mystery. The womb surrounds and gives life to the child exactly that he should be an other, but neither the separation of birth nor the coming of age and independence of the child end the womb's trembling for him. Nor do apostasy, exile, and death end the mother's compassionate embrace. Rachel continues to weep for Ephraim. Her loaded tears from the grave along the way and his pleading in exile issue from the word of God that surrounds them. God cannot speak of Rachel and Ephraim except to give them voice and so hear her and remember him with motherly love. He gives voice and response to the weeping of Rachel that his hearing raises from her grave. "Female surrounds man."

The poem performs a final knotting of the mystery that exactly enacts the dialectic and wonder of the word of God surrounding and enabling the human voice. Rachel weeps, but her weeping in the poem is God's utterance; the entire poem is what He says. Even so, God's speaking in the poem is the writing of the poet. It is God's word and the poet's work, and equally the poet's word and God's work, in the same way that Moses' entreaties are both his intercessions and God's words and in the same way that God both stands over against Israel and shares enabling identity with her. [10] "Female surrounds man."

God repeatedly says that His people are to be holy, for He is holy. To be holy is to be set apart and never completely settled. This is true for the people as a whole and particularly true for those who represent Israel to God: the closer to Him, the more separate from others.

How terrible this is for Rachel. She lies forever lonely and suffering in her grave along the way in order that, from there, she may be movingly close to God. What has God done to her? What does He require? And yet: What has God not suffered with her? The suffering of God the mother encompasses the suffering of Rachel's grief and gives it expression.

Perhaps we can say something similar about Miriam. She, too, is buried along the way. Earlier, God had unfairly ordered her out of the camp. But Katherine Doob Sakenfeld says that the larger biblical tradition presents God as the one "who stands close to and defends those on the 'outside.' . . . Miriam outside the camp may point us not only to the painful arbitrariness of her situation but also, however indirectly and allusively, to the suffering of God." [11]

Perhaps, too, we can then say that Moses' consignment to an unknown grave outside the promised land is not unique. It is a sign of proximity to God. The mystery is that, in death and separation, he, Rachel, and Miriam are adjoined and lie within the womb of God.

III

The Gospel According to John

In the stories of Moses, God is characteristically present as word. The word is powerful, dangerous, consuming. In order not to destroy his people by His presence, God places Himself in their midst by law and the mouth of Moses.

In *The Gospel According to John,* the Word has become flesh. That is how God now places Himself—encamps—among His people. John is steeped in the Jewish tradition. In the gospel's language, imagery, and associations, Moses is everywhere at hand, and so is law.[1] As I came to understand in working on this chapter, law is a primary medium for the gospel, and John's freedom to employ it is a gift with liberating consequences for the reader.

The received symbol for the Gospel of John is the eagle. This is so not because people associated with law are bound to be birds of prey but because of the gospel's elevated theology and language. It opens with a majestic prologue:

1 In the beginning was the Word,
    and the Word was with God,
    and the Word was God.
2 He was in the beginning with God.
3 All things came into being through him,
    and without him not one thing came into being
    that has come into being.
4 In him was life,
    and the life was the light of mankind.
5 And the light shines in the darkness,
    and the darkness did not overcome it.

6 There was sent by God a man named John.
7 He came as a witness
    to testify to the light
    that all might believe through him;
8 to *testify* to the light
    for He was not himself the light.
9 The true light which enlightens every man
    was coming into the world.

10 He was in the world,
    and the world was made by him;
    and the world knew him not.
11 He came to his own;
    and his own received him not.
12 But all who did receive him
    he empowered to become children of God:
    those who believe in his name,
13 those who were begotten,
    not by blood or the will of the flesh or the will of man,
    but by God.

14 And the Word became flesh,
    and dwelt among us.
    And we have seen his glory,
    the glory of an only Son from the Father,
    full of grace and truth.

15 John testified to him and cried out:
    "This is he of whom I said:
    'The one who comes after me ranks ahead of me,
    for he was before me.' "
16 And from his fullness
    have we all received—
    love in place of love:
17 for the law was given through Moses,
    grace and truth came through Jesus Christ.

18 No one has ever seen God;
    God the only Son,
    who is in the Father's bosom,
    he has made him known.

The poem sets up a play, plainer in the Greek, between "was" and "became" (or "came into being"), between *en* and *egeneto*.[1] In the beginning the Word was (*en*). Through him all things came into being (*egeneto*). And then the Word that *was* God *became* flesh. The Word, which in the beginning was, intersected the world that became.[2]

In the midst of this great drama of eternal Word and temporal world and of the astonishing entry of the Word into the world, John the Baptist arrests the eye and the mind's eye.[3] There is no fully satisfactory way to render in English the Greek words *egeneto anthropos* introducing him: "Became a man"; "Became a man sent by God, named John." Or, "There came into existence a man sent by God." John belongs to *egeneto*, the becoming world, but within that world he points to the Word.[4] He was a "witness" who "testified" to the coming light. A witness who testifies is a figure in a legal process. Right away the reader has the sense that a trial is underway, and as the gospel unfolds the trial-like atmosphere intensifies.

The challenge lies in discerning just who is on trial in which judicial process and to what effect.

The trial of Jesus is climactic in all four of the gospels.[5] In the Gospel of John's account, a contingent of Roman soldiers and Jewish police arrest Jesus in the night, bind him, and take him to Annas, formerly a high priest. Annas interrogates him and sends him to his son-in-law Caiaphas, the present high priest. They then take him to Pilate's headquarters early in the morning. Pilate emerges to ask "the Jews" what charges they bring and then tells them to judge Jesus according to their own law. They say that they are not permitted to put anyone to death. Pilate enters his headquarters and after examining Jesus returns to tell the waiting crowd that he finds no case against him. Because it is Passover, he says, they may have Jesus released, but they choose another prisoner, Barabbas, instead. Then Pilate has Jesus flogged and brings him before the crowd. They insist that he be crucified. Pilate tells them to crucify Jesus themselves and repeats his conclusion that there is no case against him. They say that their law requires his death because he claims to be the Son of God. Pilate reenters his headquarters, interrogates Jesus further, and is eager to release him. But the crowd forces his hand. They fill the air with hints of charges to be filed against him in Rome for setting free a person who claims to be king and who is therefore a threat to the emperor. In response, Pilate takes his place on a judge's bench and, apparently finding Jesus guilty of treason, sentences him to crucifixion (John 18:1–19:16).

There can be no gospel without an account of this trial. But law and legal process are more pervasive in John than they are in the other gospels, more pervasive than is necessary simply to recount the events that take place in Jerusalem. This abundance of law has various extratextual explanations, including the needs of the Church at the time the gospel was assembled and circulated.[6] Such explanations are drawn from the interaction between the text and the situations in which it was written. They are essential to scholarly study of the early Church and of the compilation of the text, and they can be useful, too, for understanding the text itself. The interaction that is my primary focus here, however, is that between the Gospel of John and its present readers. I basically take the text as it has come to us with its own integrity as a literary whole.[7]

One function of law in John is to serve the writer in the work of writing.

Near the conclusion, the author[8] explicitly addresses the difficulties of composition: "Now Jesus did many other signs in the presence of his disciples, which are not written in this book. But these are written so that you may come to believe that Jesus is the Messiah, the Son of God, and that through believing you may have life in his name" (20:30–31). The available material was daunting.[9] The last verse of the gospel adds that if all the things Jesus did were written down, "the world itself could not contain the books that would be written" (21:25). Every memory would have been treasured and worthy of preservation in the gospel. To choose among them meant exercising authorial jurisdiction over the Messiah's works. It was a complex and humbling responsibility.

Also, to say that the world could not contain all the books is to comment on more than shelf space. The Word, through whom all things came to be, is other than books can realize. The Word is the transcendent other who can and cannot be contained in writing. Even a world of words won't do. The writer had to make complex professional judgments about which of the accessible linguistic resources, in which combination, would make for him the least inadequate statement of his subject.

Then there is the difficulty in purpose. The author writes "in order that you may come to believe."[10] To write so as to induce belief is challenge enough, but before writers can induce belief they must first make themselves understood across differences in worlds. What is seen in one world may be out of view in another. Karl Mannheim observed that people in one world — "ideology" was his term — "are simply no longer able to see certain facts" accessible to those in another.[11] An example of the phenomenon is Joseph Priestley's blindness to oxygen. Thomas Kuhn describes how a shift in scientific worlds — a "paradigm shift" — "enabled Lavoisier to see in experiments like Priestley's a gas that Priestley had been unable to see" and was "to the end of his long life, unable to see."[12]

What could Lavoisier say to Priestley that would enable Priestley to see the oxygen he had discovered? Persuasion may have been necessary, but it would have been insufficient. Priestley was not simply unpersuaded; he was unable to be persuaded. He couldn't believe. That was the challenge put to the gospel writer. How to write that readers may come to believe? This was no puzzle for idle teasing in the afterhours. To the writer it was a matter of life and death: "That through believing you may have life . . ."

Given the huge amount of material and the limits of language's capacity to convey transcendent realities, together with the aim of delivering readers' belief and the available choices for the craft of gospel writing,[13] the author must have been tempted by hyperbole and vigor:

go after the audience. Instead, he writes artfully and with reserve and follows a strategy of economy in execution and plainness in presentation. (Rough edges still show in the final product.)[14]

His laconic handling of the crucifixion is illustrative. John omits many of the details of the passion story found in the other gospels[15] and employs clean simplicity of statement for the enormity of Jesus' torture: "Then [Pilate] handed him over to them to be crucified. So they took Jesus; and carrying the cross by himself, he went out to what is called Golgotha. There they crucified him" (19:16–18). The lines are evocatively spare.

Law helps satisfy the need to select and order the material of the story, and its evocative capacity advances the strategy of restraint by allowing the writer to say more with less.

In this, law works like the liturgical calendar in the gospel. On one level the principal festivals of the Jewish liturgical year are an organizational device for the story: Miracles and pieces of narrative are gathered into liturgical-chronological sections. The text emphasizes seven principal signs performed by Jesus and, as a rule, appends explanatory material to each. Some signs and their related material are associated with particular Jewish feasts: the healing of a sick man with the Sabbath (5:1–47); the miraculous feeding of a large crowd and Jesus' walking on water with Passover (6:1–71); and the healing of a blind man with the aftermath of Sukkot (7:1–9:41). (A confrontation between Jesus and "the Jews" is joined to the festival of Hanukkah [10:22–39].)

On another level, employment of the liturgical calendar serves the economy of presentation. It allows the author, in Frank Kermode's phrase, to "release into his text many unspoken suggestions."[16] Each association of Jesus' signs with a festival has this effect. The walking on water and feeding of a great crowd at the time of Passover, for example, release suggestions of the crossing through the sea and of the wilderness manna that the Passover liturgy celebrates.[17]

The trial performs the same double service. First, it is a structuring device. Much of the gospel builds toward the arrest, trial, and crucifixion in chapters 18–19. Jesus' extended discourse in chapters 13–17 belongs to the trial material because it is Jesus' effort to help the disciples understand what is about to take place. It is a pretrial interpretive guide for them.[18]

Anticipation of the trial is actually set in motion much earlier. In chapter 12 Jesus agonizes over the "coming hour" (12:27).[19] In chapter 11 plans are made to put him to death (11:51, 53). Still earlier, the text tells of attempts to arrest him in Jerusalem during Hanukkah (10:39) and Sukkot (7:32–44, 7:30).[20] In chapter 9, a blind man healed by Jesus is twice subjected to investigative questioning (9:13–17, 24–34). Before that, in chapter 8, Jesus is challenged on the legal validity of testifying on his own behalf (8:13; see also 5:31–38), and the episode is drawn out through a legal contest. Plots to kill Jesus are introduced in 7:25, 7:19, 7:1, and notably in 5:18.[21]

The latter instance occurs in conjunction with the healing of a sick man on the Sabbath. On that occasion "the Jews started persecuting Jesus" and began "seeking all the more to kill him" (5:16, 18). A. E. Harvey identifies this episode as the narrative initiation of the formal process against Jesus. Responsible Jews could not let his violation of law pass without response and would fail "in their duty if they did not see to it that the offender was convicted and punished."[22] The series of legal encounters between Jesus and Jewish lawyers that follows after chapter 5 may then be read as a drawn-out legal proceeding that is repeatedly frustrated until it can be properly brought to a conclusion in Jerusalem.[23]

As the narrative and substantive culmination of a series of legal skirmishes that begin early in the story, the Jerusalem trial provides structure to much of the gospel. It also has the added function of releasing unspoken suggestions into the text. It recalls the trials of the faithful Job and the testing of the people of Israel in the wilderness, and it may summon an underlying sense of the Hebrew Bible as a whole whose theological substance, Walter Brueggemann finds, is best conveyed in the metaphor and imagery of courtroom trial.[24] There are further, critically important, specific associations with prophetic lawsuits, and I shall return to them.

19. The Gospel Trial: A Divine Lawsuit

Jesus' trial is not the only one. There are others, and they involve the Paraclete, a figure who occupies four singular passages of Jesus' last discourse (John 14:16–17, 26; 15:26; 16:7–15) and whom John sometimes refers to as the Spirit.[1]

Jesus explains: "I will ask the Father, and he will give you another Paraclete, to be with you forever. This is the Spirit of truth" (14:16–17). The text speaks of "another" Paraclete as though Jesus himself is one. The two are closely aligned: "It is to your advantage that I go away, for if I do not go away, the Paraclete will not come to you; but if I go, I will send him to you" (16:7). The Paraclete is the continuing presence of the risen Jesus: "He abides with you, and he will be among you" (14:17).[2]

The New Revised Standard Version translates the Greek *paraclete* as "advocate" (14:16–17). This is yet another figure in a legal process.[3] Jesus promises that the Paraclete "will teach you everything, and remind you of all that I have said to you" (14:26). What the disciples did not understand or believe in the circumstance and did not remember afterward,[4] the Paraclete will bring to mind and belief. That is how the disciples are to be led at last to an understanding of the trial. In Raymond Brown's terms, in "a rerun of the trial of Jesus," the Paraclete allows its truth to emerge for the disciples.[5]

The Paraclete actively participates in separate legal proceedings as well.

Three judicial processes may be discerned in the text. They are related but distinguishable. Prominent is the trial of Jesus and the series of legal skirmishes that lead to it. For this proceeding, the Paraclete is the post-trial commentator who will fix in the disciples' understanding the trial's meaning as Jesus had explained it to them in advance.

A second legal process, or series of processes, is anticipated for Jesus' followers. The disciples and successive communities of believers will be put on trial. Theirs will be types or repetitions or extensions of Jesus' trial: "If they persecuted me, they will persecute you . . . But they will do all these things to you on account of my name" (15:20–21). The disciples fled at the critical hour of Jesus' trial in Jerusalem, but through the Paraclete they will become participants in trials yet to come. The Paraclete will equip them to be witnesses. They "also are to testify" (15:27)[6] in proceedings beyond the pages of the gospel.[7] The Paraclete is a commentator on the trial of Jesus and will be an actively supportive presence in the trials of Jesus' followers.

The Paraclete has a third, more direct role in another trial. Jesus says that the Paraclete "will testify on my behalf" (15:26) and "will prove the world wrong about sin and righteousness and judgment" (16:8). He seems to have in mind a judicial proceeding in which the Paraclete acts as a prosecutor or prosecuting witness.[8]

Attention to this third legal process takes the reader more deeply into the text and its involvement with law.

This other trial is introduced in the beginning in chapters 1–4.

Brown helpfully refers to John as "the great trial of the Word."[9] We sense the atmosphere of a trial right away. We recognize the trial of Jesus as the trial of the Word. And insofar as the projected trials of his followers will be aimed at Jesus, we understand that they, too, are a trial of the Word.

Brown's description is helpful, but it could misdirect the reader. His comment is made in reference to John the Baptist. He says that the Baptist is "the first witness in the great trial of the Word." The problem with the statement is that it may place John the Baptist in the wrong court.[10] Herod beheaded John during Jesus' lifetime. John had no direct association with the trial of Jesus or the anticipated trials of his followers. He drops out of the narrative at the end of chapter 3.[11] He is not involved in the trial of the Word.

He figures in another legal proceeding. When the prologue first mentions John the Baptist (1:6–9), he is described as a witness; when he first appears (1:19–28), he is depicted testifying. A trial is underway as the gospel begins, but John the Baptist is not on trial, Jesus has yet to appear, and only later will the trial of the Word commence.[12]

The Baptist is the opening witness in a trial of the *world*. This proceeding belongs to a category known as the prophetic *rîv,* or divine lawsuit. Commentators on John, beginning with Bultmann, have remarked on "the great lawsuit between God and the world,"[13] but only in a general and unexplored sense. It is specifically and extensively helpful to read the gospel against the background of the prophetic lawsuit.

In the books bearing their names, the classic prophets of the eighth century B.C.E.—Isaiah, Micah, Amos, and Hosea—are portrayed in part as court messengers.[14] God was understood to rule in a heavenly assembly. When the assembly convened as a court, God was judge and prosecutor. He summoned, indicted, and sentenced various nations, but His judgment was primarily aimed at His own people. They had broken their covenant with Him by their idolatry and injustice. God admitted the prophet to the heavenly assembly at some point in the proceeding. The prophet heard or saw what God spoke and was commissioned to deliver to the people the words of God, usually words of unalterable doom. Isaiah 6 constitutes such a commissioning: "Then I heard the voice of the Lord saying, 'Whom shall I send, and who will go for us?' And I said, 'Here I am; send me!' " (Isa. 6:8). God sends him with the words of forthcoming destruction (Isa. 6:9–13).

The first four chapters of John do not expressly mention a divine lawsuit, and the apparatus of a heavenly assembly is missing, but something like a *riv* is underway.

Like Isaiah, John the Baptist is said to be sent from God.[15] And his self-description as a voice crying in the wilderness is a quotation of the words given to Isaiah in his capacity as a messenger from the heavenly assembly (Isa. 40:1–5).[16] However, instead of bearing words of judgment from a trial that has already taken place in a heavenly assembly, John the Baptist announces a trial that is underway in the here and now.

The prologue sounds themes of paired opposites: *en/egeneto,* light/darkness, grace/law, Word/world. As the gospel proceeds, the opposites are understood to be dynamically related. Light is breaking in upon darkness, day is superseding night, grace is replacing law, and the Word that was in the beginning is intersecting the world that became. This intersecting or cutting into is a crisis—a crisis in the sense of the Greek *krisis,* which can mean judgment or separation as well as the condemnation that results from a trial.[17]

On the first day of the text, the Baptist testifies that one "is coming after me" (1:19–28). On the second day he identifies Jesus as the coming one. On the third day he repeats the identification, and his testimony is corroborated by three witnesses—Andrew (1:41), Philip (1:45), and Nathaniel (1:49).

Beginning with chapter 2, Jesus offers his own testimony about himself, first with signs (2:11, 23) and then by what he says (3:11–18, 4:26). And his testimony, too, is confirmed by the belief of an ever-widening circle of believers. This testimony and its corroboration are functions of chapters 2–4, which compose a unit.[18] Throughout the initial chapters there is repeated talk about disbelief (1:10–11, 3:11, 18–20, 36), but it is disbelief in general.[19] The narrated specifics emphasize corroborating belief.

A case has been established that accords with the opening statement: The Word who was in the beginning came to his own, and his own received him not. To establish the affirmative part of the case (the Word came to his own), chapters 1–4 adduce testimony, corroborated within the story, that the Word is indeed the Word and that the Word became flesh in Jesus.

Chapters 5–19 more elaborately make out the negative part of the case (his own received him not). The primary business of these chapters is the people's disbelief and rejection of Jesus.[20] A reflective evaluation at the close of the public ministry summarizes: "Although he had performed so many signs in their presence, they did not believe in him" (12:37). What they should and could have done, they did not. And "not even his brothers believed in him" (7:5). The trial in Jerusalem is the culmination of disbelief and rejection. The prosecution rests with the crucifixion and burial.

The trial of Jesus in Jerusalem is a trial within the larger trial of the world. It does not result in an explicit verdict and sentence. It does not have to. We understand that the judges condemn themselves in condemning Jesus.[21] And the text is clear about who these judges are.

Chief Priests, Pharisees, and Jewish police play a prominent role and head the roster of "the Jews" who are antagonists. The term *the Jews* has been variously interpreted. These characters in the story may be depictions of real people who opposed Jesus during his ministry. They may be representations of Jews or Jewish Christians engaged in community controversies at the time the gospel was being written. Or they may be symbols of the world opposed to Jesus.[22] In the gospel, Jesus and most of his followers as well as his opponents are Jews.[23]

"The Jews" do not stand alone in opposition. (This point is immensely important to understanding the text and to resistance of abuse of the text by anti-Semites.)[24] The list opens to include Pilate and the Romans. Their addition drives straight to the point underscored in the prologue: The *world* did not know him.[25] It is the world who sits in judgment.

Remarkably, the world in the text also includes the disciples. They, too, are implicated. The text leads in this direction with its portrait of them.[26] At the beginning of the story, the disciples have some form of belief in Jesus and follow him (1:35–51, 2:11). But when Peter affirms, "We have come to believe and know that you are the Holy One of God" (6:69), Jesus is unimpressed: "Did I not choose you, the twelve? Yet one of you is a devil" (6:70). Later, Jesus' question to one of the twelve is aimed at all: "Have I been with you all this time, . . . and you still do not know me?" (14:9). Although Jesus has carefully gone over everything with them in advance, the disciples grasp nothing of the trial's meaning. Only two disciples follow Jesus to the trial, and one of them, Peter, three times in the event denies association with him (18:17, 25–27). Almost all are absent from the crucifixion, and none protests it. The only recognition of who has been condemned is the cynical inscription ordered for the cross by Pilate as a show of his authority and of his contempt for the Jews: "Jesus of Nazareth, the King of the Jews" (19:19).

The disciples are portrayed as insiders who betray Jesus in his hour of greatest need. The gospel is unsparingly inclusive. The gospel's "world" did not know the Word. It is they who are put on trial, and it is they who judge themselves.[27]

The trial of the Word is a trial within the trial of the world in which the world — Jews, disciples, Romans — condemn themselves.

The Gospel of John never expressly condemns the judges of Jesus. We are led to do so by the understood irony. Irony works this way. It allows an author to make a statement without affirmatively articulating it. I can say someone is "bad" in such a way as to mean he is good without saying so. If I do so successfully, I draw on both words and enrich them. I also challenge a way of thinking. Someone who is judged bad may instead be "bad," and my saying so invites a reconsideration of the judgment. The danger in irony is that it may not be recognized and that the statement will not then be understood as meaning its opposite. This danger is not present in the irony of Jesus' trial. From the beginning the text provides the information that the defendant is the Word. We read the trial to mean that those who judge him judge themselves. We are meant to do so.

The text makes no express judgment and never editorially censures the participants. The silence is conspicuous for Americans, who routinely criticize court actions and trials, especially infamous trials. We are left with the irony of the judges' self-judgment. But it is an irony, and our conclusion is held in suspension.

This is no ordinary divine lawsuit. In place of the traditional finding of guilt and pronouncement of terrible punishment, the Gospel of John provides a wholly different conclusion for which the prophetic literature offers a precedent. When the gospel's first chapter has John the Baptist invoke Isaiah — "I am the voice of one crying out in the wilderness" — it alerts the reader to the possibility of a redemptive lawsuit. The quoted line is taken from a proceeding in the heavenly assembly that is unlike any other. The message given the prophet for the people is one of tenderness and restoration:

> Comfort, O comfort my people,
>   says your God.
> Speak tenderly to Jerusalem,
>   and cry to her
> that she has served her term,
>   that her penalty is paid,

that she has received from the Lord's
    hand,
  double for all her sins.

A voice cries out:
"In the wilderness prepare the way of
    the Lord,
  make straight in the desert a highway
  for our God.
Every valley shall be lifted up,
  and every mountain and hill be made
    low;
The uneven ground shall become level,
  and the rough places a plain.
Then the glory of the Lord shall be
  revealed . . ."
    (Isa. 40:1–5)

The prosecutor has become Israel's advocate, and the proceedings end in renewal.

This lawsuit of redemption is precedent for John's great trial of the world.[1] The reader has known from chapters 1–4 that the divine lawsuit underway is not a prosecution designed to destroy the defendant world. Chapters 20–21 now complete the lawsuit, and the resurrection places the trial of Jesus in a new context for the reader just as it had done in the understanding of the disciples. The Jerusalem trial is now to be seen as an element in the larger proceeding against the world. And the larger action is now to be seen as breaking down and reconstituting the meaning of trials and judgment.

In consequence, readers must rethink their implied conclusion that the judges of Jesus are condemned. John leads us to this conclusion and now unsettles it. Chapters 20–21 take nothing back. They do not show the judges to have been right after all. They do not ask us to change our minds about the judges' action. They ask us instead to see it in a new light.

In the customary prophetic lawsuit, the case is tried before the heavenly assembly with God acting as both prosecutor and judge. In John there is no heavenly assembly. At the end, the text makes it plain that the Paraclete's case against the world is tried before the reader.

When it is at last given to the disciples to grasp the significance of the empty tomb, Thomas is absent from the scene. Soon afterward, the risen Jesus dispels Thomas's continuing doubt by inviting him to touch the fatal wounds. "Do not doubt but believe," Jesus says, and adds, "Blessed are those who have not seen and yet have come to believe" (20:27, 29). It is as though Jesus has turned from the disciples to readers. He addresses the appeal and beatitude to us.[2] In the next sentences the author explicitly addresses us, the readers for whom he has written "that you may come to believe" (20:31).[3]

We are the court who conclude that the judges of Jesus condemned themselves. The resurrection disturbs our judgment, and we discover that our judgment has more to do with us than with them. There is not an us and a them.

The writer does not write from the heights. The gospel may soar, but the author's feet are firmly planted on human ground. The beloved disciple's behavior is not more exemplary than that of Peter or the other disciples or, for that matter, the judges. Nor does now looking back at the past make the author superior by the passage of time. There is no moral or chronological high ground to occupy. The writer never explicitly condemns the judges. He is in no position to judge. More than that, where he now stands, after the resurrection, judgment is no longer the point.

He would have readers understand that the same is true of us. The text has made us judges like the Jewish authorities and Pilate. Their world extends from the page to embrace the reader, and the here and now in the text becomes the here and now of the reader's interaction with the text. The divine lawsuit is tried before us. But at its conclusion, after the resurrection, the author would have from us belief and not judgment.

If the Gospel of John were an appeal in a death penalty case, it would argue for the life of the condemned. Here, capital punishment has already been carried out, and the plea is made to the judges for the judges' life. We, too, belong to the world on behalf of whom the *krisis* has come.

21. The Power of the Word: Two Women

The author brings his appeal "so that you may come to believe . . . and that in believing you may have life" (John 20:31). This is not an entreaty. It is the language of causation: *hina,* in order that you may believe. It carries the sense of fruitful action. The gospel's performance of trials on the page is intended to be performative. It is to animate belief in the reader.

As a messenger who bears belief engendering words, the writer of John follows the example of two women in his text.[1] One is Mary Magdalene. She and the beloved disciple are among the few who stand near the cross as Jesus dies. It is she who goes to the dark cemetery by herself, discovers the empty tomb, and runs to Peter with word of it. She returns to the tomb and remains there alone after Peter and the beloved disciple leave. It is she who is then the first to see the risen Jesus: "Jesus said to her . . . 'go to my brothers and say to them, "I am ascending to my Father and your Father, to my God and your God." ' Mary Magdalene went and announced to the disciples, 'I have seen the Lord'; and she told them that he had said these things to her" (20:17–18).

Her words have no immediate effect, but the reader anticipates that they will soon bear fruit. She is the first bearer of the words of the risen Jesus. In The Gospel According to Luke she is identified as an early follower of Jesus who had been cured of acute demon possession. In John she is introduced into the text late and abruptly, and we are told no more about her than we are told about the beloved disciple. She is an apostle and a leading example of who the author will be and what he will do.[2]

A Samaritan woman in chapter 4 is an earlier, preresurrection example. She is nameless. So is the beloved disciple. He shares that silence with her. He is identified as the author of the gospel, but only later tradition supplies the name John. Whether this is a correct identification is no more certain than which John he might be.[3] The care and space the nameless author devotes to this nameless woman may indicate either an aspiration to share her role or an understanding that he does so.

She is the only figure in the gospel who bears the words of Jesus to others and in doing so produces a harvest of believers. She enters the text as Jesus passes through Samaria on the way to Galilee from Judea. He stops to rest at Jacob's well. "A Samaritan woman" from the nearby city comes to draw water, and Jesus initiates a conversation with her. In the economy of the gospel, it is an extended conversation.[4] The first half revolves around the image of Jesus as the source of "living water" (4:7–15). In the second, Jesus discloses prophetic knowledge of her life: "You have had five husbands, and the one you have now is not your husband" (4:18). At the end of it, he reveals himself to her as the Messiah in the critical formula "I am he" (*ego eimi*) (4:26). The disciples appear and interrupt the exchange. They are shocked that he is speaking with a woman. Rabbis avoided public conversation with women. Moreover, this is a Samaritan woman, and the Jews held Samaritans to be apostate.[5]

The woman abandons her water jar to return to the city with the message: "Come and see a man who told me everything I have ever done! He cannot be the Messiah, can he?" (4:29). The townspeople flock to the well and invite Jesus to stay. He accepts. "And many more believed because of his word. They said to the woman, 'It is no longer because of what you said that we believe, for we have heard for ourselves, and we know that this is truly the Savior of the world' " (4:41–42).

Whatever may be said of the woman's numerous husbands, she is clearly a person at the margins, and she belongs to a people who are not Jesus' own. But she takes on an apostolic role. Jesus needs her. The testimony she bears has an immediate and considerable impact.[6] The effect is achieved by the words rather than by her belief and any infectious quality her belief may have. Jesus has revealed himself to her as the Messiah in the special formula: "Ego eimi" (I am he). But the most that she can say to the townspeople about this critical point is a question: "Could this possibly be the Messiah?" The uncertain status of her belief highlights the fact that the productive power lies in the story and in her telling it.

As the writer of John knows sympathetically, it is in the nature of apostleship that this should be so. The Word goes out and returns as a harvest. The effect is in the Word. In making his appeal—in replaying the trial of Jesus as a trial of the World, in representing the broken *riv* to belief—John puts the effective words to the reader and thus follows the example of the Samaritan woman.

22. The Power of the Word:

Moses and the Spirit

The Gospel of John's anticipation of the effectiveness of its story in generating belief is not premised upon a power inherent in the words. The power is that of the Word. The relation between the written words and the Word that makes them productive takes form in the text as the Spirit, or Paraclete.

The gospel enlists Moses' aid in presenting the subject. It does so first in a poem that is strategically placed at the end of chapter 12, where Jesus' public ministry concludes. I shall return to the poem later for what it has to say about condemnation and disbelief, but I call attention to it now for its allusions to Moses. The poem can be translated:

44 Whoever believes in me
   believes not in me
   but in Him who sent me.
45 And whoever sees me
   sees Him who sent me.
46 As light I have come into the world
   in order that all who believe in me
   remain not in darkness.
47 And if anyone hears my words and keeps them not,
   I do not condemn (*krino*) him,
   for I did not come in order to condemn (*krino*) the world
   but in order to save the world.
48 Whoever rejects me and does not receive my words
   is already subjected to his judge (*krinonta*);
   the word that I have spoken,
   that word will judge (*krinei*) him in the last day;
49 for not on my own have I spoken,
   but the Father who sent me
   has Himself commanded me
   what to say and what to speak.
50 And I know that His commandment is eternal life.
   Thus what I speak,
   I speak just as the Father has told me.

The notions of being sent and being sent with words suggest a prophet as messenger from the heavenly assembly. Especially given the references to command and commandment, they particularly suggest Deuteronomy's prophet-like Moses: "I will put my words in the mouth of the prophet, who shall speak to them everything that I command. Anyone who does not heed the words that the prophet shall speak in my name, I myself will hold accountable" (Deut. 18:18–19).[1]

In addition and more extensively, the poem's notions of keeping words and of commandment as life recall Moses' last remarks to Israel.[2] Moses said that if the people obey the commandments they will live; if they do not they will perish (e.g., Deut. 30:15–18). And he instructs them: "Take to heart all the words that I am giving in witness against you today; give them as a command to your children, so that they may diligently observe all the words of this law. This is no trifling matter for you, but rather your very life" (32:46–47).

The Gospel of John's allusions to Moses establish an interpretive link between Moses' last address to Israel and the last discourse of Jesus that soon follows. The link is strengthened by allusions to Moses within the last discourse itself. For example, Jesus tells the disciples that if they love him they will keep his commandments (John 14:15), and he continues to speak of keeping his commandments and of keeping his words and of life (14:18–24). These are very like the statements Moses makes.[3]

There are two critical differences between the speeches, however: Moses says to take his words to heart (Deut. 32:46; see also 6:6, 30:2, 6, 17), and he writes them down (31:9, 19, 22, 24).[4] Jesus does neither. These omissions make room in the text for Jesus to address the role of the Spirit.

Although Jesus makes no reference to the heart, where his commandments are to be kept, he says something similar: He talks about the Spirit, who will abide with and be in the disciples (John 14:17). To keep the words, to have them in the active center of one's being, to have them by heart, is to be the abode of the Spirit.

John Ashton observes that there is little mention of the Spirit in John except in association with words.[5] At one point Jesus says explicitly: "It is the Spirit that gives life; . . . The words that I have spoken to you are both Spirit and life" (6:63). The connection is repeated when Jesus talks to his disciples about keeping his commandments and adds the first mention of the Paraclete: "And I will ask the Father, and he will give you another Paraclete. . . . This is the Spirit of truth. . . . You know him, because he abides with you, and will be in you" (14:16–17).[6]

Words and Spirit go together. It is by the power of the Spirit that the commandments of Jesus are kept in the heart.[7]

In addition to speaking, Moses writes his words. Jesus does not.[8] He leaves the writing to the disciples.[9] This is another opening to the Spirit.[10]

The Gospel of John portrays Jesus' followers as ordinary at best. They may or may not be literate, but they are certainly mundane. They abandon Jesus at the worst of moments, and the discovery that his body is missing does not make them more reliably robust. Peter sees the empty tomb, and nothing indicates that the sight makes him believe Jesus has risen from the dead. An unnamed disciple, the beloved disciple, also sees the tomb. He "believes," but returns home and soon thereafter huddles in fear with other disciples behind locked doors (20:3–10, 19). When the risen Jesus appears, the disciples rejoice, but Thomas, who was absent, typifies their doubt. He will not believe until confronted by Jesus and invited to touch the mortal wounds (20:24–28).

As the story continues in chapter 21, the disciples have some form of hesitant, provisional belief, but they know neither what to do nor what to say and return to their old trade of fishing.[11] They do so at night, in the darkness that the prologue opposes to the light of the Word. Their sojourn with Jesus has not made them more successful fishermen, and they catch nothing. When Jesus appears on shore just after daybreak, none recognizes him. Recognition comes only when, at Jesus' bidding, some of the disciples cast a net and retrieve an impossibly large number of fish. Even then, the gospel depicts the disciples as dazed and uneasy: "Now none of the disciples dared to ask him, 'Who are you?' because they knew it was the Lord" (21:12). This group includes the "beloved disciple," who is said in the last verses of the gospel to be the one "who is testifying to these things and has written them" (21:24).[12] For all that this disciple is beloved, his belief is not depicted as sufficiently strong or enduring for him to have discerned the meaning of the trial of Jesus.

The resurrection is critical, but the disciples' understanding of its significance is fragile all the way through to the end of the text. These people are capable neither of gospel writing nor of the bold activity they will subsequently undertake, hinted at in chapter 21 and recounted in The Acts of the Apostles, which follows John in the canon.

In John, the Spirit is the source of testimony. The Spirit at last gives the disciples memory and understanding. The Spirit writes the words of Jesus on the hearts of the disciples, enables them then to write the words on pages, and will write them on the hearts of believers.

Ashton notes that in John "works have been transformed into words, spoken in the one case, written in the other. With Jesus' passing, the chance of witnessing his signs has gone forever. This is not a matter of regret: 'It is good for you that I go.' "[13] In writing, the disciples do works greater than those of Jesus (14:12). Their writing fulfills the promise.

Earlier, in discussing the challenges faced by the gospel writer, I cited his statement of the problem of selecting material: "Jesus did *many other signs. . . . these* are written in order that you may come to believe." The statement can be read with a different emphasis: "Jesus *did* many other signs. . . . these *are written* in order that you may come to believe." Jesus had done signs and miracles without collaborators or intermediaries, and people believed. After the resurrection, belief will be a function of the Spirit's labors in and with the writings of Jesus' followers. In his final prayer, offered in the pretrial discourse, Jesus intercedes for "those who will believe in me through [the disciples'] word" (17:20). The disciples' word will be pivotal as the medium for belief.[14] Following the resurrection, Jesus "breathed on them and said to them, 'Receive the Holy Spirit' " (20:22). The Word of the beginning is powerfully committed to writing at the end, and this is the work of the Spirit.

The disciples' words have no power of their own, and their welding with the empowering Spirit is neither a magical nor a mystical process. The author of John is frank. He did not receive his book from the hand of an angel. He wrote it, and he omitted a lot of good material. Moreover, he wrote within a particular community with a particular history, and his words and references depended on that community. That he and his writing had a locus among immediate friends is clear from the affidavits, added by another hand, that vouch for him and his testimony (19:35, 21:24). That he is positively dependent upon the Jewish community is patent. He can be no anti-Semite.[15] He enacts his dependence: He has no way to tell his story without the language of Jewish liturgy and Jewish stories and without Isaiah and Moses. This is a representation that the Word became flesh. The continuing presence of the Word — the Spirit — is embodied in words in communities in histories, as it always has been.

23. The Power of the Word: Disbelief

The Word goes forth and does not return empty but prospers in the thing for which it is sent. The written gospel is a medium of believing. The author anticipates that, following the example of the Samaritan woman and with the postresurrection gift of the Spirit, the words will be performatively effective — "in order that you may come to believe."

But people do not believe.

The divine lawsuit leads to the resurrection, the Spirit is given without measure, and the gospel is written. All resources are now fully committed to belief and life. Nothing is held in reserve. Disbelief is impossible. But it happens. It is the impossible possibility.[1]

The author had lived with disbelief, his own and that of his fellow disciples as well as that of Jesus' antagonists. John would continue to live with disbelief if the Epistles of John may be taken as a guide. They indicate that the very community that was the gospel's matrix itself suffered schism, deception, and either failures of believing or conflicts in believing. Even among the gospel's own, the impossible took place.[2]

There is a pattern in John's response to the impossibility of disbelief: he confronts the difficult questions but does not allow them to determine the answers. The pattern exhibits a simplicity that deserves close attention.

Earlier I turned to the poem that ends chapter 12 to take note of its allusions to Moses. I now return to that poem and its context to take note of the characteristic pattern of its response to disbelief. In chapter 12, Jesus ends his public ministry and then hides. At that strategic point, the Gospel of John inserts an editorial reflection on the plain, foundation-shaking fact that disbelief, including perhaps the author's own and that of other disciples, had already been a common reaction to Jesus' signs.

The text quotes Isaiah (53:1): "Lord, who has believed our message, and to whom has the arm of the Lord been revealed?" (12:38). The answer is a second quote from Isaiah (6:9–10), and the reader recoils from its ruthlessness: "He has blinded their eyes and hardened their heart, so that they might not look with their eyes, and understand with their heart and turn — and I would heal them" (12:40).[3] People do not believe because God prevents them from believing.

People are condemned by their failure to believe. If this be self-judgment, it constitutes a power of self-condemnation greater than God's power to save, and darkness is then greater than light. If disbelief is God's doing, His power to foreclose saving belief is at war with His power to give eternal life. Either way, or both ways, what kind of God is this?

The writer offers no mitigating interpretation of the terrible statement from Isaiah and does not try to resolve the contradictions and revulsion it arouses. The text moves briskly to the concluding poem:

Then Jesus cried aloud:
"Whoever believes in me
believes not in me
but in Him who sent me.
And whoever sees me
sees Him who sent me.
As light I have come into the world
in order that all who believe in me
remain not in darkness.
And if anyone hears my words and keeps them not,
I do not condemn him,
for I did not come in order to condemn the world
but in order to save the world.
Whoever rejects me and does not receive my words
is already subjected to his judge;
the word that I have spoken,
that word will judge him in the last day;
for not on my own have I spoken,
but the Father who sent me
has Himself commanded me
what to say and what to speak.
And I know that His commandment is eternal life.
Thus what I speak,
I speak just as the Father has told me."

The introduction to the poem is striking. Jesus "shouts" it, or "cries it aloud." This is an odd formula. It is also oddly placed. According to the preceding narrative, Jesus concluded his public performance of signs, then departed and hid from his followers. There is no one in the text for him to shout the poem to. The awkwardness contrasts with the finely wrought poetry in the Greek.[4] This combination of factors supports

John Ashton's conclusion that the text is meant "to draw the reader's attention to the particular importance of what follows."[5]

I think that Isaiah's awful saying about God hardening people's hearts has already aroused the reader's attention. It certainly stimulates in my mind questions about human belief and the terrible power and suffering of God. The poem does not answer such questions. It begins to reconfigure them instead. It moves away from the repellent, puzzling dilemma to the responsible action of telling a story told in hope.

The poem recapitulates essential elements of the prologue to the gospel. The prologue's language and themes have coursed through the intervening chapters to give and to gather meaning[6] and now reemerge once more. The development of the contrasts belief/disbelief, light/darkness, life/condemnation does not issue in a simple, symmetrical duality: those who believe are saved for the light; those who do not believe are lost to darkness.

Disbelievers are assigned no new or particular status in the poem. At the "last day"—in the future? the day of *krisis* that is already underway?—they will be judged by Jesus' word. His word will condemn them, but he has come to save, not condemn. The condemning word comes from the Father and is the command of eternal life. What sense does this make? Is life rather than condemnation the concluding, prevailing word, or is it not? Although I would have felt personally and professionally compelled to pursue these questions and attempt a logical resolution of them, the poet takes a different, aesthetic tack.

The poem associates the action of believing with receiving and keeping words. In the poem, the essential, self-described action of Jesus is speaking. (Note the density of the use of the verb *speak* in the concluding verses of the poem.) He does not judge/condemn or speculate; he gets on with the business of speaking. He speaks what the Father commands him, and the Father's commandment is eternal life. Disbelief is not replaced by belief, nor are judgment and condemnation replaced by acquittal. Along with abstraction, disbelief and condemnation are supplanted by the specific activity of speaking the only words that Jesus is authorized to speak. They are living words: The light has come into the world; those who believe in him need not remain in darkness.

The poem works down to Jesus speaking. It provides neither analysis nor answers in what we think of as the traditional form—no systematic reconciliation of contradictions, no closure, no apologetic theory, no exposition of a neutral principle. It concludes with Jesus speaking about speaking what he is told.

The poem addresses belief and disbelief and their consequences. Irreconcilably, it speaks of the judge of disbelievers, the condemning word whose content means eternal life and therefore, presumably, cannot condemn the disbeliever. It opposes those who believe and receive Jesus' words to those who reject him and do not receive his words. Are the latter to be condemned? How and to what? These verses contain no opposite to eternal life. They leave the reader with Jesus affirming that the commandment given him for utterance is, exactly, life. And then the text turns toward the death of the life-giving Word.

This is a characteristically Johannine pattern: Confront the hard questions and fundamental contradictions of belief and disbelief and their entailments. And then, because they cannot be resolved from within the limits of their own terms, place them in a wholly different context, a performance that offers answers that really are answers, but not those originally sought and not in the forms anticipated.

This is the pattern followed in the poem. It is repeated throughout the gospel,[7] and it is a basic pattern of the gospel as a whole. The text builds to the trial and execution of Jesus with its ironies of the trial judges' self-condemnation and of the status of a world that rejects the Word. There is a pause at the tomb, a disjunction. At that point, after the fashion of Jesus in the poem, the author says all that he is authorized to say. He tells the story of the resurrection. And his words have to do with life and not death. Altogether missing are words of condemnation. Nothing of punishment or heroic revenge. No eye for an eye. Missing also are words of speculation and explanation. No exposition of judgment, justice, or mercy. In their place John provides an account of confrontations with the risen Jesus and his speaking: "Peace be with you" (20:19, 21).

The pattern continues beyond the pages of the gospel. As I noted, the Epistles of John give evidence of continuing disbelief within John's own community. The Epistles' basic response to this seeming triumph of failure among its own is to repeat the story: "We declare to you what was from the beginning. . . . God is light and in him there is no darkness at all" (1 John 1:1, 5). The author confronts the impossible—inexplicable because it is impossible—and in response repeats his performance. He tells once more the story that is to generate belief but has often not done so.

The gospel and the Epistles do not keep on retelling the story with mad determination or with gleeful, triumphal aggression to promote self-condemnation, so that, every time people hear or read the story and disbelieve, darkness will be compounded. The gospel is written to believing for life. It has no other intention. It is not written for disbelief and death. It hasn't the power to condemn.

Nor does the author write out of naïveté, as though disbelief will dissolve at the wave of a story. The gospel and its tradition are not naive. The beloved disciple had, after all, witnessed the crucifixion and knew enough of disbelief, including his own. Still less does he write pitiably against nothingness, writing hopelessly exactly because it is hopeless, repeating the story despite the loss of meaning because the repetition is all that is left except the craft of storytelling and the self-righteousness of continuing failure.[8]

Nor does he write tentatively, with eroded confidence. And, in any event, there is no necessary connection between the power in the words and the state of his confidence. He simply does what he is authorized to do. He tells the story that represents the risen Jesus.

24. John's Freedom from and for Law

The Gospel of John appropriates the language of law as the medium for its performance. This would be wholly unremarkable for an appeal from a lower-court judgment to a higher court. It would also be unremarkable for a novel or film because law lends itself easily to storytelling, with its clash of opposites, conflicting narratives, investigation, argument, courtroom drama, suspense, a concluding judgment, and resolution. In fact, the language of law is unremarkable generally in the way we Americans talk about ourselves and our life together: "I've got my rights"; "I'll take it all the way to the Supreme Court." We take pride in the rule of law and hope for it for others. The Jews of the gospel's day may themselves have been saturated with the thoughtforms and language of law.

But the abundance of law in the gospel *is* remarkable. Jesus was executed by law. Law should be regarded as cursed. It is not. The author puts it to use. Strange to say, he makes out a lawsuit against law. This exhibition of his freedom to employ the medium of Jesus' death enacts his subject.

The prosecution's case against the world focuses on the rule of law.

A. E. Harvey points out that the sequence of events in the gospel is rooted in the normal observance of the Jews' own legal system.[1] The healings on the Sabbath and Jesus' statements that he was the Son of God, taken as blasphemy, provide a basis for prosecution on a capital charge.[2] And Alan Watson notes that belief in Jesus as the Messiah could ignite an uprising that the Romans would have to put down (see 11:48). Fears for the loss of the Temple and Jerusalem would justify the Sanhedrin in seeking to put Jesus to death.[3] From the perspective of the text, for its purposes, the law of the Jewish community appears to have been correctly upheld.[4]

At the eleventh hour Roman law, too, is drawn into events. The Gospel of John emphasizes the role Roman law plays in Jesus' execution. This emphasis was carried forward in the early statement of Christian faith known as the Apostles' Creed: Jesus "suffered under Pontius Pilate"—under Pilate, not the Jews. Pilate is the officer of the law who did this thing, but the gospel does not portray Pilate as an enemy of Jesus. At first Pilate finds that there is no case against Jesus and looks for a way to release him. But when Pilate hears the crowd crying out the language of treason and invoking the emperor, he brings Jesus outside and then delivers him to crucifixion (19:12–16). It is an act of juridical condemnation. Pilate convicts Jesus of what Watson calls "the most serious Roman crime of all."[5] Pilate is—to use a term favored by American judges—powerless to do otherwise. He acts according to Roman law, and the text does not question the assumption that Roman law is a politically necessary, culturally impressive creation.

From all appearances, in the instance of those who sat in judgment of Jesus in John, the system worked as it was supposed to do. Within the ordinary administration of that system, Harvey says, due process was observed when Jesus was found guilty.[6] The text offers no grounds to conclude that the judges defaulted in their responsibility to the law. The Jews were justified in forcing Pilate to act, and Pilate acted according to law. The text never questions the validity of the action as a matter of law, and it never questions the validity of law itself as a matter of politics.

Nevertheless, the institutions of law—functioning normally and without express criticism in the text—are put in issue.[7] No less than their officers, the institutions condemn themselves. The point is simple to state, but difficult to accept. The temptation is to blunt the force of it.

It would be easier if the text were to identify a defect in the judges or the law and to explain Jesus' crucifixion as a consequence of this shortfall—bad judges, bad law: Jesus was wrongly convicted. In this event, the offending instance could be separated and the fabric of the law mended so as to allow continued assertion of its goodness. Or it could be assumed that the Roman version of law was an early stage in an evolutionary process and that qualitatively different, higher forms have appeared since then. American law could then be distinguished from the Roman version, and readers could be excused from taking the full force of John's story.[8] The text provides no support for such a move.

The gospel has no quarrel with the quality of Roman law. The law could not have been reformed and made better in a way that would escape the self-condemnation presented by the gospel. Jesus is executed by law. The law rejects the Word and condemns itself. The judgment runs not to the goodness or badness of the law, but to its foundations in a world that rejects the Word.

The text never pronounces a judgment upon the law for the condemnation of Jesus. It suspends that judgment and instead tells the story of the resurrection, the event that places the preceding events and the law in a wholly different context.[9] The author's freedom to use the language of law — the words, forms, methods of presentation, ways of thinking — is the witness he bears to the difference.[10]

This freedom is characteristically extravagant. The gospel introduces the *krisis* in the prologue and then gives it narrative form in chapters 2–4. The stories in those chapters indicate what happens when the Word becomes flesh. As his first sign, Jesus turns water to wine (2:1–11). He is attending the celebration of a wedding. There is reference to drunkenness. The wine runs short. At the instigation of his mother, Jesus directs servants to fill stone water jars. The text is specific. There are six jars. The servants fill them to the brim. Each holds twenty or thirty gallons. The water turns to wine. Jesus has instantly produced something on the order of 150 gallons of wine for an already well-watered wedding party. The great quantity is matched by its high quality. The expert praises it. If, as George Macrae avers, John is singularly humorless,[11] its author has nonetheless traveled with the spirit of comedy. He knows the joyful, expressive value of excess.[12] The intersection of *en* with *egeneto* is transfiguring. Water is changed into wine, an exorbitant amount of good wine, freely drunk.

It belongs to this exuberance that, subsequent to Jesus' execution according to law, the language of law is turned into a medium for the gospel.[13] After the resurrection, obedience to the state's law is a tactic and not an obligation.[14] The disciples are free to obey the law as Jesus did. They are also free to break the law as Jesus did. They are free to suffer the consequences as he did, perhaps in the same form (21:18–19). And they are free to make use of law as Jesus did. This is so because Jesus accepted, suffered, took upon himself the goodness as well as the evil, the upholding peace as well as the violence of law — both, together the indicia of its fallenness — and triumphed over them. The resurrection is the ultimate that makes law penultimate, like all things of the political and natural worlds.[15] The resurrection both assures law a place and places limits on it. Law is to be respected, even celebrated, for the sake of the ultimate. But it cannot rule because it is penultimate.

The relation of the penultimate to the ultimate — the dialectics of saying both no and yes to law — takes form in the text of John in the never-stated, suspended condemnation of the legal system in combination with liberal use of the forms and language of law. The dialectics does not mean proceeding by halves. Like Jesus, the author is freely, fully involved in law but not of it.

The author of the gospel makes much of law because he and his enterprise cannot be determined by it. This freedom is not the same thing as the professional independence prized by lawyers, and I must explore the difference.[1]

Professional ethics require that a lawyer exercise independent professional judgment.[2] The thought is that a lawyer should be subject to no outside influence that might dilute her loyalty to a client. She is to maintain independence for investment in the client's cause.

But the matter is not so simple. Another kind of independence pulls an attorney in the opposite direction: A lawyer is supposed to reserve a measure of independence from her client as well. She must fulfill a higher duty to the law and the legal system.[3] Accordingly, a government lawyer is to serve the people and not a particular officer of the government.[4] And a public prosecutor's duty "is to seek justice, not merely to convict." [5] No less importantly, Robert Gordon observes, the small but significant segment of the bar who service large, powerful corporations "must be committed to helping maintain . . . the rules and institutions of the legal framework, even when doing so hurts their clients." [6] The hope is to provide some form of moral constraint on amoral corporations and powerful people, an end that finally serves such clients' best interest by supporting the general conditions in which they may continue to prosper.[7]

So lawyers should be independent of power in order to serve their clients, but they should be independent of clients in order to serve the higher purposes of law.

There are still more complications. Where a client, like the government or a large corporation, is a wielder of great power, there are good reasons for insisting that the attorney maintain professional distance from the client. Even in these circumstances, however, it is unclear that distance is always fitting.[8] Independence from clients is improper for most lawyers in most of their professional involvements where independence stands for a lack of empathy,[9] or distance from persons as well as interests,[10] or knowing better than the client what the client wants and needs.[11]

The independence I address here is the aspiration, described by Gordon, that "a part of the lawyer's professional persona must be set aside for dedication to public purposes":[12] Attorneys should be free of undue, outside influence in order to devote themselves to clients, but they should always be bound to the higher purposes of law. To make such a statement, standing alone or in a Law Day speech, is to say very little, however. What are improper influences? What are the higher purposes of law? Should an attorney serve different kinds of clients, say a cigarette manufacturer and a poor criminal defendant, with the same qualified devotion? Is a scorched-earth, all-out defense of an individual against the power of the state never right? Might not such a defense serve the higher purposes of law?

To represent both people and public interest with integrity may require continuing, contextually complex judgments. There is some opinion that lawyers are not successfully navigating the complexities.[13] Marc Galanter notes that "laments about commercialization and the loss of professional virtue have recurred regularly for a century," but the question now is whether, as he puts it, "the present 'crisis' is the real thing." [14] If recent consensus documents produced by the American Bar Association are a guide, the bar certainly appears to be troubled about a crisis or the perception of one, and the response of these documents is to promote greater professionalism.

I think that this response is inadequate and largely misdirected. To avoid misunderstanding, I emphasize my beliefs that the rule of law is a genuine, public good and that lawyers should be skillful professionals. In my own observation, the clients most likely to have incompetent representation are those in the worst situations to have to suffer it. This is wrong. It should not be allowed. However, the professionalism campaign is an unsatisfactory response; competence ought to be the point of departure and not the goal, ought to be the entry-level requirement for all and not the upper limit of our longing. More important, much of the campaign is self-defeating. Because professionalism is an "ism" of the intrinsic, it cannot direct us beyond itself. Law and the legal profession at their best will not finally serve as sources for the perspective and sense of direction that are needed.

In 1984 the ABA established a commission—the Stanley Commission—in response to Chief Justice Warren Burger's anxiety that "the Bar might be moving away from the principles of professionalism." [15] The commission hastened to investigate the subject and two years later returned a report: ". . . *In the Spirit of Public Service*": *A Blueprint for the Rekin-*

dling of Lawyer Professionalism.[16] The title's mixture of metaphors accurately reflects the tenor of the contents. Spirit is overtaken by engineering, and the public is thought to be served by our becoming what we were, only more so. Thomas Shaffer accurately distills the propositions of the report: "The way to be a good person and a lawyer is (i) to be professional and (ii) to be *in* the profession, to be *of* it."[17]

Subsequently, another ABA group, this one a "task force," examined how best to develop professionalism.[18] It produced the professionally celebrated MacCrate Report.[19] The task force spent many of the pages of its report, and presumably much of its time, dealing with the prior question of what constitutes the professionalism to be developed. The answer, titled "Statement of Fundamental Skills and Values," divides lawyering into discrete parts and then subjects them to a form of diluted social-scientific analysis. The task force came to its assignment as a task to be solved, and that is what came out of its work: lawyers as task-consumed, problem-solving technocrats.[20] Its report portrays the skills and values of attorneys in the way that a descriptive inventory for an auto parts shop would list the contents of its shelves. Not only does it separate values from skills, it places a much greater emphasis on skills— ten of them as compared to four values, sixty-six pages as compared to fourteen.

The difference in emphasis is qualitative as well as quantitative. The first and primary of the four values is to have and apply the ten skills. The fourth and last is to improve the skills that it is the first value to have. As part of what the report calls the skill of recognizing and resolving "ethical dilemmas," the report does say that lawyers should be familiar with "sources of ethical rules," including "aspects of ethical philosophy" and a "personal sense of morality."[21] And it includes a little section on the value of promoting justice, fairness, and morality.[22] Professionalism-as-technique, however, is the central trope of the report. The task force undertook a preparatory survey of law schools to examine the way they teach skills. A footnote reveals that it did not trouble to ask about ethics or values education, which the report refers to as "values training."[23] Even as a subject for training, ethics and values were not in mind. The report proceeds as though the professionalism it commends is not itself an affirmation of desiccating values.

A more recent installment in the professionalism serial is more encouraging.[24] This one was written by a committee asked to determine how the new, celebrated sense of professionalism is to be inculcated.[25] It embraces the "Statement of Fundamental Skills and Values" and refers carefully to certain pages in the statement as though all that remained for the committee to do was to work out details for instilling the values contained in those pages. In fact, there is almost no substantive correspondence between the report and the statement. The report is written in a different language, with different metaphors and a wholly different image of lawyering. It says that a professional lawyer is "an expert in law pursuing a learned art in service to clients and in the spirit of public service; and engaging in these pursuits as part of a common calling to promote justice and public good." [26]

Included among the indicia of *this* professional lawyer are a capacity for moral dialogue with clients, prudential wisdom, and economic temperance (!). The report suggests that teachers may teach professionalism by themselves being and being seen to be professionals of the desired sort. In this committee's hands, the technocratically proficient problem solver is reborn as a learned artist called to serve others in all that she does. [27]

This portrait of a lawyer is an improvement even on Robert Gordon's affecting notion of a lawyer reserving part of her persona for public purposes. The committee's learned servant is a whole person, all of whose professional life — and not only a piece of it — belongs to public service whatever the setting of her practice. The independence of such a lawyer lies in "dedication to certain ideals as a way of life as part of a specialized group." [28] This dedication requires forswearing the pursuit of other possibilities, hence the mention of economic temperance.

That no lawyer known to you fits the image does not impugn its validity. The point is what we would become. "Myth," Robert Cover said, "is the part of reality we create and choose to remember in order to *re-enact*. . . . History is a countermove bringing us back to reality. . . . Only myth tells us who we would become; only history can tell us how hard it will really be to become that." [29]

As it happens, however, there are such lawyers, historical and not mythological, more than might be suspected. They are public-spirited and learned. Some of them are also loving and economically temperate to a fault. I have written the stories of a few, and many more are or are becoming publicly familiar. [30] Some represent clients who are poor, others are in government service, and still others engage in the private practice of general or business law. One unacceptable quality of the technocrat–problem solver image is that it breaks faith with these lawyers.

The image of the learned artist whose independence derives from dedication to public service is a good and inspiring one. It inspires me, and I have urged it upon colleagues and students. It is nonetheless limited because it, too, is ultimately bound by law—what the committee refers to as ideals as a way of life at the bar and others call "norms supplied by traditional and technocratic legalism" (Robert Gordon)[31] or the rule of law.[32] This limit it shares with Chief Justice Burger, the Stanley Commission, and the MacCrate Report.

Justice is one ideal sometimes promoted as a key aspect of professionalism, but lawyers generally think of justice as dependent upon law. For example, an inscription on the Supreme Court building announces: "Equal Justice Under Law." And the preamble to the Model Code of Professional Responsibility holds, in words that can scarcely be read aloud sensibly: "The continued existence of a free and democratic society depends upon recognition of the concept that justice is based upon the rule of law grounded in respect for the dignity of the individual and his capacity through reason for enlightened self-government. Law so grounded makes justice possible."[33] With more blunt, Gallic simplicity, Charles DeGaulle said: "I have no need to tell you that justice of any sort, in principle as in execution, emanates from the State."[34] Justice so conceived is, like professionalism at its best, unable to generate the lift and momentum necessary to give the lawyer exit velocity from the gravitational pull of a law-bound system of values.

Judge Richard Posner observes that lawyers tend to think of law as self-enclosed and self-sustaining and that they then surrender the ability to gain distance from it. The study of law presents its subject, he says, "as something not to be questioned, as something that has always existed and in approximately its contemporary form."[35] The consequence is that shortly after entering law school the student loses perspective, never to regain it.[36] Thereafter the lawyer's attitude toward law "is pious and reverential rather than inquiring and challenging."[37]

I think that the study and practice of law do indeed incline us to discard the worthy perspectives we have received from families, from communities of profoundly political commitment, and—to the extent that they are distinguishable—from communities of faith as well. Law can be deeply deracinating in this way.[38]

In the course of an ethnographic study conducted at the Harvard Law School, Robert Granfield discovered that students replace their own views, which they come to see as biased, with professional values perceived as neutral.[39] This often means absorbing a professional, detached cynicism that students adjust to by assigning it value.[40] Posner would say that they come to venerate it. One student told Granfield that since entering law school she had come to "realize that the system is set up and you can't change it. I've become really cynical. . . . I'm not sure what's right or wrong anymore."[41] Encouraging students to overcome their debilitating prejudices is a worthwhile function of professional education, Granfield observes, but encouraging them to accept the neutrality of a professional game as though it is necessary and natural has the effect of disabling the idealists. They abandon "their previous aspirations of 'doing good.'"[42] They are then forced to come to terms with what they view as selling out.[43]

There is more to be said. Granfield discovered, as have I, a minority of students who reject the dominant legal consciousness and are resistant to cynicism.[44] (In my experience they have increased in number since the early 1990s.) Granfield notes that these students do not come to law expecting to find in it the content of justice and truth. They know better. After they arrive, they are not confounded by the incoherence in law and are instead empowered by it for the greater flexibility it allows in constructing arguments. They view law as a tool to be used, and they are thereby protected against cynicism. In contrast to the majority, they identify with critical and justice-oriented approaches, and they are active in challenging the law school establishment. They are also, Granfield reports, "vehement in their criticism of law," and yet they graduate into very active practices with legal services, labor organizations, and grassroots community groups.[45] (Students of mine enter these kinds of practices but also a great variety of others, including corporate law.)

Granfield found that these people are guided by political and by theological commitments in opposition to the professional values that are pressed upon them.[46] They are vehement critics of law but not cynics, and they become vigorous practitioners of law. I suspect that it is exactly because these people are free not to be determined by law that they are free to become mistrustfully yet actively immersed in it. They develop freedom from the independence of professionalism. They are free to be in but not of the law.

The freedom realized in the Gospel of John is not derived from the rule of law or professional ideals. The penultimacy of law exposed in the resurrection allows John to be saturated with legal terms and formulas and not to be determined by them. The dialectics of this freedom evident in the text of the gospel—the no and yes—is reflected in the sharp-edged, prophetic example of William Stringfellow's relationship to law. He felt the dialectics beginning with his entry into Harvard Law School in 1953, long before Granfield's study, then during his first practice in East Harlem, and thereafter until his death in 1985.[47]

Stringfellow was struck not only by the limitations of law but also by its violent aggression as a fallen institution and instrument of death.[48] He also saw that his law practice would condone or appear to condone its violence. He could therefore never shelve the insistent, ironic question of whether he would "have to renounce being a lawyer the better to be an advocate."[49]

He could scarcely discern himself as a victim of the legal system (although discernment came more readily when the FBI put him under surveillance and examination). But his law practice provided him intimate experience with the aggressions of law against others. His first experience was with the assault of law against black people in New York, and he understood its meaning for himself: "If the American legal system seems viable for me and other white Americans but is not so for citizens who are black, or for many others, then how, as the dual commandment would ask, in the name of humanity, can it be affirmed as viable for me or for any human being?"[50]

He believed that his practice not only risked advancing the aggression of the system but also put him at risk. Law is not a neutral tool. He would say that just here is the danger for a lawyer who thinks of herself as a learned artist. She may find it difficult to recognize her participation in law as participation in politics, power, and violence.[51]

So Stringfellow was clear-eyed about law and his practice of it, about its risks to others and to himself. He always might have had to renounce being a lawyer as he was free and ready to do. But he continued freely in the work, for law is also a gift of God.[52] He said that he was not called to be an attorney, because no profession or employment in itself can constitute a vocation. He was instead called to be human—to be human, not religious—and his work as a lawyer, like any work, could be "rendered a sacrament of that vocation."[53] He celebrated this sacrament with abandon. He found himself "free to advocate the cause of one . . . as over against everyone and everything else in the world,"[54] not because the system of justice demands it but because, divested of self-interest, he could interest himself fully in his clients. He could receive them as gifts rather than as problems or bearers of problems.[55]

His freedom meant, too, that he could freely advance the rule of law, a fact that confounded people unaccustomed to a simultaneous no and yes. Robert Kennedy planned to hold a conference on how lawyers could better serve poor people. He had read one of Stringfellow's books, was moved by it, and sent around an aide to consult Stringfellow on the conference subject. The visitor began with the confidence that Stringfellow would not be invited to speak at the conference because "You're too radical." In amused reward of such honesty, Stringfellow proceeded with the interview.[56] This was not the first time he had been called radical, but he always thought the label a mistake. He maintained that he belonged solidly within the American legal tradition and offered his practice of law as verification:

> I have been an advocate for the poor, for the urban underclass, for freedom riders and war resisters, for people deprived of elementary rights: children, women, blacks, hispanics, native Americans, political prisoners, homosexuals, the elderly, the handicapped, clergy accused of heresy, women aspiring to priesthood. The consistent concerns of my practice have been the values of the constitutional system, due process of law, and the rule of law.[57]

His practice was an intoxicated exercise of the freedom to be fully in but not of law.

The word *advocate* bears emphasis in Stringfellow's thought about renouncing his profession of law the better to fulfill his vocation of advocacy. He believed that advocating the cause of the victims of society exemplifies the Church's work of intercession for anyone in need.[58] He had learned from his stay in Harlem, where he was an outsider among outsiders, "that all human beings are outcasts in one sense or another. It is only more vivid that people are outcasts in a place like Harlem." [59] All of us need an advocate, and advocacy as intercession for those in need can take lawyering as one of its several forms. Such advocacy is the Church's work, and the bar enjoys no monopoly in defining what it is and who may take part in it.

For that matter, Emily Fowler Hartigan says, the legal system has no more final say about the name *lawyer* than it does about the name *advocate*. The bar can revoke the license of a person who practices law by vocation, but it cannot rescind her being a lawyer. For her to be declared an outlaw "does not contradict the reality that it is she and true communities that have the final power of naming" who she is.[60]

Hartigan once heard Stringfellow talk about advocacy as making oneself vulnerable on behalf of another, even unto death.[61] For a long time afterward, she mostly read his work as prophetically stern and condemnatory, and so did I. She has now come to a different understanding that has given me, too, a different way to read him. We deceive ourselves, she says, when we think "that there are people who can be condemned—and implicitly that it can happen to us. The deepest truth of Stringfellow's advocacy is that he was advocating for both us and our clients to our internal Accusers." In the practice of advocacy, we "become vulnerable on behalf of another, and anOther [*sic*] becomes vulnerable on our behalf. We are advocates, and we are met by the Advocate." [62] As a consequence, Hartigan says, the "prisoner whom the lawyer sets free is, unexpectedly, most centrally herself." [63]

The lawyer becomes a witness in the midst of her lawyering in its ordinary circumstances, and her practice points beyond itself to the transcendent reality within which the person and the practice daily subsist—as though within a womb.

Andrew McThenia notes that Stringfellow offered neither programs nor prescriptions and did not exhort us to do anything: "He was merely pointing to the reality of the resurrection." [64] That reality gave him his independence and freed him to be a critical lawyer who could—exuberantly—devote himself to others in his practice. This I read as a reflection of the Gospel of John, which provides no formula for belief and no list of things that believers are to do. Instead, at the critical juncture, it represents the subversive, freeing resurrection to the reader.[65]

The Word was put to death by law. But the author of John does not reject the law. As witness to the possibilities of its transfiguration, he appropriates law as a language for the gospel. In spite of itself, law is made a medium of the transcendent. That the gospel's author writes like a lawyer offers unexpected hope for what "lawyerlike" can mean.

The Moses saga and the Gospel of John raise the question of authority, and I have given it only passing attention. I return to it now not to bring closure but to credit the continued, authorizing dynamics of the stories.

The text tells us that the Hebrew midwives feared God, but it does not say how they came to do so or how they knew it was God they feared. In their place in the exodus story, they have little to go on. God's greatest self-revealing acts—the voice from the bush, the exodus, and the Sinai encounters—have yet to take place. The midwives subvert the ruling power of the nation on meager, obscure authority.

There is far more narrative material relating to God's authority for Moses and Moses' authority among the people, but it is discomfiting and much remains inexplicable. When, from the flaming bush, God tells Moses that He is sending him to Pharaoh to bring the people out, Moses troubles about what the people will make of his claiming to speak for this voice that he cannot identify and that is, except for the flames and the bush, disembodied. He knows that his history and personal qualities will not enable the people to recognize authority in him, certainly not authority to speak for One who names Himself "I am who I am." Moses himself is unconvinced that he is or can be or should be the bearer of the office the voice would bestow. Who is this who sends him, and who is Moses that he "should go to Pharaoh, and bring the Israelites out of Egypt" (Exod. 3:11)?

To the questions of authorizing identity and capacity, God answers that He will be with Moses, "and this shall be the sign for you that it is I who sent you: when you have brought the people out of Egypt, you shall worship God on this mountain" (Exod. 3:12). The assurance Moses seeks in the present will be given only in the future, retrospectively, after the critical events, and then the history it relies upon will not be dispositive. The works and wonders and crossing of the sea that God says will happen do happen, and, for good measure, terrifying thunder, lightning, trumpet blowing, and a smoking mountain all erupt at Sinai. But none of this makes a more lasting impression on the people than the tortures God visited upon Egypt made on Pharaoh. The people find in their history no reason to refrain from devoting themselves to a manufactured calf.

For Moses and the people there is to be no determinative, external ground of certification, no overwhelming proof. The assurance sought in the present will be given only in the future, and in that later time it will come as a sign and not a certainty. And the sign itself will be circular and self-referential: only by engagement, only in the act of returning praise to God, will Moses and the people have the sign, and then, because it is a sign, it will require believing and interpreting. Now, in the present, when Moses must act, he has only word about the future: "This shall be the sign." After he brings the people out, he and they "shall worship God on this mountain," and this will be the possibility for knowing and certifying. But the worship will mean that, by then, he and they will already be in the process of believing. And, because we have read on in the story, we know from the worship at the mountain that the process of believing is intimately bound up with the process of disbelieving.

God tried to kill Moses. Pharaoh was unimpressed with his credentials. The people did not readily or steadfastly consent to his leadership. And at the end, Moses is left out. Authority is not more settled for Moses than for the people. Like the Israelites and their story, authority is always underway, always in play. The law, written on portable stones, mobilizes the people and has authority among them in its performance.

The Gospel According to John is "written so that you may come/continue to believe" (20:31). Because it is written to the end of believing, James Muilenburg says, it is "pre-eminently a demonstrative gospel. It seeks to prove and convince." [1] It is demonstrative, but I am not sure that it seeks to prove and convince, or that proving and convincing are the only or the best ways to persuade. Or that persuasion is in order. The gospel surely does not attempt to prove, convince, or persuade in scientific and social-scientific terms. John's strategy is aesthetic and representational. It is something more like Shakespeare convincing an audience of Lear's humanity and their own, something more like the convincing drama that good trial attorneys produce. But not exactly that, either.

When the prologue says that in the beginning was the Word and all things came into being through him, it does not try to establish the truth of the proposition. There are no presently available eyewitnesses. The gospel could nonetheless offer arguments in support of the assertion. It could make arguments from nature, from the things that came into being to their maker. This is the kind of argument that natural theologians and physicists sometimes make. John refuses to be drawn into it.

Nor does the prologue appeal for a willing suspension of disbelief. Quite the contrary. It is a believing affirmation, and the author very openly numbers himself among the believers right from the start. He is no disinterested witness, and he says so. The truth of the prologue is the same as that for the gospel as a whole. It is the truth of believing. It is the truth for those who believe.[2]

This is not an expression of arrogance or privilege or inside communication among a select elite. The author writes to be read and understood and to be joined by disbelievers like himself. And he writes to readers as though they are also at the same time believers like himself.

There are later instances of this kind of strategy in the Church's history, one of them provided by Anselm, the Archbishop of Canterbury beginning in 1093. His *Proslogion* offers a proof for the existence of God. Karl Barth remarked on the incredible assumption of the proof: Anselm assumed that the outsider, whose doubt or denial he sought to overcome, already held Christian dogma in common with him. He approached the unbeliever "as if there were no rejection of the revelation,"[3] a move that prompted Barth to observe: "Divine simplicity and the way of the most incredible deception have always run parallel, separated only by the merest hair's breadth."[4] But Barth concluded that the "as if" is "really not an 'as if' at all, but . . . the final and decisive means whereby the believer could speak to the unbeliever."[5]

The author of John is a gospel writer and is not the writer of a book on theology like Anselm; he is an evangelist rather than an explicator of the faith. But the approach to nonbelievers as if they are believers is the same. Any other approach would constitute a betrayal of the gospel writer's own experience and his story. Belief had been given him. It was not his doing or the fruit of argument or the product of some inspiration to self-improvement. It was a gift of words. It was a gift of the Word. If believing is to happen to others, that, too, will be such a gift.

Following the example of the one in whom he believes, the gospel writer thus assumes solidarity with unbelievers. He addresses them as equals. With artistry and without apology, he tells the story with the assurance that, when others come to believe, he will not have been the cause. He assumes the gift, as he must. Or, rather, he circulates the gift.[6] He represents it in the legal drama of his narrative. As ably as he can in words on the page, he offers what he has received in the way that he received it. This is all he can do. This is the best that he can do.

He and his story have authority in the believing for which the story is told. He has no authority to hand down and enforce commands. He has authority to author a story for the telling. Its beginning, middle, and end is the authorizing Word.

When Abraham set out from Haran in obedience to God's command, all he had to go on was a promise: "I will make of you a great nation. . . . and in you all the families of the earth shall be blessed" (Gen. 12:2–3). Abraham would have scant evidence of fulfillment. Rachel, Miriam, and Moses would have little more in their lives, and the circumstances in which the sagas leave them in death offer no more to the reader. But the promise endures and gathers believers.

John's account of Jesus' last gathering with his disciples opens with a strange scene. He washes their feet. It is a parable of his forthcoming humiliation in death and a parable, too, of the self-sacrificial humility of his life and the lives his disciples are to lead.[7] His act is introduced with an editorial statement of interpretive context: "Jesus, knowing that the Father had given all things into his hands, and that he had come from God and was going to God, got up from the table, took off his outer robe, and tied a towel around himself" (13:3–4). The Word that was sent forth has full authority and is returning. The resulting harvest that remains is a small company of servants who are pariahs, like Jesus himself and the outcasts in the sagas of the Hebrew Bible.

John's account of the crucifixion furnishes Jesus' dying words to his mother at the foot of the cross and to the beloved disciple standing beside her: "He said to his mother, 'Woman, here is your son.' Then he said to the disciple, 'Here is your mother' " (19:26–27). The company he leaves behind has the nature of a new family.[8] Their greatness is to be read not in their number or in their political, military, or economic power but in the humility of their service to others, the quality of their binding together, and the authority of their story.

So the story holds.

Acknowledgments

At the end of *The Word and the Law*, I offered a detailed account of my work's dependence upon others. Because those individuals and communities have continued to sustain me in the meantime, I gladly reacknowledge my continuing indebtedness to them, and I thank those of them and others who have contributed to this present project:

The University of Georgia School of Law and its deans, first Ned Spurgeon and now David Shipley, provided welcome research grants that made it possible for me to complete this book. I am grateful for their support.

Wallace Alston, Robert Alter, June Ball, Scott Ball, Paula Cooey, Sarah Ball Damberg, Tom Eisele, Emily Fowler Hartigan, Stanley Hauerwas, Virginia McCormack, Alexander McKelway, Charles Platter, Tom Shaffer, Moody Smith, Reynolds Smith, Aviam Soifer, James Boyd White, and Steve and Rachel Wizner read all or portions of earlier versions of this volume and offered helpful, critical comments on them. In some cases the comments were extensive, arose from very close reading, and led me to undertake major, beneficial additions and revisions. Notes to the present text specify instances where I have drawn directly upon their work. Even as I write, I am freshly reminded of the rare gift of their friendship and collegiality and am thankful. If I knew the names of two anonymous Duke reviewers I would include them as well. I do know Ted Lewis's name and thank him for his continuing, much-needed help with Hebrew. Carol Weisbrod had been a support, but her most recent book, *Butterfly, The Bride,* came into my hands too late to take it into account.

Two of the reviews of my last book were particularly imaginative and helpful. Clark Cunningham explored the notion of lawyer as witness in one; in the other, Robin West pressed the role of stories and the need to address the subject of justice. They gave good criticism. The reconsideration they prompted me to undertake helped set me on the way to this book.

By providing opportunities in the form of lectures or faculty symposia where I could put to the test early versions of parts of this book, I am indebted to the Boston College School of Law (Aviam Soifer), the University of Cincinnati School of Law (Tom Eisele and Dean Joseph

Tomain), the Columbia Law School Legal Theory Workshop (George Fletcher and Kent Greenawalt), the University of Mississippi School of Law (Michael Hoffheimer and Barbara Sullivan) (Matthews Lecture), the Northwestern University School of Law (Robert Burns), the Rutgers-Camden Law School (Ed Chase and Roger Clark), the Society of Biblical Literature's Section on Biblical Law (Bernard Levinson, Rachel Magdalene, Martha Roth), the University of Tennessee School of Law (Tom Eisele, Joseph Cook, and Dean Richard Wirtz) (Alumni Distinguished Lecture in Jurisprudence), and Trinity University (Paula Cooey) (Willson Lecture). The faculties of these institutions, and in some cases the student bodies as well, did me great honor and gave me much help. Versions of my presentations at their schools were published in the law reviews of the University of Tennessee School of Law (Jurisprudence from Below, 61 Tenn. L. Rev. 749 [1994]) and the University of Cincinnati School of Law (A Little Mistrust Now and Then, 66 Cin. J. Rev. 877 [1998]).

Tammy Mettenburger and Vicki Mullis cheerfully suffered through with me the preparation of the manuscript.

Dan and Sally Coenen and Bertis and Katherine Downs (as I have noted before) and now Addie are the locus of a community that is very like a family. They and especially my family in fact compose the matrix for my writing. I prize the added professional relationship with Sarah Ball Damberg that this project has provided.

Appendix

KA HOʻOKOLOKOLONUI KANAKA MAOLI
Verdict of the International People's Tribunal
Hawaiʻi, August 1993
(abridged, edited version)

The International People's Tribunal, Hawaiʻi, 1993, convened to consider the rights of the Kanaka Maoli (indigenous peoples of *Ka Pae ʻaina Hawai ʻi*, the Hawaiian Archipelago).

The Charges, as they were formulated and presented to us by attorneys representing the Kanaka Maoli plaintiffs, are as follows:

1. Impermissible interference in the internal affairs of a sovereign people and nation.

2. Aiding and abetting a foreign coup d'état against the government of a sovereign people and nation.

3. Annexation of a sovereign people, their nation and territory, without their free and informed consent.

4. Imposition of statehood on a people, their nation and territory, without their free and informed consent.

5. Illegal appropriation of the lands, waters, and resources of the Kanaka Maoli.

6. Economic colonization and dispossession of the Kanaka Maoli.

7. Acts of genocide and ethnocide against the Kanaka Maoli.

8. Destruction, pollution, contamination, and desecration of the environment of *Ka Pae ʻaina*.

9. Violations by the United States and its subsidiaries of their own established trust responsibilities and other obligations toward the Kanaka Maoli.

Over the course of the proceedings, the Tribunal found that it might consolidate certain of the charges. In essence, Plaintiff's Charges 2 and 3 have been combined as the Tribunal's Charge 2; Plaintiff's Charge 4 is thus the Tribunal's Charge 3; Plaintiff's Charges 5, 6, and 8 have been combined as the Tribunal's Charge 4; Plaintiff's Charge 7 thus becomes the Tribunal's Charge 5. Plaintiff's Charge 9 has been dismissed as formulated insofar as the Tribunal was unable to ascertain a lawful basis for U.S. assumption of trust prerogatives in the first place; its substance is subsumed under various of the Tribunal's restructured Charges.

The Tribunal, as its name suggests, is a People's Tribunal in the fullest sense of the term and is both an exercise of sovereign rights of the people indigenous to Hawai'i and an expression of their democratic prerogative. The inspiration, organization, and funding of the Tribunal, as well as its staffing, procedures, and operations, manifested at every stage the will, activity, and special imagination of the people of the Kanaka Maoli nation. This assertion is reflected in the sponsorship of the Tribunal by more than one hundred groups and citizens' associations, all of which are dedicated in one way or another to the recovery and exercise of Kanaka Maoli sovereignty.

It should be pointed out that the U.S. government was formally and genuinely invited to participate in these proceedings, first of all, by a letter from Dr. Kekuni Blaisdell, convener of the Tribunal, to the President of the United States, dated July 31, 1991. This included an offer of a full opportunity to respond to the charges. The invitation was renewed periodically during the formal sessions, but no response has been received. Absent U.S. governmental participation, the panel of judges tried on its own to ascertain whether there were exonerating facts and legal arguments available in relation to the charges being made on behalf of the Kanaka Maoli.

THE PANEL OF JUDGES

Milner S. Ball, Caldwell Professor of Constitutional Law,
University of Georgia.

Hyun-Kyung Chung, Assistant Professor of Theology,
Ewha Women's University, Seoul, Korea.

Ward Churchill (Keetoowah Band Cherokee), Rapporteur,
Associate Professor of American Indian Studies, University of Colorado at Boulder.

Richard Falk, Albert G. Milbank Professor of International Law
and Practice and Fellow of the Center of International Studies,
Princeton University.

Lennox Hinds, Professor of Law, Rutgers University.

Te Moana Nui A Kiwa Jackson (Ngati Kahungunu and Ngati Porou Maori), Chair, Director of Maori Legal Service, Wellington, Aotearoa ("New Zealand").

Asthma Khader, attorney, educator, journalist; member of the Palestinian Rights Society and the National Committee for the Protection of Children (Amman, Jordan).

Oda Makoto, novelist and literary critic; member of the Permanent People's Tribunal.

Sharon Venne (Cree), attorney, human rights advocate at the United Nations since 1981; Rockefeller Fellow on indigenous legal systems.

LEGAL STANDING OF THE TRIBUNAL

The authority of the Tribunal and its Verdict ultimately rest upon the mandate of the Kanaka Maoli people, the persuasiveness of the reasoning set forth, and the evidence relied upon in response to the nine charges. The Tribunal does not pretend in any sense to be a court of law that derives its authority from the U.S. government or its subdivisions, or from any organ of the United Nations. But neither should this Tribunal be viewed as an innovation conceived for this situation, that is, as being without firm and impressive precedent.

In fact, the formation of and respect for international people's tribunals is a growing practice in all parts of the world and is a sign of the deepening solidarity of transnational democratic forces. Nations and citizens have claimed the rights — following procedures outlined in international law under U.N. Resolution 1503 (XLVIII) — to sit in judgment of states and their governments, as well as of international institutions, in situations in which serious abuses of human rights and the rights of peoples seem to be occurring on a large scale.

More than fifty such tribunals have been held to date, and there exists in Rome the headquarters of the Permanent People's Tribunal.

LEGAL POSTURE OF THE TRIBUNAL

The sessions of the Tribunal began and ended with sacred ceremonies, and the panel of judges visited numerous sites of profound significance to the identity of the Kanaka Maoli. Additionally, the Tribunal heard testimony and received written and/or visual submissions from many representatives of the people. The Tribunal was also guided by experts with special knowledge relating to the various charges.

In substance, the Tribunal has been guided by reliance upon five distinct but related and mutually reinforcing conceptions of law, drawing freely from each in developing its findings on the charges, as well as its conclusions and recommendations for redress. These are:

Kanaka Maoli Law

The Kanaka Maoli ideas of law are embracing sets of convictions about right action and righteousness on political, economic, and social relations. This Kanaka Maoli conception of law bears especially on relations to land and water, which are essential to the identity and survival of indigenous peoples and their nations and which deeply moved and impressed the panel of judges. It is also relevant in giving special authority to elders (the *Kupuna*) and spiritual leaders who clarify the essence of law.

International Law

It needs to be understood as a matter of history that international law often served as an instrument to validate colonial rule and to uphold other types of exploitative economic, political, and cultural domination. But international law is also increasingly sensitive to the democratic claims of peoples and nations that insist on the accountability of states and their leaders. Especially relevant in this regard is the 1992 version of the Draft Universal Declaration on the Rights of Indigenous Peoples.

U.S. Domestic Law

As we construe the charges, they raise three issues about U.S. domestic law, including the law of the state of Hawai'i:

They challenge the validity of U.S. assertions of legal authority over the Kanaka Maoli and their lands. They claim that the law of the United States and the State of Hawai'i are not binding on the Kanaka Maoli inasmuch as neither the United States nor the State of Hawai'i have valid jurisdiction over the Kanaka Maoli and their land.

In addition and independently, they maintain that, although U.S. law is not binding on the Kanaka Maoli, it is binding on the United States and that the United States has failed to abide by its own law.

Finally they propose that, to the extent the United States and state governments have acknowledged Kanaka Maoli rights, they have not successfully protected, implemented, or nurtured those rights.

The Law of Nations and Peoples

By initiative of peoples and nations, the experience of international people's tribunals has itself become a source of law. A framework for these efforts, which emerged with the Nuremberg and Tokyo Tribunals of the late 1940s, is contained not only in the aforementioned U.N. Resolution 1503 (XLVIII) but also in the 1976 Algiers Declaration on the Rights and Duties of Peoples.

The Inherent Law of Humanity

In addition to other sources, there exists a higher law based on the search for justice in the relations among persons and peoples and their nations;

as well, there is a law establishing the conditions for harmony between human activity and nature, drawing on ideas of stewardship that exist in many of the world's great cultural traditions and that are especially embodied in the cultures of indigenous peoples.

The Tribunal will have achieved its purpose if this Verdict is empowering to the Kanaka Maoli and their inherent rights to self-determination, to survival, and to enhancement of the value and validity of their highly spiritual ways of life. It is our hope that acknowledgment of their rights will begin the process of healing the open wounds produced by the many varieties of colonial rule.

Charge 1

Impermissible Interference in the
Internal Affairs of a Sovereign Nation or People

This charge relates specifically to the actions of the U.S. government and its agents against the Lahui Kanaka Maoli between 1790 and 1892. The Tribunal viewed this charge as requiring not only factual evidence about the alleged actions but also evidence on four related issues:

1. The life, culture, and sociopolitical structures of the Kanaka Maoli peoples prior to large-scale arrival of nonnatives;

2. The existence of any pre-1790 law that may still shape the Kanaka Maoli perception of their rights;

3. The existence of any engendering effect of such law on concepts of nationhood and self-determination that would have allowed its jurisdiction to extend to nonnatives entering upon their lands; and

4. Any Kanaka Maoli exercise of self-determination in treaty-making and other international sovereign rights.

The Tribunal's response to Charge 1 will address these general issues relating to the sovereignty and self-determination of the Lahui Kanaka Maoli (the nation or people). The Tribunal reserves to Charge 2 its findings on specific actions of the United States from 1790 to 1892. (We view those actions as part of a pattern that includes the climactic 1893 coup d'état and 1898 annexation that form the basis of Charge 2.)

FINDINGS OF FACT

Kupuna and academics from many disciplines (both native and nonnative) presented detailed evidence about their society and culture developed over two thousand years in *Ka Pae ʻaina Hawaiʻi*. With a population reliably estimated at eight hundred thousand by the late eighteenth century, the Kanaka Maoli had created a sophisticated sociopolitical system that sought the protection of the *lahui* (people), their *'aina* (land), and their *wai* (water). The basis of that protection was a set of religious/legal proscriptions expressing their philosophy of *pono* (harmony, balance, correct behavior). The social structure was shaped by a sense of place within a known and *kapu* lineage that regulated rights and responsibilities.

These relationships were in turn defined by the interdependent links each had with the *'aina* and their *wai*. Thus, when the Tribunal was taken to various sites, the local people welcomed us by placing themselves within their lineage and by establishing links to the *Akua*, the land or the waters that surrounded us.

The reaffirmation of these links reflected and validated the indivisibility of Kanaka Maoli life: that nothing could exist (or be understood) in isolation. The socioreligious norms and legal system that developed within the collective were similarly inseparable from each other. In fact, law was religion, religion was law, and both were the leitmotif of Kanaka Maoli life. Just as people did not have dominion over the land and its creatures but lived in and with them, so did they not live under the dominion of their law but in and with it.

Kanaka Maoli Law

It is the considered view of the Tribunal that a further conception of the term *law* that recognizes the validity of indigenous legal processes is required if the international community is to end the oppression of native peoples. The testimony of many witnesses referred to the basic law of *Kapu*, which defined, among other things, the sacredness of land and the sanctity of burial sites and *heiau* (temple, religious site).

Other testimony explained the application of concepts such as *malama* (to care for, protect) and *kanawai* (laws, or specific law relating to water). This and other evidence clearly established the existence of a complex legal system within Hawaiian society. The observance and implementation of various laws was an inherent part of the social behavior determined by and expected within the total collective of Kanaka Maoli culture. Many examples of sanctions imposed for breaches of law were placed before the Tribunal, including instances of immediate dispatch of persons for the wrongful taking of fish or other food resources. The weight of evidence leads us to make the following statements of fact:

That a clearly identifiable legal process operated as an integral and interrelated part of Kanaka Maoli life;

That there is an acknowledgment and application of the legal philosophies that underpin that process still operating in the relationship and attitudes of Kanaka Maoli to their land and natural resources; and

That the subsequent assertion by the United States that indigenous rights (and law) were extinguished by annexation did not ipso facto make it so in the *mana 'o* (thoughts) of the people.

A Concept of Self-Determination

Two particular legal concepts of the Kanaka Maoli were helpful to the Tribunal in determining whether they recognized a concept of self-determination. The first is the notion of *ea*. The evidence of *Kupuna* and other experts illustrated an interwoven set of meanings for *ea* that illustrates again the relational nature of Kanaka Maoli life and society. At a fundamental level, *ea* is life, any life. The sanctity of life places upon the people an obligation that is a supreme, sovereign duty. When exercised through the politico-religious sanctions of the people it denoted a constitutional authority and state of independence. When exercised within the total collective relationship, it denoted the *mana* or divine power to move heaven and earth: the ultimate constitutional authority.

The second concept of relevance to self-determination is that of *malama,* or responsibility to care for and protect the land and people. Examples of the exercise of *ea* and application of *malama* by kings and *mo'i* (high chiefs) clearly show that the Kanaka Maoli regarded themselves as a nation capable of exercising the most basic powers of sovereignty: the right and ability to defend and protect the people and the sacred lands on which they lived.

What is also clear is that the nature and extent of this power was definable only by the Kanaka Maoli. It grew from the complex lineage, religion, and law that were the gifts of the *Akua* as accepted in the precedents established by *Kupuna*. Hence, the right and powers of sovereignty and self-determination were not extinguished by human acts of cession, annexation, or conquest. Within this context it is equally clear that any non-native person entering the lands of the Kanaka Maoli would be expected and could be compelled to accept the jurisdiction of the collective.

International Exercise of Sovereignty

Three major treaties entered in evidence indicate both that the Kanaka Maoli nation exercised the right of self-determination in the international arena and that other states recognized that right. Two of the treaties are particularly relevant to the Tribunal's consideration of this charge: The 1826 Convention between Commodore Catesby Jones of the United States and Kauikeaouli (Kamehameha III), King of the Hawaiian Islands; and the 1850 Treaty of Friendship, Commerce and Navigation between Kamehameha III and the United States of America.

The Tribunal finds uncontradicted and established as fact the historical descriptions of actions taken by the United States against Lahui Kanaka Maoli from 1790 through 1887 (see Charge 2).

FINDINGS OF LAW

The Tribunal finds that the Kanaka Maoli during the period in issue were a *lahui,* or sovereign nation or people, that they so considered themselves, and that they were so considered by others, including the United States. The Tribunal also finds that, during the period in issue, Lahui Kanaka Maoli exercised self-determination and were considered as having the right to exercise self-determination by themselves and by others, including the United States. The Tribunal further finds that at no time during the period in issue did the Kanaka Maoli relinquish their sovereignty and right to self-determination. Finally, the Tribunal finds that the actions of the United States that are the subject of this Charge were violations of Kanaka Maoli sovereignty and self-determination, as we shall particularly set out in the following section, Charge 2.

Charge 2

Aiding and Abetting a Coup d'Etat and Annexing a
Sovereign People, Their Nation, and Territory

This Charge concerns the fundamental sovereignty inhering in the Kanaka Maoli people with respect to the governance of their own nation. Annexation is a crucial issue because if it occurred as alleged it would purport to change the formal status of the Lahui Kanaka Maoli and the effective rights of its people.

FINDINGS OF FACT

Based upon exhaustive documentation and oral testimony, the Tribunal finds that by 1842 the United States had announced what came to be known as the "Tyler Doctrine" in its Executive Statement on Foreign Policy. This position, supported by the Congressional Committee on Foreign Affairs, unilaterally declared that Hawai'i was within "the U.S. sphere of influence." Further, the idea was articulated that the United States should pursue its own perceived national interests in Hawai'i by "virtual right of conquest," regardless of the desires of the Kanaka Maoli Nation. It should be noted that the United States had long accorded to the Kanaka Maoli nation formal recognition of its full and separate sovereignty. Not the least evidence of this recognition are the Convention between Commodore Catesby Jones of the United States and Kauikeaouli on December 23, 1826, and the Treaty of Friendship, Commerce and Navigation between Kamehameha III and the United States of America, subsequently ratified by the U.S. Senate on August 19, 1850.

Nonetheless, in 1854, the U.S. government first sought to effect the annexation of Hawai'i. This effort to directly subordinate Lahui Kanaka Maoli to the "American System" failed, largely because of massive and concerted resistance by indigenous Hawaiians combined with diplomatic (and potential military) opposition on the part of at least two European powers, France and Great Britain.

Over the next three decades, Euroamerican entrepreneurs in Hawai'i lobbied more or less continuously for another annexation effort. They were, by all appearances, concerned with avoiding U.S. sugar tariffs while promoting transpacific travel, fishing, whaling, and other commercial enterprises. In any event, their agenda meshed quite well with the U.S. War Department's desire to permanently secure a deepwater port as a base of operations in the central and eastern Pacific. The U.S. government's consistent dispatch of gunboats to enforce sandalwood and sugar contracts deemed invalid by Kanaka Maoli courts is compelling evidence of the confluence of interests between U.S. public and private sectors.

There is strong evidence that, acting in collusion, U.S. citizens and government emissaries engaged in an extended series of seditious maneuvers to undercut the viability of the Hawaiian Crown and otherwise render the Kanaka Maoli nation vulnerable to increasing Euroamerican encroachment. So successful was this program of subversion that in 1877 the U.S. Minister to Hawai'i claimed (wrongly in our view) that the Hawaiian Islands had been reduced to little more than "an American colony." By 1887, the United States had managed to impose the so-called Bayonet Constitution and to force cession of the Pearl Lagoon (now Pearl Harbor). By 1891 the Harrison administration was confident enough of eventual success to resume efforts to annex the entire archipelago.

Ultimately, a group of Euroamerican businessmen residing in Hawai'i, calling themselves the "Honolulu Rifles" and headed by the planter Lorrin Thurston, resorted to the use of armed force in 1893. They seized Kanaka Maoli governmental facilities, imprisoned Queen Lili'uokalani, and announced that she had been deposed. They anointed themselves the "provisional government" of the "Republic of Hawaii" and named Sanford Dole, a missionary's son, the new president. This action was quickly supported by the federal government, which directed the landing of a detachment of marines to "restore order." Such an instruction normally implies intervention on behalf of a recognized and legitimate governing body, but U.S. force was deployed for precisely the opposite purpose: to consummate the overthrow.

U.S. force was deployed again in 1895 to put down an attempt by the Kanaka Maoli to reinstate the queen, an action that resulted in more than two hundred indigenous leaders being imprisoned on charges of "treason." The Dole cabal consolidated its position. The federal government opted to treat the Dole group as the sole "legitimate" authority in the islands. It was this group, not the Kanaka Maoli, who approved and facilitated the long-sought annexation of Hawai'i by the United States that was confirmed by a joint resolution of Congress in 1898.

The Kanaka Maoli consented to none of these developments. It is a matter of record that resentment and resistance were intense. Unlike the citizens of Texas, the Kanaka Maoli were afforded no opportunity to disapprove of annexation by plebiscite.

President Grover Cleveland clearly acknowledged the lawlessness of the U.S. military action in 1893. In his "Message on the Situation in Hawaii" of December 18, 1893, the president said that the U.S. "armed invasion" of Hawai'i was both an illegal "act of war" and a "lawless occupation."

President Cleveland had earlier dispatched James Blount as a commissioner to investigate the situation in Hawai'i. Blount's official report said that the interaction of federal personnel with Dole's plotters amounted to "complicity with their plan" and that any future support extended by the United States to the Dole group's "provisional government" would amount to the "countenancing of a wrong."

In the judgment of the Tribunal the evidence supports the conclusions that the Kanaka Maoli did not at any time during the period in question, 1790–1898, relinquish their right to self-determination. We note that the Kanaka Maoli sense of themselves as a sovereign people in 1893 can be felt in 1993 in the vitality of the continuing devotion to Queen Lili'uokalani, which found repeated, various expression in testimony presented to the Tribunal.

The Tribunal is of the view that the destructive acts of the United States from 1790 through 1898 were aggressions against Kanaka Maoli sovereignty. Representatives of the United States finally overthrew the Hawaiian government but did not and could not end the sovereignty of the people. The Tribunal is persuaded, on the basis of overwhelming evidence—written, spoken, performed, and presented in tears and painful silences—that Kanaka Maoli sovereignty is a powerful, continuing reality. The overthrow or alteration of a government does not destroy the underlying sovereignty of the people absent their unqualified, clearly expressed consent.

It is to be noted that notions of consent have, in the application of Western colonial law, omitted consideration of whether indigenous peoples understood the implications and consequences of their consent as perceived by outsiders. The Tribunal therefore holds the view that assertions of "consent" must be judged against the procedures and law of the indigenous peoples concerned.

The Tribunal received no evidence that, in the long history of claims of Kanaka Maoli "consent," the United States gave any thought at all to Kanaka Maoli understanding of consent or Kanaka Maoli procedure and law for obtaining consent. (For example, there was no evidence that the United States ever attempted, as this Tribunal has, to obtain the views of the Kanaka Maoli at sites and through forms of their choosing, on the terms of their aloha and great generosity.)

FINDINGS OF LAW

As matters of law, the Tribunal concludes that:

Throughout the period of time in issue the Kanaka Maoli were a *lahui* or nation or people who had a sovereign right to self-determination;

The Kanaka Maoli never consented to a surrender or usurpation of their sovereignty and right of self-determination;

U.S. assertions of jurisdiction over the Kanaka Maoli and their lands were illegitimate offenses against their sovereignty and right to self-determination. Specifically, the circumstances surrounding the 1893 coup d'état, the 1898 annexation of Hawai'i, and the chain of events leading up to these acts violated the inherent and fundamental sovereign rights of Lahui Kanaka Maoli. Insofar as these rights were formally and repeatedly recognized through treaties and agreements, counterarguments based on the notion of *terra nullius* do not apply.

Hypothetically it can be argued that, under customary international law prior to the postwar decolonization movement, one sovereign could acquire "legal" sovereignty over another through conquest, cession, or adjudication. However, the Tribunal finds no evidence that Hawai'i was conquered or that the United States acquired it through adjudication.

Finally, no evidence exists that, other than in the case of the Pearl Lagoon, a deed of purchase or treaty ceding jurisdiction was executed between the United States and any lawful representative of the Kanaka Maoli people.

Additionally, the Tribunal finds that no principle of law, logic, or morality can serve to justify the unlawfulness of the United States in its violation of the sovereign rights of the Lahui Kanaka Maoli.

Further and in particular, the Tribunal finds as follows:

A. Violations of Kanaka Maoli Law

The entire pattern of conduct on the part of the United States in supporting a foreign coup d'état against Queen Lili'uokalani and annexing the Hawaiian Islands represents a gross violation of traditional Kanaka Maoli law.

B. Violations of U.S. Domestic Law

The Tribunal finds that actions of the United States during the period in issue were violations of its own fundamental law as expressed in the Declaration of Independence and the U.S. Constitution. The Tribunal finds that, since U.S. jurisdiction over the Kanaka Maoli and their lands has no legitimate basis, U.S. law is not binding on the Kanaka Maoli. Nonetheless, U.S. law is binding on the U.S. government, which describes itself as "a government of law and not of men."

The Tribunal therefore finds that the aggressive pattern of action of the United States and its agents, culminating in the 1893 coup and the 1898 annexation without Kanaka Maoli consent, was a violation of two of its fundamental commitments, expressed in its Declaration of Independence: first, that all people are "created equal" and "are endowed by their Creator with certain inalienable rights, that among these are life, liberty, and the pursuit of happiness"; and, second, that governments derive "their just powers from the consent of the governed." The independence that the United States declared for itself it denied to the Kanaka Maoli.

The Tribunal further finds that the actions by the United States and its agents also violated the U.S. Constitution in the following particulars:

1. The Constitution's Preamble states: "We the People of the United States, in order to form a more perfect union, establish justice, insure domestic tranquility, provide for the common defense, promote the general welfare, and secure the blessings of liberty to ourselves and our posterity, do ordain and establish this Constitution for the United States of America."

a. In a report to the President on the events of 1893, Secretary of State W. Q. Gresham noted that the president's commissioner to the Hawaiian Islands, James Blount, "did not meet a single annexationist who expressed willingness to submit the question to a vote of the people, nor did he talk with one on that subject who did not insist that if the Islands were annexed suffrage should be so restricted as to give complete control to foreigners or whites" (Report to the President from the Secretary of State, October 18, 1893, House of Rep., 53d Cong., 2d sess., Ex. Doc. 47, p. xx). The Constitution depends for its legitimacy on the acceptance, support, and participation of the people. "We, the Kanaka Maoli" have never consented to be governed by the United States. The Tribunal finds that the imposition of U.S. government and law upon the Kanaka Maoli without their consent is a violation of the Constitution's first premise.

b. In a message to the Congress concerning the events of 1893, President Grover Cleveland observed: "By an act of war, committed with the participation of a diplomatic representative of the United States and without authority of Congress, the Government of a feeble but friendly and confiding people has been overthrown. A substantial wrong has thus been done which a due regard for our national character as well as the rights of the injured people requires we should endeavor to repair" (President's Message to Cong., Dec. 18, 1893, House of Rep., 53d Cong., 2d sess., Ex. Doc. 47, p. xiv). Secretary Gresham, in his report to the president, asked: "Should not the great wrong done to a feeble but independent State by an abuse of the authority of the United States be undone by restoring the legitimate government? Anything short of that will not, I respectfully submit, satisfy the demands of justice" (Report to the President from the Secretary of State, Oct. 18, 1893, House of Rep., 53d Cong., 2d sess., Ex. Doc. 47, p. xxi). The Preamble to the Constitution makes it clear that one of its chief purposes is the establishment of justice. The Tribunal finds that this constitutional purpose has been subverted by the actions of the U.S. government and its agents against the Kanaka Maoli.

2. Article I, section 8 of the Constitution placed in Congress the power to declare war. President Cleveland noted that the 1893 coup against the government of the Kanaka Maoli was an act of war and that it was undertaken without the authority of Congress. The Tribunal finds that this act of war was a violation of Article I, section 8.

3. Article VI provides that the Constitution "and all treaties made, or which shall be made, under the authority of the United States, shall be the supreme law of the land." The listed aggressive actions of the United States and its agents against the Kanaka Maoli from 1826 through 1898 violated several treaties cited in Plaintiff's Charge 1 and 2 (in particular, the Treaties of 1826, 1850, and 1875). The Tribunal finds that these actions were therefore violations of Article VI of the Constitution.

4. Amendment V provides: "No person shall be . . . deprived of life, liberty, or property, without due process of law; nor shall private property be taken for public use without just compensation." The Tribunal finds that the U.S. government violated the Due Process and Taking Clauses in multiple ways in the actions under scrutiny. For example:

a. In 1826 U.S. gunboats enforced the payment of what were purported to be private debts. There is no evidence that the debt contracts were legally valid under either Kanaka Maoli or U.S. law. There is evidence that they were enforced under authority of U.S. agents without either due process or just compensation.

b. The 1893 coup by U.S. agents and the 1898 annexation not only deprived Kanaka Maoli of liberty and property but also constituted a gross offense against fundamental fairness. The Fifth Amendment has been held to require of the government not only proper procedure and payment of appropriate compensation but also fundamental fairness in its treatment of persons. This amendment says "person." It does not say "citizen." It establishes a limit on the power of the U.S. government over, and extends its corresponding protection to, any person whether a U.S. citizen or not. The United States may not deprive Kanaka Maoli of their life, liberty, or property without due process of law whether or not they are U.S. citizens. The Kanaka Maoli do not have to accede to government by the United States in order to claim the protection of the Fifth Amendment, which establishes an inherent, legal limit on U.S. power. The U.S. actions against the Kanaka Maoli violated the Fifth Amendment's requirements of fundamental fairness, due process, and just compensation.

C. Violations of International Law

The Tribunal also finds that the U.S. actions at issue violate a range of elements of customary international law, reflected in the U.N. Charter, to wit:

Article 1. The purposes of the United Nations are: (1) To maintain international peace and security; (2) To develop friendly relations among nations based on respect for the principle of equal rights and self-determination of peoples and to take other appropriate measures to strengthen universal peace; and (3) To achieve international cooperation in solving international problems of an economic, social, and cultural, or humanitarian character, and in promoting and encouraging respect of human rights and for fundamental freedoms for all without distinction as to race, sex, language, or religion.

Article 2 (4). The Organization and its Members, in pursuit of the Purposes stated in Article 1, shall refrain in their international relations from the threat or use of force against the territorial integrity or political independence of any state, or in any other manner inconsistent with the Purposes of the United Nations.

Article 55. With a view to the creation of conditions of stability and well-being which are necessary for peaceful and friendly relations among nations based on respect for the principle of equal rights and self-determination of peoples, the United Nations shall promote: (a) higher standards of living, full employment, and conditions of economic and social progress and development; (b) solutions of international economic, social, health, and related problems; and international cultural and educational cooperation; and (c) universal respect for, and observance of, human rights and fundamental freedoms for all without distinctions as to race, sex, language, or religion.

Article 73. Members of the United Nations which have or assume responsibilities for the administration of territories whose peoples have not yet attained a full measure of self-government recognize the principle that the interests of the inhabitants of these territories are paramount, and accept as a sacred trust the obligation to promote to the utmost, within the system of international peace and security established by the present Charter, the well-being of the inhabitants of these territories.

Further, as is stipulated in the Charter of the Organization of American States:

Article 17. Respect for and the faithful observance of treaties constitute standards for the development of peaceful relations among States.

Article 18. No State or groups of States has the right to intervene, directly or indirectly, for any reason whatever, in the internal or external affairs of any other State. The foregoing principle prohibits not only armed force but also any other form of interference or attempted threat against the personality of the State or against its political, economic, and cultural elements.

Article 19. No State may use or encourage the use of coercive measures of an economic or political character in order to force the sovereign will of another state and obtain from it advantages of any kind.

Article 20. The territory of a State is inviolable; it may not be the object, even temporarily, of military occupation or of other measures of force taken by another State, directly or indirectly, on any grounds whatever. No territorial acquisitions or special advantages obtained either by force or by other means of coercion shall be recognized.

[Additional violations include those of Article 1 of the International Covenant of Civil and Political Rights and International Covenant on Economic, Social and Cultural Rights and of Article 1 of the 1933 Montevideo Convention on the Rights and Duties of States.]

Charge 3

Imposition of Statehood on a People, Their Nation, and
Territory, Without Their Free and Informed Consent

Throughout the proceedings, abundant testimony, supported by considerable documentary evidence, was entered to the effect that the Kanaka Maoli never desired that their territory be subsumed by the United States as a State of the Union. To the contrary, numerous statements were made asserting that many indigenous Hawaiians still do not wish to be construed as part of the United States. The Tribunal has considered this in light of its understanding that the coerced or otherwise unconsenting incorporation of any people or their territory into the political-geographic corpus of another represents a fundamental breach of international law.

FINDINGS OF FACT

In 1959, Hawai'i, formerly a Pacific trust territory held by the United States, was designated the fiftieth State of the Union. There is exhaustive evidence that, in effecting this alteration in Hawaiian political status, the United States failed to comply with U.N. requirements. Essentially, the United States manipulated the procedure by which Hawai'i was removed from an internationally recognized list of Non-Self-Governing Territories—on which it had been placed by the U.N. in 1946—and scheduled for formal decolonization. In the process, the United States conducted a fraudulent referendum, from which the Kanaka Maoli voice was largely excluded, and in which the nonnative population was inappropriately included, in order to create the illusion that "the people" had democratically determined they wished to become an integral part of the United States.

Although the illegality of the U.S. maneuvers attending Hawai'i's statehood has been amply documented by Valentine Mamokukaua Huihui Sr., Mililani Trask, and others, both the federal government and the government of the State of Hawai'i officially persist in their contention that the result is "binding." Meanwhile, it is unquestionable that many grassroots Kanaka Maoli, notably the members of the Ka Lahui Hawai'i (Sovereign Hawaiian Nation), Ka Pakaukau (a coalition of Hawaiian independence groups), and similar organizations, manifest a growing and ever more determined opposition to such pretenses.

The Tribunal finds that the imposition of U.S. statehood on the Kanaka Maoli without their free and informed consent was, as a matter of fact, a replication and extension of those aggressive actions of the United States during the nineteenth century that culminated in the 1893 coup and 1898 annexation.

FINDINGS OF LAW

The Tribunal finds as matters of law that:

Throughout the period in issue the Kanaka Maoli were a *lahui* or nation or people who had a sovereign right to self-determination;

The Kanaka Maoli never consented to a surrender or usurpation of their sovereignty and right to self-determination;

U.S. assertions of jurisdiction over the Kanaka Maoli and their lands were illegitimate offenses against their sovereignty and right to self-determination; current assumptions or assertions of such jurisdiction are without a legitimate basis and are a continuation in the present of the offenses against the Kanaka Maoli committed in the nineteenth century;

Imposition of statehood was offensive to law in particular, as follows:

Kanaka Maoli Law

The Tribunal finds that the U.S. performance in imposing statehood upon Hawai'i represents an extraordinarily grave breach of Kanaka Maoli law insofar as it was accomplished without the consent of indigenous Hawaiians and over their express and sustained objections.

U.S. Domestic Law

As the example of Texas demonstrates, an existing sovereign can be admitted to the Union, but only upon the prior, free, and informed consent of the people. No such consent was given by or appropriately sought from the Kanaka Maoli. In this regard, President Cleveland noted the marked contrast in relations between the United States and Texas on the one hand, and the United States and Hawai'i on the other (President's Message to Cong., Dec. 18, 1893, House of Rep., 53d Cong., 2d sess. Ex. Doc. 47, p. xiv).

The imposition of statehood, no less than the coup and annexation, violated the fundamental commitments and law of the United States expressed in the Declaration of Independence and the Constitution's Preamble and Fifth Amendment (see Charge 2).

International Law

The tribunal further finds that the United States has violated several elements of international law in the course of making Hawai'i a state. [These include Article 73 of the U.N. Charter, setting forth the treatment to be accorded Non-Self-Governing Territories; the U.N. Declaration on the Granting of Independence to Colonial Countries and Peoples (1960); the Declaration on Principles of International Law Concerning Friendly Relations and Co-operation among States in Accordance with the Charter of the United Nations (1970), setting forth the duty to promote the principle of equal rights and self-determination of peoples; and Article 14 (2) of the U.N. Universal Declaration of Human Rights (1948), which holds that people are not to be arbitrarily deprived of their nationality.]

Charge 4

Appropriation of the Lands, Waters, and Natural Resources, and Economic Colonization of the Kanaka Maoli

During the course of the proceedings, the Tribunal heard substantial testimony, well supported by documentary evidence, concerning the vital importance of *malama 'aina* (care for the land) and *malama kai* (care for the sea) in the traditional Kanaka Maoli worldview. A consistent theme of the testimony has been that the political-economic order that the United States imposed upon the Kanaka Maoli by annexation and colonization has made it virtually impossible for indigenous Hawaiians to fulfill their obligations as human beings to practice *malama 'aina* and *malama kai*. These obligations are plainly fundamental to the Kanaka Maoli individual and collective sense of being. The massive and systematic U.S. intrusions bespeak a pattern of crimes against Kanaka Maoli humanity and their world.

FINDINGS OF FACT

Witnesses devoted much testimony to explaining that a complex of related activities on the part of the United States, its corporations, and its citizens has been responsible for the damage sustained by the Kanaka Maoli and their environment. Witnesses devoted an almost equivalent amount of testimony, all of it borne out by ample documentation, to demonstrating how the Kanaka Maoli have sought in all good faith, over an extended period and to no avail, to obtain at least minimal redress through the courts of the United States and State of Hawai'i.

Lands Designed for Kanaka Maoli Homesteading

Beginning in the early decades of the nineteenth century, U.S. citizens, with the direct or indirect support of their government, began to replace and therefore destroy the traditional Kanaka Maoli land tenure system. They did so through such acts as the Great Mahele of 1848. Their approach was to advance the Western legal concept and practice of property ownership. This is the tactic employed against American Indians and given expression in the 1887 General Allotment Act. The collectively held land of Lahui Kanaka Maoli was converted into separate parcels that could be individually owned and transferred.

A powerful, few nonnatives took over the bulk of the land. By the 1960s 47 percent of Hawaiian land was held by only seventy-two private owners and 49 percent by state and federal governments. Of the 47 percent held by seventy-two owners, "18 landholders, with tracts of 21,000 acres or more, owned more than 40% . . . and . . . on Oʻahi, the most urbanized of the islands, 22 landowners owned 72.5% of the fee simple titles" (*Hawaii Housing Auth. v. Midkiff*, 467 U.S. 229, 232 [1984]). (Subsequent actions have dispersed land ownership but have done so without material change in Kanaka Maoli holdings and participation.)

In 1921, for complex reasons including paternalism and economic self-interest, the United States declared two hundred thousand acres of land in the Hawaiian Islands to be set aside for homesteading by Kanaka Maoli. These homelands have been the occasion for abuse of the Kanaka Maoli in four ways, two at the beginning of the program and two in the way it has been administered since:

1. The original acreage set aside was largely from "the worst lands in the territory. It was remote, inaccessible, arid, and unsuitable for productive development" (Hawaiʻi Advisory Committee to the U.S. Comm'n. On Civ. Rts., A Broken Trust, Dec., 1991, p. 2). The Tribunal's own site inspection (in one instance the only access was by helicopter) revealed homelands located on hillsides that had been denuded by pre-1921 exploitation under Western economic interests and that were now robbed of water by present Western and Eastern economic interests (contiguous pineapple plantations, golf courses, and resorts).

2. Congress limited access to the homelands by establishing blood quantum eligibility. Only those who can prove that they are of "50% or more Hawaiian blood" qualify for homesteads. The Kanaka Maoli did not define themselves by blood quantum, a definition imposed from the outside. Testimony before the Tribunal revealed that, of those who are Kanaka Maoli by this imposed definition, many find it impossible to produce the kind of written documents required by Western law to prove their heritage. Testimony given the Tribunal also revealed that the blood quantum standard has a pernicious effect that may also indicate an originally pernicious intent. While the Kanaka Maoli presently constitute some two hundred thousand of the one million island population, only five thousand are "pure" Kanaka Maoli by the U.S. standard, and they are expected to be reduced to almost none by the year 2044. In another fifty years, there may be few people remaining who are eligible for the homelands under the imposed blood quantum standard.

3. In 1991, seventy years after they were set aside, distribution and use of the homelands remained a scandal. According to one official investigation, only 17.5 percent of the total available lands have actually been placed in the hands of homesteaders, although there is a waiting list of some twenty thousand. "At the same time, over 62 per cent of the lands are being used by non-natives, often for minimal compensation. Espe-

cially egregious is the continued questionable use of valuable homelands by the U.S. Government, with virtually no compensation to the trust. These include some of the most suitable lands for development of homes" (Hawai'i Advisory Committee to the U.S. Comm'n on Civ. Rts., A Broken Trust, Dec. 1991, Letter of Transmittal, unpaginated). Of the homelands that are productive and well located, all that the Tribunal saw are in the hands of the nonnatives.

Not the least painful testimony received by the Tribunal concerned the denial of their lands to the Kanaka Maoli, the frustration of their repeated attempts to live on their lands, and the massive, ecologically incompatible use of their designated lands by others. The Tribunal was especially moved by the very real pain felt by the Kanaka Maoli in consequence of the state and federal practice of dangling before them the promise of their homelands but denying to them meaningful, real opportunity to homestead it.

Continuing to deny that opportunity while punishing those who make their own way onto their land — jailing "squatters," tearing down their homes and cultural centers, destroying their gardens — is a form of persecution especially acute for a people whose being and spirituality is so intimately bound to their land and water. Juridical means of relief for the Kanaka Maoli in this situation appear to be either severely restricted or nonexistent. For example, the Tribunal found it remarkable that a state "Judicial Relief Act" provides for aggrieved Kanaka Maoli to bring a homelands suit but mandates that any land or money recovered is to be awarded, not to the successful plaintiff, but to the land trustees who are likely to be the defendants. ("Actual damages" may be awarded to successful plaintiffs, but it appears that "actual damages" do not cover either the land sought or such things as thirty years of unsuccessful waiting for a parcel. That is, actual damages as defined in Western common law are likely to be either irrelevant or difficult of proof or both.)

Currently, there is no indication that the governments of the United States or the State of Hawai'i evidence a meaningful intent to restore any significant amount of property to Lahui Kanaka Maoli or even to offer compensation for it. To the contrary, substantial evidence suggests that, under the rubric of "law and order," both state and federal authorities have set out on a course of visiting ever harsher penalties upon indigenous Hawaiians who attempt to live on or otherwise use land set aside for them.

Desecration of Sacred Sites

Many indigenous peoples hold land to be sacred. In this, the Kanaka Maoli are no exception. However, certain locations carry a special spiritual significance for the Kanaka Maoli. The designation of Hawaiian Trust Lands evidences no concern for the relative sacredness of various sites throughout the islands. Indeed, the great majority of such locations were left outside the trust area boundaries with devastating results. For example:

On the island of Maui, there is an important burial site in the dunes at Waiheʻe. A Japanese corporation, operating under sanction of the State of Hawaiʻi, is constructing a golf course at this location. Already considerable excavation has occurred, and the sand has been sold to various resorts to improve the sand quality of tourist beaches. The Kanaka Maoli have sought unsuccessfully to enjoin this unearthing of the *na iwi* (bones) of their ancestors. More broadly, indigenous Hawaiians have pursued, with equal lack of success, a legislative remedy that would create buffer zones against development around all traditional burial sites in the islands.

The recently constructed Kauaʻi Test Facility (KTF) at Barking Sands on the island of Kauaʻi, along with portions of the adjoining Pacific Missile Range Facility, was built directly atop the Nohili Sand Dunes, perhaps the most important Kanaka Maoli burial complex in all of Hawaiʻi. The obliteration of graves in the areas where construction has occurred is virtually complete.

The sacred island of Kahoʻolawe, impounded by the Navy as a bombing range during World War II, has been subjected to more or less continuous saturation with high explosives and other ordnance ever since. Even a series of physical interventions by the Kanaka Maoli have failed to slow the process of systematic devastation.

Given that these examples are drawn from several dozen comparable situations reviewed by the Tribunal during the proceedings, the scope of the problem of desecration is readily apparent. The Tribunal notes that a recent U.N. study entitled *Cultural Property of Indigenous Peoples* deals quite specifically with the question of preserving sacred sites in the face of nonindigenous development schemes. The study leaves no doubt that spiritual values attached to such sites by native peoples should receive priority over the "use values" assigned them by others.

Military Use of Lands

Since its inception in 1778, when a U.S. warship first arrived in Hawaiian waters, the federal relationship to Hawaiʻi has been military at its crux. Approximately one-quarter of the island of Oʻahu is presently reserved for use by the military, as is about 10 percent of the surface area of the archipelago as a whole. Concentrations of U.S. military personnel in the islands have served to inflate housing and other prices and thereby create further material disadvantages to the Kanaka Maoli. Aside from its monopolization of a disproportionate quantity of land, the military's use of land has negative consequences. For example:

The Pearl Lagoon is Hawai'i's largest estuary and is the location of the sixty-acre Pearl Harbor National Wildlife Refuge. However, a report published in *Environmental Hawai'i* indicates that activities in the contiguous Pearl Harbor Naval Base have made the entire area "one of the most polluted sites in the state." Pearl Harbor is currently on the list of Federal Environmental Superfund sites, but only six of several dozen known sources of such contamination are slated for cleanup. The processes generating the pollution remain as active now as they have been in the past. To date, all Kanaka Maoli efforts to address the problem through U.S. courts have been rebuffed under the rubric of "National Security."

The ancestral *ahupua'a* of Mana, in Kaua'i's Polihale State Park, is considered by the Kanaka Maoli to be a prime location for reestablishment of a traditionally oriented indigenous community. Efforts to establish such a community have been blocked by the desire of the military to utilize the same land as a safety zone around the Pacific Missile Range Facility. Among the reasons this zone is needed is the periodic release of substantial quantities of freon gas during firing exercises. Kanaka Maoli attempts to halt such releases have been rejected by the courts on the basis of military arguments that the emissions take place outside the jurisdiction of the state legal system.

On balance, the Tribunal's examination of the circumstances attending U.S. military utilization of the Kanaka Maoli landbase leads unerringly to the conclusion that the archipelago has already been affected by or is presently vulnerable to wholesale pollution by pesticides, herbicides, waste oil, asbestos, chromic acids, PCBs, solvents such as TCE, and solid nuclear waste. It must be noted in this connection that the Environmental Protection Agency currently lists thirty-one federal sites in the islands as extremely hazardous. This conservative, official count affords Hawai'i the dubious distinction of having the highest concentration of such sites of any state.

Tourism

The first hotel in Waikiki, the Moana, was constructed in 1901. By 1993, the volume of tourists exceeded seven million a year. The infrastructure required to accommodate them utilizes vast quantities of land, water, and other natural resources.

Most consumptive have been the forms of entertainment and recreation peddled as "paradise" by nonnative interests to tourists. Golf is one example:

A report published by the Office of State Planning of Hawai'i in 1992 indicates that there were 65 eighteen-hole golf courses in operation throughout the islands, each encompassing from 150 to 200 acres of land. The report also indicated that the state intended to encourage the establishment of a further 102 golf courses as rapidly as possible.

A recent study released by the College of Tropical Agriculture and Human Resources at the University of Hawai'i determined that each eighteen-hole golf course required, depending on the season and other factors, between five hundred thousand and one million gallons of water *per day* to be maintained in playing condition.

This and other studies have also found that golf course maintenance also requires use of highly toxic substances, including a broad range of pesticides, herbicides, and fungicides. For 1992, it is calculated that an aggregate of 94,025 pounds of such herbicides as MSMA, glyphosate, oryzalin, oxidiazon, and metribuzin were dispersed across the imported lawns of Hawaiian golf courses. Not only have these chemicals evidenced a significant negative impact on Hawai'i's natural vegetation, they have also demonstrated a noticeably negative impact on birds, land animals, and freshwater fish in areas proximate to the greens.

The magnitude of such tourism-related environmental devastation shows plainly that tourism is almost as great a threat to the well being of the Kanaka Maoli as the U.S. military.

Nor can it be said that the Kanaka Maoli are to some extent compensated for the loss and damage to their land by employment in the tourism industry. Several studies indicate clearly that, aside from a relatively small number of the most menial occupations, native Hawaiians are almost entirely absent from the business. Indeed, as resorts have steadily bought up Hawai'i's beaches, indigenous people have been increasingly denied access to such "privileges" as swimming and surfing in their own waters. On the related issue of impacts on Kanaka Maoli health, see the following charge.

Plantations

Traditionally, a major aspect of the Kanaka Maoli economy devolved upon the growing of taro, from which highly nutritious *poi* is made. Because taro is central to native Hawaiian well being, it is considered an older brother and a god and is thus of utmost significance to Kanaka Maoli spirituality. It is reliably estimated that more than 9,000 acres were under taro cultivation prior to the arrival of the first European in Hawai'i.

By 1876, some twenty-five years after a treaty allowed Hawaiian-grown sugar to be imported duty-free into the United States, the land devoted to taro had been reduced to approximately 2,000 acres, and an estimated 12,000 acres of Kanaka Maoli territory had been consigned to the growing of sugarcane in areas taken over by Europeans and Euroamericans.

In 1900, only about 1,300 acres remained of the original taro fields, while more than 128,000 acres were given over to sprawling sugar plantations.

By 1991, with more than 90 percent of the archipelago's agribusiness controlled by a handful of giant transnational corporations like Del Monte and Dole, only 310 acres remained under taro cultivation. Over 220,000 acres were in sugar production, and another 130,000 acres were devoted to producing pineapple and other alien cash crops. It must be noted that Hawai'i's is the only irrigated sugarcane in the world. Water for sugar was taken from the wetland taro farms. At present rates of diminishment, the last taro patch will have gone out of existence in Hawai'i before the end of the decade.

Fishing Rights

Fishing was the second mainstay of the traditional Kanaka Maoli economy. In preinvasion times, indigenous Hawaiians relied not only on open sea- and freshwater, but also, more importantly, on fishponds specially built along the shore. These ponds, maintained for centuries, ranged in size from less than an acre to several hundred acres. Their construction required monumental labor by the people as a whole. A large pond on the western side of Moloka' is a salient example. It was built with hundreds of thousands of stones carried over steep mountains from the eastern side. So important were these efforts to the Kanaka Maoli that the ponds came to occupy a vital niche in their spiritual life.

While it is true that traditional fishponds have not as yet completely disappeared—the Tribunal visited a functioning one of approximately fifty acres—it is equally true that the great bulk of them have been destroyed as nonnatives bought up prime beachfront properties throughout the islands. For example, in 1901, O'ahu had over one hundred fishponds. By 1993, only two remained. The future of the ponds is anything but secure. Property rights to the ponds are unsecured, and concentrations of pollutants threaten their viability.

Freshwater and open sea fishing are not now viable options. The former has been virtually destroyed by water diversion. The latter is constrained by a combination of state and federal licensing requirements and the impact of commercial and tourist fishing.

FINDINGS OF LAW

Kanaka Maoli Law

It is beyond dispute that the U.S. policy of near-total expropriation of Kanaka Maoli territory has violated every conceivable aspect of traditional Hawaiian law pertaining to the relationship of the people to their landbase. And it has violated Kanaka Maoli law concerning the burial grounds of their ancestors and ceremonial sites.

U.S. Law

Alexis de Tocqueville observed about U.S. treatment of American Indians that "it is impossible to destroy men with more respect for the laws of humanity" (*Democracy in America*, 355 [Henry Reeve text, rev. by Francis Bowen, 1948]). Much the same may be said of U.S. treatment of the Kanaka Maoli. The Tribunal is of the view, however, that the wrongs set forth in this Charge do betray a fundamental lack of respect for law, U.S. law as well as the law of humanity.

1. Due Process. By force or fraud, the United States or its citizens with direct or indirect U.S. support wrested from the Kanaka Maoli all of the natural resources and most of the labor that has produced the wealth of Hawai'i. The Kanaka Maoli have received almost nothing in return. This appropriation continues that of the nineteenth century and is no less a violation of the U.S. fundamental law than those found under Charge 2.

Specifically, these wrongs, when taken separately but more so when taken together as a whole, contravene the commitments to equality and to life, liberty, and the pursuit of happiness expressed in the Declaration of Independence as well as the commitment to justice embodied in the Preamble to the U.S. Constitution. These wrongs — separately but more so as a whole — also specifically violate the Fifth Amendment to the Constitution. As noted in Charge 2, the Fifth Amendment prohibits the government from denying due process of law to any person and from taking property without just compensation. The Tribunal finds that the United States has denied due process of law to the Kanaka Maoli in two ways.

a. The United States has denied due process of law in the substantial sense. As the discussion of U.S. law under Charge 2 explains, the Fifth Amendment requires fundamental fairness of the U.S. Government in its treatment of any person. "Fundamental fairness" has been defined in a variety of ways by the United States. Suffice it to say that the Tribunal concludes that the massive appropriation set forth in this Charge is wholly out of keeping with the exemplary traditions of the people of the United States, the positive aspects of their history, and their realizations

of ordered liberty. We cannot escape the conclusion that this appropriation, either effected by the United States or condoned by it, is a violation
of the Fifth Amendment's guarantee that the U.S. government shall act
with fundamental fairness.

b. As explained in the discussion of the Fifth Amendment under Charge
2, that amendment also guarantees legitimate process and just compensation. The Tribunal concludes that the life, liberty, and property taken
from the Kanaka Maoli was effected without legitimate process and without just compensation. The Tribunal notes that the emphasis in the Constitutional language should fall on the word "just." The appropriations
outlined under this charge raise the question of what just compensation
may require in the circumstances of the Hawaiian Islands. According to
the law, customs, and traditions of the Kanaka Maoli, money is no compensation for the seizure of the various kinds of property in issue. Moreover, what is "property" in Western legal concepts may be quite different
from the Kanaka Maoli equivalent to "property." No compensation can
be just that fails to take Kanaka Maoli traditions into decisive account or
that fails to take a form suitable to the Kanaka Maoli.

2. Equal Protection. The equal protection of the law mandated by the
Fourteenth Amendment, like the protections of Fifth Amendment due
process, is owed to "any person." But this duty, unlike that under the Fifth
Amendment, is owed to any person "within its jurisdiction." The Kanaka
Maoli deny that the United States and the State of Hawai'i have jurisdiction over them. The Tribunal has found that there is no legitimate basis
for such jurisdiction. To cite the United States and the State for violations
of the Equal Protection Clause does not entail acceding to or legitimating
such jurisdiction. It is only to point out that the United States is in double
default: It unlawfully claims jurisdiction and then unlawfully implements
the jurisdiction that it unlawfully claims.

In establishing a blood quantum criterion for Kanaka Maoli homesteading of their homeland, the United States has created a racial classification.
This is the sort of act that the Fourteenth Amendment was specifically
adopted to outlaw. The U.S. Supreme Court has found that similar clas-
sifications applied to American Indians are political rather than racial in
nature and are thus constitutionally permissible. Even if these decisions
are law within the United States, we find them inapplicable to the Kanaka
Maoli blood quantum classification. We so find on two grounds.

a. There is a substantial history of U.S. documents drawing a distinction between "native Hawaiians" and "whites." That is, the history of
U.S.-Kanaka relations is marked by documented, official, U.S. distinctions
based on race.

b. The imposed Kanaka Maoli blood quantum standard does not arise out of any political consideration. In the instance of American Indians, blood quantum relates to tribal recognition. In Hawai'i, the standard has no such political referent and can be explained as arising out of and functioning towards a racial division. The Tribunal concludes that the blood quantum standard would be a violation of the letter and spirit of equal protection if the United States had jurisdiction of the Kanaka Maoli. Because there is no such legitimate jurisdiction, the Tribunal can only point out the consistency of illegality in United States treatment of the Kanaka Maoli from illegitimate assertion of jurisdiction to illegitimate implementation of it.

3. Thirteenth Amendment. The Thirteenth Amendment states: "Neither slavery nor involuntary servitude, except as a punishment for crime whereof the party shall have been duly convicted, shall exist within the U.S., or any place subject to their jurisdiction." This amendment applies not only against federal and state governments but also against private parties. Slavery and involuntary servitude are plainly outlawed. Even so, this amendment again raises the question of jurisdiction.

It can be argued that the Kanaka Maoli — as an independent, sovereign, self-determined entity — are located within the borders of the United States but are not within its jurisdiction for Thirteenth Amendment purposes. However, notwithstanding such jurisdictional arguments, the Tribunal believes that the people of the United States would not countenance their government enslaving people or subjecting them to involuntary servitude anywhere.

The wrongs set forth in this Charge appear to the Tribunal to constitute exactly the kind of subjection of the Kanaka Maoli to involuntary servitude that the Thirteenth Amendment was adopted to prevent.

It may be that the injuries discussed in this Charge constitute wrongs that are not cognizable in the U.S. legal system at its present state of development or that cannot be fully repaired by the legal remedies currently available. This is not to say that the U.S. legal system cannot grow to encompass them. We do not foreclose the eventuality that, at some future time, redressable wrongs can be identified and cured in a manner not presently obvious.

International Law

The Tribunal finds that the United States is in violation of Article 17 of the U.N. Universal Declaration of Human Rights (1948), which holds that "(1) Everyone has the right to own property alone as well as in association with others" and "(2) No one shall be arbitrarily deprived of his property." Further, the Tribunal finds that the actions and policies at issue violate Article IX of the American Declaration of the Rights and Duties of Man (1948): "Every person has the right to the inviolability of his home." Article XXIII of the American Declaration also states, "Every person has a right to own such private property as meets the essential needs of decent living and helps to maintain the dignity of the individual and the home."

As pertains especially to the federal imposition of blood quantum standards for purposes of identifying indigenous Hawaiians and curtailing their property rights, the United States stands in violation of customary international law as codified in the U.N. International Convention on the Elimination of All Forms of Racial Discrimination (1966). Although the United States is not a signatory to this Convention, the Nuremberg Doctrine may be invoked as binding all governments, whether or not they are signatories to specific instruments, to adhere to certain basic standards of comportment. From this perspective, it must be observed that Article 2 of this Convention requires all States to:

(a) . . . undertake to engage in no act or practice of racial discrimination . . . ;

(c) . . . amend, rescind or nullify laws and regulations which have the effect of creating or perpetuating racial discrimination wherever it exists;

(d) . . . prohibit and bring to an end . . . racial discrimination by any person, group or organization;

(e) . . . discourage anything which tends to strengthen racial division.

Article 4 (c) of the Convention also stipulates that States shall "not permit public authorities or public institutions, national or local, to promote or incite racial discrimination."

The uses to which expropriated Kanaka Maoli territory have been put by the U.S. military, various businesses, and the more general influx of non-natives onto native lands violate provisions of the Universal Declaration of Human Rights:

Article 18. Everyone has the right to freedom of thought, conscience and religion; this includes the freedom to change his religion or belief, and freedom, either alone or in community with others and in public or private, to manifest his religion or belief in teaching, practice, worship and observance.

Article 27 (1). Everyone has the right to freely participate in the cultural life of the community, to enjoy the arts and to share in scientific advancement and its benefits.

Similarly, U.S.-sanctioned military/corporate usage of Kanaka Maoli land contravenes the principle advanced under Article XIII of the American

Declaration on the Rights and Duties of Man proclaiming, "Every person has the right to take part in the cultural life of the community, to enjoy the arts, and to participate in the benefits that result from intellectual progress, especially scientific discoveries."

Along with the expropriation of their land and concomitant obliteration of their traditional economy, indigenous Hawaiians have been consigned to employment, when they have been employed at all, that bespeaks further violations of international law. Article XIV of the American Declaration holds, "Every person has the right to work, under proper conditions, and to follow his vocation freely, in so far as existing conditions of employment permit. Every person who works has the right to receive such remuneration as will, in proportion to his capacity, and skill, assure him of a standard of living suitable for himself and his family." This principle conforms closely to elements of the Universal Declaration of Human Rights:

Article 4. No one shall be held in slavery or servitude; slavery and the slave trade shall be abolished in all their forms.

Article 23. (1) Everyone has the right to work, to free choice of employment, to just and favorable conditions of work and to protection against unemployment.

(2) Everyone, without any discrimination, has the right to equal pay for equal work.

(3) Everyone who works has the right to just and favorable remuneration ensuring for himself and his family an existence worthy of human dignity, and supplemented, if necessary, by other means of social protection.

Given the root level at which U.S. juridical doctrine and judicial practice deviate from international standards on matters of import to indigenous people, the Tribunal is of the view that it will be necessary for the Kanaka Maoli to pursue legal venues outside the framework of the present U.S. system, as well as within it, until such time as U.S. law achieves sufficient maturity and scope to respond fitly to their property related claim.

Charge 5

Acts of Genocide and Ethnocide against the Kanaka Maoli

The testimony received by the Tribunal, and much of the written material submitted in support and amplification of this testimony, made continual, specific reference to "genocide" to describe the ongoing processes visited on the Kanaka Maoli. Although witnesses addressed many different aspects of the issue and approached it from many different perspectives, they identified as genocide the complex, sustained series of actions and policies on the part of the United States that has caused catastrophic damage to Kanaka Maoli society in its religious and national dimensions and that threatens the very existence of indigenous Hawaiians as an identifiable human group.

FINDINGS OF FACT

During the century following initial U.S. contact with the Kanaka Maoli in 1790, the native Hawaiian population, which numbered some eight hundred thousand at the outset, was reduced to fewer than forty thousand. Much of the loss resulted from epidemics unleashed when Europeans and Euroamericans introduced a variety of pathogens to which the Kanaka Maoli had not been exposed and had no immunity.

Such bacteriological/viral contamination was not necessarily inadvertent. The effects of disease introduced by nonnatives into pristine environments was known and had been widely reported upon with regard to the Americas by 1790. (There are accounts of a 1763 instance in which a British military commander, Jeffrey Amherst, issued written orders to his subordinates to dispense smallpox-laden blankets to a group of Ottawa Indians for the express purpose of "extirpating this execrable race.")

Despite the outbreak of several major epidemics in the wake of early nonnative incursions into Kanaka Maoli territory and despite general knowledge of the sources of the disease, Euroamerican missionaries and entrepreneurs advocated an increased rate of Euroamerican immigration to the islands. Correspondingly, the rate of Kanaka Maoli attrition through disease was accelerated. Outsiders' correspondence, diaries, and other records contain statements of satisfaction with this circumstance, and a tone of celebration at the prospect of the total disappearance of native Hawaiians may sometimes be detected.

Many nonnatives took active steps to exacerbate the impact of disease. For instance, during the middle of the nineteenth century, a group of missionaries banded together on the island of O'ahu to block construction of a hospital that would have provided medical assistance to unChristianized natives.

Euroamerican businessmen impressed thousands of Kanaka Maoli into veritable slave labor in order to develop the lucrative sugar trade. The rigors and deprivations attending work in the sugar camps rendered those forced into it far more susceptible to the ravages of illness. Throughout the entire period, the United States did not intervene on behalf of the victims. Instead it intervened in support of some of the victimizers. For example, between 1824 and 1844 United States gunboats were repeatedly sent into Hawaiian waters to enforce payment on sandalwood contracts involving private American interest.

As the Tribunal has already noted, the United States and its citizens have come to Hawai'i with a primary interest in securing the islands' lands, waters, and attendant resources for their own use and profit. While the exact nature of this interest has varied from group to group, a common denominator has been the systematic and near-total dispossession and displacement of the Kanaka Maoli from their traditional territories.

In thus pauperizing a people who had not only been entirely self-sufficient, but in fact wealthy by any reasonable standard, the United States has placed them as a group in a situation of perpetual physical degradation. According to testimony, corroborated by both official and unofficial studies and reports, as of 1988 40 percent of all Kanaka Maoli families — including the vast bulk of those evidencing prominently native features — lived at or below the poverty line. Correspondingly, indigenous Hawaiians chronically suffer all the standard indicators of poverty-generated health problems, many of them directly related to poor diet and environmental contamination.

As one analyst recently put it, "Native Hawaiians live in the . . . healthiest state [in the U.S.], but they have the shortest life-span among the country's ethnic groups." They have been forced away from traditional Kanaka Maoli foods such as *poi* and fish and enticed into a high-cholesterol, high-calorie Western "junk food" diet. In consequence, poor diet and obesity affect an estimated 65 percent of the native population. The following points highlight the results:

Although indigenous people make up only 20 percent of the present population in Hawai'i, they suffered 44 percent of infant mortality in the state during 1990.

In 1920, when indigenous Hawaiians still retained a sufficient landbase to feed themselves in accordance with traditional dietary preferences, they accounted for 4.8 percent of all deaths from heart disease in the islands. By 1980, after the loss of their taro and fish economy, they suffered 31.5 percent of such deaths.

Also in 1920, as the U.S. colonial system took firm hold in Hawai'i, the indigenous population accounted for 3.3 percent of all deaths from cancer in the islands. In 1987, the rate of death from cancer was 299.1 per 100,000 among indigenous Hawaiians, as compared to an average of 132 per 100,000 among all the other population groups in the islands.

As compared to the general U.S. population, according to one report, indigenous Hawaiians are "three times as likely to die of heart disease, . . . twice as likely to die of cancer or a stroke. And they are six times as likely to die of diabetes."

Such physical ravages, endemic and structurally induced as they are, should be considered in conjunction with U.S. political and economic policies that have served over an extended period to supplant Lahui Kanaka Maoli's social, economic and political institutions, obliterate the preponderance of indigenous Hawaiian material culture, and undermine its capacity to sustain its spiritual belief system.

Taken as a whole, the situation is such that the Tribunal has no alternative but to conclude that the United States has relegated the Kanaka Maoli to a de facto status of expendability in its own interest if it has not consciously and deliberately targeted them for eventual eradication.

FINDINGS OF LAW

Kanaka Maoli Law

The Tribunal cannot imagine a greater transgression against the tenets of traditional Kanaka Maoli law than to engage in the physical and cultural destruction of indigenous Hawaiians themselves, whatever the motivation and whether accomplished directly or indirectly.

U.S. Domestic Law

The Tribunal is of the view that there is no greater departure from the fundamental commitments of the people of the United States to liberty and justice, expressed in their Declaration of Independence and Constitution, and no greater offense against their Constitution's promises of due process and equal protection, than to conduct or allow the physical and cultural destruction of the Kanaka Maoli.

International Law

The Tribunal finds that the U.S. actions and policies that have resulted in the present circumstances suffered by the Kanaka Maoli represent a violation of international law. The 1948 U.N. Convention for Punishment and Prevention of the Crime of Genocide is pivotal. Article II of that convention holds that it is a crime to commit the following acts "with intent to destroy, in whole or in part, a national, ethnical, racial or religious group, as such":

(a) Killing members of the group;

(b) Causing serious bodily or mental harm to members of the group;

(c) Deliberately inflicting on the group conditions of life calculated to bring about physical destruction in whole or in part;

(d) Imposing measures intended to prevent births within the group.

Article III of the Genocide Convention makes it clear that conspiracy to commit and complicity in genocide are also criminal. The Tribunal finds the U.S. government culpable with respect to each of these criteria.

It follows that, with respect to its record regarding the Kanaka Maoli, the United States stands in violation of the U.N. Universal Declaration of Human Rights (1948). Article 3 of that Declaration stipulates, "Everyone has the right to life, liberty and security of person." Article 5 of the Universal Declaration further states, "No one shall be subjected to torture or cruel, inhuman or degrading treatment or punishment." And Article 25 holds:

(1) Everyone has the right to a standard of living adequate for the health and well-being of himself and his family, including food, clothing, housing and medical care and necessary social services, and the right to security in the event of unemployment, sickness, disability, widowhood, old age or other lack of livelihood in circumstances beyond his control.

(2) Motherhood and childhood are entitled to special care and assistance. All children, whether born in or out of wedlock, shall enjoy the same social protection.

The United States is also in violation of its solemn commitments made as a signatory to the 1948 Declaration of the Rights and Duties of Man.

RECOMMENDATIONS

Having heard extensive and compelling testimony on the islands of Oʻhau, Maui, Molakaʻi, Kauaʻi, and Hawaiʻi from August 13–19, 1993, having received voluminous documentary evidence in support and corroboration of the testimony, and having engaged in a number of site inspections during the same period, the People's International Tribunal, Hawaiʻi, 1993, has arrived at the findings delineated above and advances the following recommendations:

1. The United States and the world should immediately recognize the sovereignty and right to self-determination of Lahui Kanaka Maoli under provision of the U.N. Charter, Universal Declaration of Human Rights, American Declaration of the Rights and Duties of Man, International Covenant on Civil and Political Rights and the International Covenant on Economic, Social and Cultural Rights, among other elements of international law.

2. The United States and the community of nations should immediately acknowledge the right of Lahui Kanaka Maoli to decolonization under provision of U.N. Declaration on the Granting of Independence to Colonial Countries and Peoples.

3. Kanaka Maoli lands, including all ceded lands, Hawaiian Home Lands, and all other lands to which they have an historic claim, should be

returned to the control of Lahui Kanaka Maoli without delay. Return of lands should be construed to include restoration of water and other associated rights. Compensation of Lahui Kanaka Maoli for the deprivation of use of and damage to its territory during the period of U.S. occupation should be considered as a separate but closely related matter.

4. Jurisdiction over restored lands should be bindingly recognized as belonging to Lahui Kanaka Maoli at the time of restoration. The terms under which nonnatives might be allowed to remain on indigenous Hawaiian land should from that point forward be defined exclusively by Kanaka Maoli law, in accordance with international law, custom, and convention.

5. In compliance with its own Constitution and the International Convention on the Elimination of all Forms of Racism, the United States should immediately suspend utilization of "blood quantum standards" for purposes of identifying native Hawaiians. Lahui Kanaka Maoli itself must determine the composition of its citizenry in accordance with its own traditions, free from external interference.

6. The United States, in negotiations and other interactions with Lahui Kanaka Maoli, should observe the provisions of the U.N. Declaration on the Rights of Indigenous Peoples as the minimum standards to be applied.

7. The United States should immediately effect a valid ratification of and adherence to the 1948 Convention on Punishment and Prevention of the Crime of Genocide. Indemnification of the Kanaka Maoli for their human losses during the period of U.S. occupation should be treated as a separate but closely related matter.

8. All other wrongs suffered by the Kanaka Maoli at the hands of the United States and its subsidiaries should be rectified in a manner deemed satisfactory to the people themselves.

Notes

Prologue

1 The idea of the challenge of the Bible's story-worlds comes from Walter Brueggemann, *Theology of the Old Testament* (Minneapolis, Minn.: Fortress Press, 1997), 19, 712–29; and Leo Perdue, "Adhering to Israel's God," *Christian Century,* May 20–27, 1998, 525 (reviewing Brueggemann).

2 Robert Cover drew prophetically from the narrative of the Judaic tradition in his legal scholarship. Too soon dead, he set an example now followed by, among several others, Aviam Soifer, Martha Minow, Joseph Singer, and Suzanne Last Stone. In the Christian tradition, William Stringfellow long, faithfully, and affectingly followed the biblical stories in his writing about and practice of law. Since Stringfellow's death, Thomas Shaffer has led theologically based exploration of the moment narrative has for law. He has been joined by a growing company, including Frank Alexander, Emily Fowler Hartigan, Andrew McThenia, and those members of the Hamline Law School faculty who produce the *Journal of Law and Religion.* The size and range of work in the field is indicated by the latter journal, by the Fordham Symposium on the Relevance of Religion to a Lawyer's Work (papers published in 66 Fordham L. Rev. 1075–1641 [1998]), and by the editors of and contributors to *Can a Good Christian Be a Good Lawyer?* ed. Thomas Baker and Timothy Floyd (Notre Dame, Ind.: University of Notre Dame Press, 1998).

The kind of attention Clark Cunningham, Richard Weisberg, Robin West, and James Boyd White give to stories is formal precedent for the way I follow biblical stories here, although their approaches are not expressly based in theology and although I flatter myself in making the claim to companionship with them in the work. My oldest and most rewarding debt among them is to White.

Artful storytelling—as practiced by Derrick Bell, Richard Delgado, Mari Matsuda, Martha Minow, and Patricia Williams—has now joined studies of economics, narrative, religion, and theology as a medium for legal scholarship.

3 Paul Lehmann, *The Decalogue and a Human Future* (Grand Rapids, Mich.: William B. Eerdmans, 1994), 23.

4 Arthur Danto, *The Transfiguration of the Commonplace* (Cambridge, Mass.: Harvard University Press, 1981), 202.

5 Ibid.

6 Ibid.

7 The stories authorize my retelling them and my receiving from others the retelling of their stories and the stories of their authority. They also authorize my radical, vulnerable openness to whatever may follow from the sharing.

The stories hint intriguingly at a kind of courtesy extended by the God of Israel to other gods and other gods' people. Israel is certainly not to worship other gods, for Israel belongs to YHWH. But the ban may not apply to other nations.

For example, Deuteronomy offers several clues in this direction. "When you look up to the heavens and see the sun, the moon and the stars, all the host of heaven, do not be led astray and bow down to them and serve them, things that the Lord your God has allotted to all the peoples everywhere under heaven. But the Lord has taken you and brought you out of the iron-smelter, out of Egypt, to become a people of his very own possession, as you are now" (Deut. 4:19–20). Israel is not to worship other peoples' gods (Deut. 29:16, 26), but God himself allotted the other gods to the other peoples: "When the Most High apportioned the nations, when he divided humankind, He fixed the boundaries of the peoples according to the number of the gods; the Lord's own portion was his people, Jacob his allotted share" (Deut. 32:8–9). (Except where otherwise indicated, biblical quotations are taken from the New Revised Standard Version as published in *The New Oxford Annotated Bible* [New York: Oxford University Press, 1991].)

Patrick Miller observes that "the other nations of the world are clearly understood as having been created by the Lord, with each apportioned its territory and each allotted to one of the gods, that is, set under the aegis of one of the gods. . . . Here is the strange word that only vis à vis Israel are the other gods idols and condemned. . . . from the perspective of the other nations and in the divine economy, it is another matter. They are accepted as belonging to the divine world ruled by the Lord of Israel even though they are criticized; indeed they are actually allotted to the other nations by the Lord. . . . Those gods that function as center of value and meaning for other nations have their place. The religions of that world were a part of the order set by the God of Israel. Not much is said in these verses, but a note is sounded" (*Deuteronomy*, Interpretation: A Bible Commentary for Teaching and Preaching, ed. John Mays [Louisville, Ky.: John Knox Press, 1990], 229).

8 See Miller, *Deuteronomy*, 88–89; David Tracy, *The Analogical Imagination: Christian Theology and the Culture of Pluralism* (New York: Crossroad, 1981).

9 Paul Lehmann, *The Transfiguration of Politics* (New York: Harper and Row, 1975), 24.

1. Law and the "Mouth" for God

1 Peter Steinfels, "Looking Away from DeMille to Find Moses," *New York Times*, April 7, 1996, sec. 2, p. 36, col. 1. It is better for me to perform my method of reading than to talk about it, but full disclosure requires a word about my approach. I first learned the biblical sagas from my mother and grandmother in a small Southern Baptist Church in a small central Georgia town. And from there I carry and continue to be affected in reading by love for the words and the wonder of them. But I can no longer read only precritically.

My teachers at Harvard introduced me to "higher" criticism and taught me to analyze biblical texts with an eye for their sources and their history. And I remain deeply grateful to them for the gift of their rich, heady education. They continue to guide me, although I can no longer read only in their critical mode either. Most recently, biblical texts have been freshly opened to me by practitioners of literary and of feminist criticism. The literary critic Frank Kermode describes his own reading as "postcritical" (*The Literary Guide to the Bible*, ed. Robert Alter and Frank Kermode [Cambridge: Harvard University Press, 1987], 441). But that won't do as a description for mine because I cannot and would not fully shed my precritical and critical educations. Nor can I avoid bringing to the Bible what I have learned in the meantime from both Karl Barth and Paul Lehmann about theology and from American law about how to read texts closely to the ends of action, argument, and earning a living. Meir Sternberg concludes that what contemporary reading of the Bible needs is "a community or overlap rather than a division of labor" (*The Poetics of Biblical Narrative* [Bloomington: Indiana University Press, 1985], 15). My own reading is communal and layered. It is precritical, critical, and postcritical—and theological and lawyerly to boot.

So I come to the text with all of my accumulated educations in reading and with all of my accumulated experiences in living and with all of the colorings, enrichments, shortcomings, and distortions of both. In short, I come as who I am, and I cannot draw any meaningful distinction between my method and my identity, between my way of reading and my way of being and acting.

2 Sternberg, *Poetics of Biblical Narrative*, 31.

3 In order to qualify as a pharaoh, a candidate had to be the child of a marriage between a man and his father's sister.

4 When I read this passage to Henry Schwarzschild over the telephone, his response was: "What does it mean: God *tried* to kill him?"

5 I discuss Moses as prophet and judge below in notes 8 and 16.

6 There is a certain amount of risk in the use of the translation "mouth

for." It may entail a prejudicial assumption of meaning. The Hebrew *peh*, "mouth," may well have been something very different in ancient Israel than the mouth is for us. In addition, "mouth for" may elicit misleading or limiting associations: the lawyer as mouthpiece. The *Oxford English Dictionary* indicates that "mouthpiece" is a late-developing word, especially as slang for a solicitor. And "mouth for" scarcely has the original sense of that part of a musical instrument made for blowing through.

The image of the mouth was employed by Judge Learned Hand in a more elevated sense. He said that "the judge's authority depends upon the assumption that he speaks with the mouth of others" (quoted in William J. Brennan, "The Role of the Court—The Challenge of the Future," in *An Affair with Freedom*, by William Brennan, ed. Stephen Friedman [New York: Atheneum, 1967], 324). Hand's point was that judges are charged to decide cases according to law and not simply according to the politics of the moment. They must therefore draw around themselves the legitimating figures of the past. As Hand's sentence develops, however, various mixings of metaphors underscore his idea that judges must enrobe themselves in something other than a contemporary politics: "The judge's authority depends upon the assumption that he speaks with the mouth of others, that is to say, the momentum of his utterances must be greater than any which his personal reputation and character can command, if it is to do the work assigned to it—if it is to stand against the passionate resentments arising out of the interests he must frustrate—for while a judge must discover some composition with the dominant trends of his times, he must preserve his authority by cloaking himself in the majesty of an overshadowing past." Judge Hand's use of the image of a "mouth of" is more ennobling than "mouthpiece," but it is nonetheless different from the Mosaic "mouth for." Moses' authority depends upon his serving as mouth for another greater than himself, but unlike Hand's judge, he does not "cloak" himself with this mouth. Among other differences, the active party is God. God makes Moses His mouth. And the act is not an attempt by God to preserve His authority. It is an act of courtesy.

"Mouth for God" has the advantage of some relation to but no exact match with other conventional terms for the lawyer. For example, it does not exactly fit within any of Thomas Shaffer's (and Robert Cochran's) categories: the lawyer as godfather, or as hired gun, or as guru, or as friend. See Thomas Shaffer and Robert Cochran, *Lawyers, Clients, and Moral Responsibility* (St. Paul, Minn.: West, 1994) (a useful book that, like Shaffer's work generally, is a welcome broadening of the way we customarily think about lawyers).

On the notion of representation, see Hanna Pitkin, *The Concept of Representation* (Berkeley: University of California, 1967); J. Roland Pennock and John Chapman, eds., *Representation, Nomos X* (New York: Atherton, 1968).

7   On Aaron see chapter 6.

8   Moses is also "God for" Aaron. Although the designation elevates him above Aaron, it also a reminder that Moses is, in turn, subordinate to God. The texts later describe Moses as a prophet, but this is to specify one of his functions as mouth for God. The nature of prophecy is thereby clarified: a prophet is one who speaks the word of God and is not necessarily one who predicts the future. God says to Moses: "I have made you like God to Pharaoh, and your brother Aaron shall be your prophet" (Exod. 7:1). As Moses is prophet for God, Aaron is prophet for Moses. "Whatever the derivation of the word *nabhi,* prophet, the emphasis is upon speaking not prediction" (D. M. G. Stalker, "Exodus," in *Peake's Commentary on the Bible,* gen. ed. Matthew Black [New York: Thomas Nelson and Sons, 1962], 213). Patrick Miller points out that "the central characteristic that identifies Moses as the ideal prophet is his function as the mediator of the divine word" (" 'Moses My Servant': The Deuteronomic Portrait of Moses," *Interpretation* 41 [1987]: 245, 248). The "mouth for" metaphor comes from sentences attributed to the underlying J source, the so-called Jahwist (Stalker, "Exodus," 213); the later "prophet" identification is attributed to P, the priestly editors (ibid., 215).

9   The presence of God "is the basis of civilized life if handled properly, but a raging, destructive force if misused" (David Damrosch, "Leviticus," in Alter and Kermode, *Literary Guide to the Bible,* 70). I have relied upon Damrosch's suggestive work here and later. But I do take issue with his notion of "misusing" the presence of God. God is not a fissionable quantity of uranium for the using or misusing. To think of God as usable is to make the religious and false assumption of human ascendancy over God. We do not "use" the power of God. See also Damrosch's question about how the holiness, the power of God, is to "be contained, so that the people may be led and nurtured without being consumed?" (ibid., 79). In the biblical stories the power of God is not contained after the fashion of a controlled nuclear reactor.

10   See also Exod. 33:5. In some cases, the issue is how one stands with respect to God ontologically, not geographically. A visitation, *paqad,* by God might be looked on with either great anticipation or fear depending on one's faithful righteousness or standpoint (as among or not among the chosen).

11   It is in the same manner that Bezalel (and Oholiab) is to be understood: "I have filled him with divine spirit, with ability, intelligence, and knowledge in every kind of craft, to devise artistic designs, to work in gold, silver, and bronze, in cutting stones for setting, and in carving wood, in every kind of craft" (Exod. 31:3–5). If Moses is mouth for God, Bezalel

may be thought of as hand for God. His handiwork is a medium for the powerful presence of God.

No less than Moses, Bezalel and his construction crew worked with exacting care (Exod. 36–39). "In this way all the work of the tabernacle of the tent of meeting was finished; and the Israelites had done everything just as the Lord had commanded Moses. . . . When Moses saw that they had done all the work just as the Lord had commanded, he blessed them" (Exod. 39:32, 43).

It is to be noted that craftsmanship—discipline, artistry—signifies, arises from, and is directed toward the presence of God. In the same sense that God gives speech to mortals, he also gives them art, culture, and craft. The latter are forms of the former.

12 This is what Patrick Miller describes as "teaching to do" (*Deuteronomy*, 247).

13 Perhaps this is a very different practice of due process than Grant Gilmore had in mind when he proposed that in "Hell there will be nothing but law, and due process will be meticulously observed" (*The Ages of American Law* [New Haven, Conn.: Yale University Press, 1977], 111).

14 God first speaks to Moses from a bush. The bush burns but is not consumed. No one shall see God and live (Exod. 33:20). Similarly, when Moses has been in conversation with God, his face shines and he must wear a veil before the people (Exod. 34:29–35).

15 This first encounter was not preceded by a specific, authorizing injunction "Go to Pharaoh and say . . ." Was Moses' first visit *ultra vires?*

16 After the exodus from Egypt and before the encounter at Sinai, Moses acts as judge for the willing people. His caseload increases to become a great burden. His father-in-law Jethro proposes that Moses appoint other judges to decide the easy cases and to reserve to himself only the hard cases. Jethro puts it this way: "You should represent the people before God, and you should bring their cases before God" (Exod. 18:19). Such "representation before God" may constitute a form of mouth for the people. However, Moses' own explanation of his office is that "the people come to me to inquire of God. . . . I decide between one person and another, and I make known to them the statutes and instructions of God" (Exod. 18:15–16). That is, his own understanding is that as judge he represents God to the people.

17 Compare Deuteronomy 5:4–5 ("I was standing between the Lord and you to declare to you the words of the Lord") and Deuteronomy 5:22–27 ("Go near, you yourself, and hear all that the Lord our God will say. Then tell us everything that the Lord our God tells you, and we will listen and do it").

18 As would also be true of a treaty of the time, the writing preserves the terms and allows them to stand as a reminder of the obedience

due. On the relation of the Deuteronomic covenant to contemporaneous treaties, see Moshe Weinfeld, *Deuteronomy*, vol. 5 of The Anchor
Bible (New York: Doubleday, 1991), 1–11, 6–9. See also E. W. Nicholson,
"Covenant in a Century of Study since Wellhausen," in *Crises and Perspectives*, Oudtestamentische Studien, no. 24 (Leiden: Brill, 1986), 54;
A. D. H. Mayes, "Deuteronomy 4 and the Literary Criticism of Deuteronomy," *Journal of Biblical Literature* 23 (1981): 100.

19 Arthur Jacobson, *The Idolatry of Rules: Writing Law according to Moses,
with Reference to Other Jurisprudences*, 11 Cardozo L. Rev. 1079 (1990).

20 Exod. 24:12. The tablets of stone are the Bible's third reference to writ-
ing. The second precedes it in the same chapter (Exod. 24:4), when
Moses writes the book of the covenant, the covenant code spoken in
Exodus 20:22–23:33.

   When God first speaks the law at Mt. Sinai, the people "witnessed
the thunder and lightning, the sound of the trumpet, and the mountain
smoking" (Exod. 20:18), and it is then that fear drives them to ask Moses
to speak for God because they cannot bear the words when they are spoken immediately by God. God deliberately speaks terrifyingly in this instance to establish the authority of Moses — "that the people may hear
when I speak with you and so trust you ever after" (Exod. 19:9).

   So Moses "drew near to the thick darkness where God was" (Exod.
20:21), and there God speaks the law to him. When Moses subsequently
returns to deliver the words to the people, he speaks them. When, after
hearing the words, the people agree to do them, Moses writes them
down (Exod. 24:3–4). Oxen are then sacrificed, half their blood is
dashed against the altar, the book is read, the people again promise to
do the words, and the remainder of the blood is dashed on them (Exod.
24:5–8). The writing, like the companion blood shower, is sure to be
remembered.

21 Jacobson, *Idolatry of Rules*, 1108–9.

22 Jacobson's point can be established in a different way by comparing the
Exodus version with that of Deuteronomy. The Deuteronomic sequence
begins in the same way. God writes the Ten Commandments on two
stone tablets (Deut. 4:13, 5:22, 9:10), Moses smashes them (Deut. 9:17)
and later makes two more (Deut. 10:1). However, in the Deuteronomic
account, *God* writes the second edition as well as the first (Deut. 10:2,
4). Afterward, Moses deposits the stones in the ark, "and there they
are" (Deut. 10:5). Although the Exodus text is not ambiguous, there is
nevertheless ambiguity in the differing accounts offered by Exodus and
Deuteronomy.

23 Jacobson, *Idolatry of Rules*, 1095. His argument is considerably more
elaborate than I have indicated. For example, he reads in Exodus two
designations of God: Elohim, who unilaterally hands down rules, and

Yahweh, who interacts with other characters in the story. "If only Elohim writes, then characters have no role in creation. Moses must write in order to befriend Yahweh, He must destroy and replace Elohim's writing [even as he destroyed the golden calf]. But if Moses writes, then people will bow down to the text as a graven image [as they bowed down to the calf]. They will want Moses to be Pharaoh. . . . Yahweh/Moses must write a second time what Elohim wrote first and Moses destroyed [thereby erasing it and demonstrating the possibility of collaboration]. Moses must write as a collaborator of Yahweh not as Elohim/Pharaoh" (Jacobson, *Idolatry of Rules*, 1084). Jacobson refers to a third writing, Exodus understood as authored by Moses, "which records the struggle over the first two" (ibid., 1095). He also seems to have in mind another kind of third writing, the people's rewriting of the propositions in their deeds (ibid.). He then draws a lesson for analysis of modern secular law: "Naturalism requires only one [writing]. . . . Positivism requires two, a procedure for marking rules as law and the actual markings of rules according to the procedure" (ibid.). Common law requires three, as does the jurisprudence of rights (ibid., 1096, 1125ff.). The law that counts is collaborative.

24 Idols are silent. Moses grinds the idol to dust, then makes the people consume it. The act is a parody of receiving the law into their hearts.

25 Jacobson, *Idolatry of Rules*, 1079.

26 Ibid.

27 Ibid.

28 Brandeis held: "The great achievement of the English-speaking people is the attainment of liberty through law" ("The Opportunity in the Law," in *Business — A Profession* [Boston: Small, Maynard, 1914], 314). But the great achievement of the Hebrew-speaking people was the achievement of law through liberty.

29 Karl Barth put it this way: "There is no abstract cult-regulation, no abstract legal norm, no abstract moral law. Everything that God wills is an exact expression of the fact that those of whom He wills it are His own — an exact counterpart of the 'great and terrible things' which God had already done for [this people]. . . . The Ten Commandments and the various ceremonial, legal and moral enactments, are not independent and cannot be separated from this antecedent. They receive and have from it their specific content. They are merely part of the law of the life of the people led by God out of Egypt and into [the promised land]. It is because it is this people, because it would not exist without these 'great and terrible things' done by God, because it owes its existence to these acts of God, that it is bound and obliged to keep the command of its God. And in content each of the commands reflects and confirms the fact that Israel is this people, the people created and maintained by

these acts of God. *Thou* shalt! means, *Israel* shall! and everything that Israel *shall* is only an imperative transcription of what Israel *is,* repeating in some sense only what Israel has become by God, and what it must always be with God" (*The Doctrine of God,* vol. 2 of *Church Dogmatics,* pt. 2 [Edinburgh: T. and T. Clark, 1957], 572). See also Milner Ball, *The Promise of American Law* (Athens: University of Georgia Press, 1981), 65–66, 16–63. (I would not presently express the subject matter as I did in those pages.)

2. Intercession

1 See the references to a similar office in The Book of Job: 16:19 (witness?); 33:23 (mediator, interpreter?); 19:25 (vindicator, advocate, redeemer?). See Marvin Pope, *Job,* vol. 15 of The Anchor Bible (New York: Doubleday, 1975), 146. On Moses and Samuel as intercessors, see Jer. 15:1, Ps. 99:6, and below in part 2.

2 a. The first is not clearly intercessory, since God evidently hears the people's accusations directly without their being routed through Moses. "As Pharaoh drew near, the Israelites looked back, and there were the Egyptians advancing on them. In great fear the Israelites *cried out to the Lord. They said to Moses,* 'Was it because there were no graves in Egypt that you have taken us away to die in the wilderness?' . . . But *Moses said to the people,* 'Do not be afraid, stand firm, and see the deliverance that the Lord will accomplish for you today. . . .' *Then the Lord said to Moses, 'Why do you cry out to me?* Tell the Israelites to go forward' " (Exod. 14:10–15, emphasis added).

b. The second is less intercession than a quick aside fired off by Moses in a tight spot. After three dry days, the people discovered a spring, but the water was too bitter to drink. "And the people complained against Moses, saying, 'What shall we drink?' He cried out to the Lord; and the Lord showed him a piece of wood; he threw it into the water, and the water became sweet" (Exod. 15:24–25).

c. Hunger for meat and bread shortly followed thirst, and complaints "against Moses and Aaron" erupted once more (Exod. 16:2). Moses identifies the complaining as "not against us but against the Lord" (Exod. 16:8). And, without intervention by Moses, God hears and promises food (quail and manna) in response.

d. The people grow thirsty again, and water is provided from a rock (Exod. 17:2), an episode that I shall return to later.

3 Numbers 11:4–35 may be a narrative representation of God's being fed up with complaints about hunger and with Moses' complaining about the complaints. See the interesting interpretation in James S. Ackerman,

"Numbers," in Alter and Kermode, *Literary Guide to the Bible*, 80–83. In response to the people's craving for meat, God sends an excessive amount. In response to Moses' request for help with his burden, God sends an excess of spirit. It is on the order of: "You want quails? I'll give you quails. You want spirit? I'll give you spirit."

4 There are also later intercessions on the way to Canaan: on behalf of Miriam after her rebellion (Num. 12); on behalf of the people in conjunction with Korah's rebellion (Num. 16:22); for relief from snakes (Num. 21:4–9); and on behalf of the people at the border of Canaan that a successor to himself be appointed lest the people be sheep without a shepherd (Num. 27:16–17).

5 For an interesting account of Moses' argument see Yochanon Muffs, *Love and Joy* (New York: Jewish Theological Seminary of America, 1992), 12–13. (God refers to the Israelites as "your" [Moses'] people; Moses refers to them as "your" [God's] people.)

6 One of the intercession's arguments is based on the covenant: if you destroy this people, you will default on your promises. Another relates to reputation: what will the Egyptians say? This argument will be repeated and elaborated in a later intercession for Israel when, after advance spies return from the promised land with unflattering, fearful reports of what awaits them, the people attempt a democratic rebellion: "Let us choose a captain, and go back to Egypt" (Num. 14:4). Moses and Aaron entreat them to desist, they do not, and, in terms reminiscent of the Mt. Sinai episode, God vows to do away with them (Num. 14:12). Thereupon Moses argues to God that "the Egyptians will hear of it . . . and they will tell the inhabitants of this land . . . then the nations who have heard about it will say, 'It is because the Lord was not able to bring this people into the land that he swore to give them that he has slaughtered them in the wilderness' " (Num. 14:13–16). Rumor and public relations have their uses and together with covenantal promises persuade God to change his mind in the Numbers as well as the Exodus text.

7 Caleb and Joshua are the sole exceptions (Num. 32:11–12, Deut. 1:35–38).

8 Muffs reads God's statement somewhat differently: God agrees here only to send His angel, not Himself (*Love and Joy*, 14–16).

9 "What is clear from the motivating appeals of Moses is that the prayer is not for an arbitrary or inconsistent action on God's part. It is a prayer for God to act according to the divine will and purpose as it has been manifest over and over again" (Miller, "Moses My Servant," 245, 253).

10 "Then the Lord said to me: Though Moses and Samuel stood before me, yet my heart would not turn toward this people" (Jer. 15:1). This text is discussed later, in part 2.

11 Deut. 5:5. See Michael Walzer, *Exodus and Revolution* (New York: Basic Books, 1985), 95.

12 My recognition of the fact that I was bound to take up lawyering for the situation came in a specific moment. I had talked briefly to the faculty of the Boston College School of Law about my early work on the Moses story, and, in the conversation with them that followed, I and the dean, Aviam Soifer, had a simultaneous "aha" experience: Is Moses at Sinai counsel for a situation after the fashion of Louis Brandeis?

Some years ago, I explored American law's dependence on story and then the possibility that the story of America's beginning can be related to the biblical story of beginning as one type can be related to its fundamental antetype (*Promise of American Law*, 7–28). The present enterprise is not an exercise in typology.

3. Counsel for the Situation

1 John Frank, *The Legal Ethics of Louis D. Brandeis*, 17 Stan. L. Rev. 683, 697 (1965).

2 See, e.g., Thomas Shaffer, *The Legal Ethics of Radical Individualism*, 65 Tex. L. Rev. 963 (1987). See also David Luban, *Lawyers and Justice* (Princeton, N.J.: Princeton University Press, 1988); William Simon, *Visions of Practice in Legal Thought*, 36 Stan. L. Rev. 469 (1984); David Wilkins, *Who Should Regulate Lawyers?* 105 Harv. L. Rev. 799 (1992). Other sources are discussed later.

Clyde Spillenger has a good description of lawyering for the situation: "It is to recognize and respect certain organic bonds, like family and other relationships, as deserving of representation. It is to suggest that the lawyer should be able to act as intermediary in situations that involve multiple but not necessarily adverse interests. . . . Sometimes the phrase refers to the role of lawyers as social reformers — making 'the situation' synonymous with 'the public' or 'the public good' " (*Elusive Advocate: Reconsidering Brandeis as People's Lawyer*, 105 Yale L. J. 1445, 1502 [1996]).

3 See John Dzienkowski, *Lawyers as Intermediaries*, 1992 U. Ill. L. Rev. 741, 748–53; Frank, *Legal Ethics of Louis D. Brandeis*, 698–703; Spillenger, *Elusive Advocate*, 1504–5 and n. 208. For a very interesting reflection on Brandeis in relation to Moses, see Robert Burt, *Two Jewish Justices* (Berkeley: University of California, 1988), 124–26.

4 Brandeis said: "We hear much of the 'corporation lawyer,' and far too little of the 'People's lawyer.' The great opportunity of the American Bar is and will be to stand again as it did in the past, ready to protect also the

interests of the people" ("Opportunity in the Law," 321 [1905 address to the Harvard Ethical Society]). On images of Brandeis as "attorney for the people," see Spillenger, *Elusive Advocate*, 1471 and n. 83, 1481 and n. 121, 1502–3.

5 See generally, e.g., Luban, *Lawyers and Justice;* Spillenger, *Elusive Advocate.*

6 See Alpheus Mason, *Brandeis, A Free Man's Life* (New York: Viking, 1946), 491–508; Philippa Strum, *Louis D. Brandeis: Justice for the People* (Cambridge: Murrand University Press, 1984), 291–308; A. L. Todd, *Justice on Trial* (New York: McGraw-Hill, 1964), 96–237.

7 Geoffrey Hazard, *Ethics in the Practice of Law* (New Haven, Conn.: Yale University Press, 1978), 58–59.

8 See Frank, *Legal Ethics of Louis D. Brandeis,* 699–703; Dzienkowski, *Lawyers as Intermediaries,* 750–53; Spillenger, *Elusive Advocate,* 1505–11.

9 Hearings before the Subcommittee of the Senate Committee on the Judiciary on the Nomination of Louis D. Brandeis to Be an Associate Justice of the Supreme Court of the United States, 64th Cong., 1st sess., 1916, ser. 6926, 287.

10 Frank, *Legal Ethics of Louis D. Brandeis,* 702.

11 Ibid.

Dzienkowski says: "One could interpret [it] in many different ways" (*Lawyers as Intermediaries,* 752). Spillenger believes it "was not the expression of a lawyering metaphysic but a hurried and embarrassed response to a question put to him by hostile counsel" (*Elusive Advocate,* 1507).

12 The charge against Brandeis "did not so much collapse as become submerged in concessions from other reputable lawyers that they had often done exactly as Brandeis" (Hazard, *Ethics in the Practice of Law,* 61). Lawyers told Hazard that lawyering to the situation described settings in which they had found themselves (ibid., 61–62).

13 Ibid., 65, see also 7, 61–62; Spillenger, *Elusive Advocate,* 1503–4.

14 American Bar Association, *Canons of Professional Ethics* 6 (1908).

15 American Bar Association, *American Bar Association Model Code of Professional Responsibility* (1982), DR 5-105 (C). The "ethical considerations" that accompanied the rule expressed concern for a lawyer's independence of judgment and loyalty to her client but accepted the propriety of representing multiple clients with differing interests outside the context of litigation so long as there was full disclosure and client consent (EC 5-14 to 5-16).

16 Ibid., EC 5-20.

17 See Hazard, *Ethics in the Practice of Law,* 62–64; Dzienkowski, *Lawyers as Intermediaries,* 759–62.

18 Hazard, *Ethics in the Practice of Law,* 62.

19 American Bar Association, *Model Rules of Professional Responsibility* (1992), Rule 2.2. Consultation and consent are required. There are other conditions, including reasonable beliefs that the undertaking will be successful and that there is little risk of prejudice to the clients' individual interests if it is not (ibid., Rule 2.2.a.1–3). Each client must be able to make informed decisions, and the lawyer must believe that her representation will be impartial as well as compatible with her responsibilities to the individual clients.

Rule 1.7 is the general conflict of interest rule. For commentary on that rule and its relation to Rule 2.2 see Russell Pearce, *Family Values and Legal Ethics: Competing Approaches to Conflicts in Representing Spouses*, 62 Fordham L. Rev. 1253 (1992); Teresa Collett, *The Ethics of Intergenerational Representation*, 62 Fordham L. Rev., 1453 (1992). One learned commentator believes that the rule constitutes an improvement but that it "leaves many fundamental questions unresolved" (Dzienkowski, *Lawyers as Intermediaries*, 745).

An ABA commission reevaluating the Model Rules proposes eliminating Rule 2.2 and the language of "intermediation." It would instead cover what it refers to as a "joint representation" under Rule 1.7. See note 22.

20 My representation of Shaffer is drawn from my correspondence with him and from his well-taken, influential treatment of the subject in *The Legal Ethics of Radical Individualism*.

21 American Law Institute, "Restatement of the Law Third: Restatement of the Law Governing Lawyers, Proposed Final Draft No. 1," March 29, 1996, sec. 211, cmt. a. That comment also states: "Although its terminology might be thought to imply otherwise, Rule 2.2 addresses a particular setting for applying the general rules governing conflicts" (ibid.).

22 See Commission on Evaluation of the Rules of Professional Conduct, "Draft for Public Comment," March 23, 1999, Proposed Rule 1.7 — Public Discussion Draft, Comments 27–32; ibid., Model Rule 1.7 — Reporter's Explanation of Changes, Comments 27–32; ibid., Model Rule 2.2 — Reporter's Explanation of Changes (http://www.abanet.org/cpr/ethics2k.html). See note 19.

23 The Restatement basically returns to the 1969 Model Code's requirement of consent and adequate representation. Sections 209 and 210 cover, respectively, representation of multiple parties in civil and in criminal litigation. Section 211 covers multiple representation in nonlitigation contexts. All three allow for representation of multiple parties where the clients consent. Client consent is covered by section 202, which requires that a client's consent be based on "reasonably adequate information about the material risks of such representation." This section also provides that, consent notwithstanding, it must nevertheless

be "reasonably likely that the lawyer will be able to provide adequate representation."

24 Hazard, *Ethics in the Practice of Law*, 64.

25 Dzienkowski warns that Brandeis's concept is "no longer viable in the modern legal profession" (*Lawyers as Intermediaries*, 748).

26 Hazard notes that bar association advisory opinions are abstract and dogmatic and, as "clean-cut answers to hypothetical problems," not really illuminating "for the messy ethical questions of real life" (*Ethics in the Practice of Law*, 60).

27 He simply "saw himself," Robert Burt suggests, "standing alone at the margin of his society," where he resisted affiliation with groups, causes, and clients, and preserved his autonomy (*Two Jewish Justices*, 9).

28 Spillenger, *Elusive Advocate*, 1509. This is to specify and extend Robert Burt's observation that "Brandeis always turned away; he always found a place to stand alone" (*Two Jewish Justices*, 9).

29 Dzienkowski notes that, in these instances, "the clients bear a risk that is not present in other types of representations. The risk relates primarily to the fact that the lawyer does not owe his or her loyalty exclusively to one client's interests. Further, most intermediations arise outside the litigation context, and thus are not supervised by an impartial trier of fact or law" (*Lawyers as Intermediaries*, 775 n. 184).

Derrick Bell noted about civil rights lawyers in the 1970s: "Idealism, though rarer than greed, can be especially hard to control" and can be especially dangerous (*Serving Two Masters: Integration Ideals and Client Interests in School Desegregation Litigation*, 85 Yale L. J. 470, 505 [1976]).

Owen Fiss noted about one lawyer for the situation in the abolitionist cause: "In invoking humanity's interest in freedom, Dana [stood] in danger of substituting his own conception of the good — or that of the privileged group to which he belongs — for that of the collective he [purported] to represent" (*Can a Lawyer Ever Do Right?* 17 Cardozo L. Rev. 1859, 1862 [1996]).

30 Rule 2.2, comment. The rule itself provides that, before a lawyer acts as an intermediary, she must believe that there is little risk of prejudice to client interests if she fails to achieve success.

31 Such detachment is not on its face an unsound idea. There are circumstances when an attorney should be independent. But Spillenger makes a well-taken point: "The Lennoxes of this world probably fall in the vast middle of a universe of clients bounded by 'powerful, amoral corporations' (from which a lawyer should exercise independence), on one side, and 'disempowered individuals' (with whom a lawyer should engage in empathetic dialogue), on the other. A lawyerly ethic that counsels independence from a client's unlawful or immoral goals does little to explain Brandeis's instincts in the Lennox case — his lack of interest in solutions

other than his own" (*Elusive Advocate*, 1510–11). For more on the independence of the lawyer, see part 3.

32 Hazard, *Ethics in the Practice of Law*, 67.

4. The Word in Moses' Situation

1 Hanna Pitkin establishes and elaborates two basic types of representation: that of mandate and that of independence (*Concept of Representation*). In speaking for God and the people, Moses performs in both instances a role that is sometimes following a mandate and sometimes an exercise of creative independence.

2 Jacobson's underlying point is that Freud got it backward. Freud proposed in *Moses and Monotheism* (1939) that Moses was a distinguished Egyptian who joined a group of culturally inferior immigrants. "The text is not hiding the secret that Moses was an Egyptian prince. Moses is telling us that he risked setting up as Pharaoh" (*Idolatry of Rules*, 1097–98).

3 Christian tradition singles out for celebration and memory Moses' resistance to forms of the pharaonic temptation: "By faith, Moses, when he was grown up, refused to be called a son of Pharaoh's daughter, choosing rather to share ill-treatment with the people of God than to enjoy the fleeting pleasures of sin" (Heb. 11:24–25).

   Moses' resistance to the pharaonic temptation renders especially ironic the claims of the rebels that he had engineered the exodus for his own purposes (Num. 16:12–14). Compare Numbers 10:29–32, the stories in Numbers 13, and the comments on them by Ackerman ("Numbers," 80, 83). See also Numbers 11:11ff.

4 God's response begins: "Whoever has sinned against me I will blot out of my book" (Exod. 32:33).

5 Yochanon Muffs proposes that the prophet is not only the messenger from the heavenly court but also an independent advocate to the court whose prayer and intercession seek rescission of the "evil" decree: "He is first the messenger of the divine court to the defendant, but his mission boomerangs back to the sender. Now, he is no longer the messenger of the court; he becomes the agent of the defendant, attempting to mitigate the severity of the decree" (*Love and Joy*, 9). God is then imagined as subject to conflicting emotions of justice and mercy: "If there is no balance in the divine emotion, if justice gets the upper hand over mercy, then the world is placed in great danger. Therefore, God allows the prophet to represent in his prayer His own attribute of mercy, the very element that enables a calming of God's feelings" (ibid., 33).

6 The ear of God is a metaphor primarily of petition in the Psalms: "Give ear to my prayer."

In a 1985 letter, my teacher James Luther Adams wrote: "My memory took me back to the writings of Thorkild Jacobsen, my colleague for twenty years in Chicago and then for two decades at Harvard, an eminent authority on the religion of Mesopotamia." Jacobsen had written an essay in which he "argues that the Council of the Gods was a projection of the primitive democracy of the Mesopotamian village. No god or goddess was to undertake action without first consulting the Council. The god or the goddess must first listen to the discussion in council. After reading the article I talked with him, and said that I wanted to venture to state a major theme in the article. 'Would you mind my risking an oversimplification?' 'Certainly not.' 'A major inference to be drawn from the account of this 'primitive democracy' is this: the sign of the god or goddess is the capacity to raise the hand to the ear and hear what another was saying.' 'That will do very nicely.' "

7 Gen. 12:1–3, 15:1–21, 17:1–27.

8 The poetic link between God passing before Moses and Israel in the company of God passing before other peoples is suggested by the juxtaposition of 34:6–7 and 34:8–14.

9 To be sure, the text has yet to give us the making of the tabernacle and vestments. But what reader does not gladly pause for the prejourney nourishment of the text's wonderful description of the extraordinary tent and its covering, the ark and mercy seat, the altar, the lamps, and hangings, the finely worked garments, and the robe finished all around the hem with alternating bells of gold and pomegranates of blue, purple, and crimson yarn. The details delight the imagination, and the reading time passes quickly.

10 What is to be made of the fact that Moses, in smashing the stones, erases God's words written by God? Is this an act extending God's wrath: Moses destroys that which would have mobilized and animated the people? Is this an act of mercy: If the words God has written enter the camp at the moment Israel is in the midst of its festival of idolatry, the word will break out and consume them? Is this a pedagogical act, as Arthur Jacobson proposes: Moses' smashing the stones to teach the people that this engraved stone is not an idol?

11 In the Christian tradition, believers return God's express words to him in the Lord's Prayer.

12 Jonathan Edwards: "The emanation or communication of the divine fullness, consisting in the knowledge of God, love to him and joy in him, has relation indeed both to *God* and the *creature:* but it has relation to God as its *fountain,* as the thing communicated is something of his internal fullness. The water in the stream is something of the fountain; and the beams of the sun are something of the sun. And again, they have relation to God as their *object:* for the knowledge communicated is

the knowledge of God; and the love communicated is the love of God; and the happiness communicated is joy in God. In the creature's knowing, esteeming, loving, rejoicing in, and praising God, the glory of God is both *exhibited* and *acknowledged;* his fullness is *received* and *returned.* Here is both an *emanation* and *remanation.* The refulgence shines upon and into the creature, and is reflected back to the luminary. The beams of glory come from God, are something of God, and are refunded back again to their original. So that the whole is *of* God, and *in* God, and *to* God; and he is the beginning, and the middle, and the end" ("Dissertation concerning the End for Which God Created the World," in *The Works of Jonathan Edwards* [Edward Baines, 1806], 1:462, 529).

5. The Risks

1 Robert Jenson, *Systematic Theology* (New York: Oxford University Press, 1997), 1:94.

2 Jenson, *Systematic Theology,* 217.

3 Ibid., 222. "God is not God in spite of changing his mind, in spite of answering prayer or failing to do so; he is God because he does and can do such things wholeheartedly" (ibid.).

4 Brueggemann, *Theology of the Old Testament,* 144.

5 Ibid., 83.

6 Ibid.

7 Jenson, *Systematic Theology,* 76 (quoting Mekhilta Y to Exodus 12:41).

8 Ibid.

9 Israel needs "to speak of God as a 'settled' participant in her story with him, who is yet other than the perpetrator of the identification" (ibid.). "God is identified *with* Israel in that he is identified *as* a participant *in* Israel's story with him" (ibid., 77).

10 Numbers 12.

11 See, e.g., Sternberg, *Poetics of Biblical Narrative,* 107; Ackerman, "Numbers," 84, 85; N. H. Snaith, "Numbers," in *Peake's Commentary,* 264.

12 Repeated at Numbers 27:14 ("you rebelled against my word, you did not show my holiness").

13 Deuteronomy ends on what Patrick Miller describes as "a subversive note." *Deuteronomy,* 244.

14 Damrosch, "Leviticus," 74.

15 Jenson, *Systematic Theology,* 231.

16 Ibid., 222; see also ibid., 80.

17 Damrosch, "Leviticus," 74.

18 Miller, "Deuteronomy," 50–51.

19 Brueggemann, *Theology of the Old Testament,* 83.

20 Ibid., 567.

21 In *The Practice of Justice* (Cambridge, Mass.: Harvard University Press, 1998) William Simon argues that lawyers should practice justice and that they should do so contextually. His emphasis on these subjects is a welcome addition to the literature on lawyering. It is also a welcome challenge to the established view according to which legal ethics and professional responsibility are reduced to little, categorical rules that leave scant room for the exercise of discretion. Simon's approach is limited, however, by his limited notions of justice and context. He presents justice as no more than the values of the legal system and the context as no more than the individual attorney's assessment of the relevant circumstances of the particular case and their relation to legal merit.

22 I draw upon Paul Lehmann: "Obviously the kind of ethical literalism which aims at a one-to-one correlation between a specific word of Jesus and a specific action misses the point of Jesus teaching. Decision making as the Christian understands it goes on in quite another way. For the Christian the *environment* of decision, not the *rules* of decision, gives to behavior its ethical significance. If . . . God is at work in this world, doing what it takes to make and to keep human life human, no specific action can be said to express or fulfill an ethical principle in a literal way. Telling the truth is, [for example], not identical with optimal verbal veracity. It is a matter of saying the 'right' word. The 'right' word, however, is a *sign* that human relations are going on in an environment of trust. . . . a human action has occurred which *indicates* or *points to* fundamental human relations which are both fundamental and human because of what God is doing in the world" (*Ethics in a Christian Context* [New York: Harper and Row, 1963], 346–47).

23 Ibid., 347.

24 Brueggemann, *Theology of the Old Testament*, 723.

25 Ibid.

26 Ibid., 713 (emphasis omitted).

6. The Promise of Succession

1 Earlier, at the base of Mt. Sinai, Aaron had committed the gravest of offenses. It was he who made the calf and led the people's worship of it. The other idolaters were punished for their sin: They perished in the desert before they could reach the promised land. Aaron was not included in this punishment. (He would also conspire with Miriam to rebel against Moses, an act for which Miriam but not he was punished [Num. 12:1–16].)

There are two explanations for God's excepting Aaron. According to

Deuteronomy, Moses successfully interceded on Aaron's behalf (9:20). According to Exodus, after Moses interrupted the calf worship, the entire House of Levi redeemed itself by leading the bloody purge: "Moses said, 'Today you have ordained yourselves for the service of the Lord, each one of you at the cost of a son or a brother, and so have brought a blessing on yourselves this day' " (Exod. 32:29). On this explanation, Aaron brought an atoning blessing on himself. Either way Aaron is not sentenced. Not for that transgression.

(It is possible that he was punished for that transgression. David Damrosch suggests a causal link between Aaron's idolatry and the death of his eldest sons, who were consumed by fire when they made the improvised offering [Lev. 10:1–3] ["Leviticus," 66, 69–71]. See also Jacob Milgrom, *Leviticus 1–16*, vol. 3 in The Anchor Bible [New York: Doubleday, 1991], 628–35.)

However, Aaron is ultimately punished in the same way as the others but for a different reason. It is the same reason that Moses must die outside the promised land: the incident at Meribah. Meribah is made the sentencing equivalent of the idolatry at Mt. Sinai. However, at Mt. Sinai Aaron was a leader in the offense.

2 Deuteronomy offers the same explanation for Aaron's early death (32:50).

3 For a comparison of this statement with the later statement that "never since has there arisen a prophet in Israel like Moses" (Deut. 34:10), see Robert Polzin, *Moses and the Deuteronomist* (Bloomington: Indiana University Press, 1980), 35–36.

4 In the beginning of Deuteronomy Moses reviews the failures and complaints of the people in the wilderness and God's anger in response to them and says about the incident at Meribah: "Even with me the Lord was angry on your account" (Deut. 1:37)—on your account, not mine. Moses blames the people. However, toward the end of Deuteronomy, in the passage cited, God says, "You broke faith with me among the Israelites at the waters of Meribah-kadesh . . . , by failing to maintain my holiness among the Israelites" (Deut. 32:48–52). Here God says Moses is to blame.

Moses' statement is to be matched against God's. *Moses says* he is to be punished because God was angry with the people for cutting a trail of rebellious grumbling through the desert. *God says* Moses himself rebelled, and He makes no mention of anger at the people. The two are not necessarily mutually exclusive, but there is a subtle difference in the fixing of blame. And there is no doubt about which account the text would have us believe is the more credible.

If only in the smallest way the reader is led to questions about Moses. Are his statements about Meribah (understandably) self-serving? Are they a reflection or repetition of the self-serving offense committed at Meribah? Is this a way of allowing readers to witness a version of the offense for themselves? Is Moses at last like Adam in pointing to others instead of accepting responsibility ("The woman whom you gave to be with me, she gave me the fruit from the tree" [Gen. 3:12])? Does he attempt to play God as Geoffrey Hazard says lawyers for the situation do? Has he this much in common with us? Is he, after all, one of us?

5 Robert Polzin, "Deuteronomy," in Alter and Kermode, *Literary Guide to the Bible,* 94.

6 Robert Polzin, "Reporting Speech in the Book of Deuteronomy: Toward a Compositional Analysis of the Deuteronomic History," in *Traditions in Transformation: Turning Points in Biblical Faith,* ed. Baruch Halpern and Jon Levenson (Winona Lake, Ind.: Eisenbrauns, 1981), 200.

7 Polzin, "Reporting Speech in the Book of Deuteronomy," 202; republished in Polzin, *Moses and the Deuteronomist,* 27; repeated in Polzin, "Deuteronomy," 93.

On the matter of "author" and "narrator," Meir Sternberg notes that, since Wayne Booth's *Rhetoric of Fiction,* theorists have spoken of an "actual writer," an "implied author," and a "narrator" (Sternberg, *Poetics of Biblical Narrative,* 74–78). The first is the person, who, during his life, did many things, including writing. The second is the author projected by a given text as its creator. The narrator is the voice or character created by the writer to do the telling. Sternberg observes that this tripartition doesn't exactly suit the biblical texts in which, he argues, the implied author and the narrator practically merge. When he uses the word "narrator," therefore, he intends it to embrace both and means "the master of the tale in general" (ibid., 75). He notes that there remains a marked distinction between the actual writer who "lived in history" and the narrator "who comes to life in interpretation" (ibid.). The matter is not free of complication, but I tend to follow Sternberg's usage.

8 There are both "an overt, obvious voice that exalts Moses as it plays down its own role, and a still, soft voice that nevertheless succeeds in drawing attention to itself at the expense of Moses' uniqueness" (Polzin, "Deuteronomy," 94).

9 "As Moses speaks for God, so the narrator speaks for Moses" and for God and blurs "the distinction between the teaching authority of his hero and that of the narrator" (ibid., 96).

10 The assurance runs to the people and not to the individual. Any particular successor to Moses—priest, political leader, prophet, writer—will enjoy no more privilege or immunity than did he. None is to confuse himself with God. All are subject to the terrible consequences of transgression.

Writer-successors suffer a subtle temptation. Meir Sternberg says that biblical writers exhibit certain kinds of omniscience and omnipotence. Their abilities to penetrate a character's mind and to narrate widely separated events simultaneously constitute their omniscience (Sternberg, *Poetics of Biblical Narrative,* 59). Their ability to create a world on the page is their omnipotence (ibid., 99). Both powers are to serve God, who is the Omniscient and Omnipotent. Sternberg says that, at Meribah, Moses struck the rock and drew water "at the price of diminishing God" and thereby robbed "the Omnipotent of his hallmark and the demonstration of its grandeur" (ibid., 107). It is a central offense, and Aaron is guilty of it as well. The danger for the succeeding biblical writers is that they, too, will display their omniscience and omnipotence so as to diminish rather than serve the Omniscient and Omnipotent God. Writers' temptation is to replicate the core offense of Moses and Aaron and conflate being mouth for God with being God.

The Deuteronomist expressly disavows any exalted comparison with Moses in the conclusion to Deuteronomy: "Never since has there arisen a prophet in Israel like Moses, whom the Lord knew face to face. He was unequaled for all the signs and wonders that the Lord sent him to perform . . . and for all the mighty deeds and all the terrifying displays of power that Moses performed in the sight of all Israel" (Deut. 34:10–12). The Deuteronomist enacts a succession to Moses and yet depends upon the story he tells rather than upon explicit claims for the writing to establish the authority of his words.

7. The Promise of Justice

1 See also Deuteronomy 24:17–18, 27:19.
2 Damrosch, "Leviticus," 74. "The transformation of exile makes alienation the basis for a renewed ethical closeness to one's neighbors and even to strangers" (ibid.).
3 Remarkably, the bringing together continues as an obligation sufficiently radical to include even Egyptians in the assembly of the Lord: "You shall not abhor any of the Egyptians, because you were an alien residing in their land. The children of the third generation that are born to them may be admitted to the assembly of the Lord" (Deut. 23:7–8). But a memory for outrage is also to continue. Ammonites and Moabites are to be excluded "because they did not meet you with food and water on your journey out of Egypt. . . . You shall never promote their welfare or their prosperity as long as you live" (Deut. 23:4, 6). Why include Egyptians and exclude Ammonites and Moabites?

8. Psalm 114

1 These comments are made about Trible by Walter Brueggemann (*Theology of the Old Testament*, 56). I make direct use of Trible's work in part 2.

2 Ibid., 56.

3 The story of crossing the Jordan on dry ground is told in Joshua: 3:14–17.

4 Robert Alter, *The Art of Biblical Poetry* (New York: Basic Books, 1985), 210.

5 Ibid.

6 Water made to flow from a rock in the desert is an explicit image of God's redemptive nurturing of His people in Isaiah: "God has redeemed His servant Jacob, and they did not thirst in the wastelands where He led them. Water from a rock he made flow for them. He split the rock and water gushed." (This is the translation of Robert Alter, who discusses these verses helpfully in *The Art of Biblical Poetry*, 20.)

7 See Alter, *Art of Biblical Poetry;* Alter, "The Characteristics of Ancient Hebrew Poetry," in Alter and Kermode, *Literary Guide to the Bible*, 600; George W. Anderson, "Characteristics of Hebrew Poetry," in *New Oxford Annotated Bible*, 392.

8 So far as I know, a people of strange language occurs nowhere else in the Bible as a description of the Egyptians. However, Robert Alter pointed out to me in correspondence that it is quite common in the Bible to refer to foreign peoples as speakers of gibberish. It was the same for the Greeks, who regarded foreigners as uttering incomprehensible nonsense that sounded to them like "barbarabarbarabarbara" and so referred to them as barbarians. Mitchell Dahood argues that the root consonants in the Hebrew *l'z* should be translated as "barbaric" rather than as "of strange language" (*Psalms III*, vol. 17A of The Anchor Bible [New York: Doubleday, 1970], 134). I accept the usual translation rather than his and find that it performs useful work in the poem, as I shall propose below.

9 J. P. Fokkelman provides an example of the advantages of legislation in verse that employs chiasm: "Whoever sheds the blood of a human, by a human shall that person's blood be shed; for in his own image God made humankind" (Gen. 9:6). Fokkleman writes: "Verse 6a is a legal directive which prescribes an accurate balance between capital crime and punishment; 6b contains its sacral motivation . . . : shofekh dam ha'adam / ba'adam damo yishafekh (6a) for in the image of God / made he man. (6b) The first line is usually wrongly translated 'Who sheds the blood of a human being, by a human being his blood shall be shed.' The structure of the first line in Hebrew, however, reveals a symmetry, the concentric pattern *abcc'b'a'*. The purpose of this arrangement is of course to

show that the 'human being' in the first half-verse is the same person as the 'human being' (that is, the victim) in the other. The correct rendering offers a precise image of balanced legal retribution: 'Who sheds the blood of a human being, his blood (as compensation) for that human being be shed' " ("Genesis," in Alter and Kermode, *Literary Guide to the Bible,* 45).

10 Dahood employs the past tense (*Psalms III,* 133, 136).

11 In the stories of the exodus, while the water draws back there is no trembling of mountains. The shaking of the mountains takes place later when God descends upon Mt. Sinai. In Psalm 77, however, the shaking of the earth belongs to the poetic description of the mighty event of the exodus. In Psalm 114, the reference to mountains and hills may be to the Sinai events, in which case the entire sweep of stories is set out before the mind's eye: exodus, Sinai, conquest. Or the reference may be to the exodus or exodus and entry. Or it may be no reference of the sort but instead a reflection of a poetic formula. See, e.g., Alter's interesting reflections on the use of "mountains-hills" in prophetic poetry (*Art of Biblical Poetry,* 154–57, esp. 157). See also his observations on the use elsewhere of mountains-hills in the image of God's world-embracing justice (ibid., 131).

12 Robert Alter employs Deuteronomy 32:13 as an illustration of some of the dynamics of biblical poetry's parallelism. His comments about rock/flinty stone in that text apply here as well. He translates the lines in Deuteronomy as "He suckled him with honey from a rock / and oil from the flinty stone." Psalm 114's "pool of water" and "spring of water" may be substituted for "honey" and "oil" in reading Alter's comment: "Flinty stone' follows the rule of a specific instance of the category coming after the general term and by so doing effects an intensification or focusing of meaning. The first verset might even be read 'naturalistically,' as a hyperbolic poetic allusion to the discovery of honey combs in rocky crags [pools of water in the hollows of desert stone], but no such construal is allowable in the second verset, both because here it is oil that is provided and because the focusing effect of 'flinty stone' leaves no alternative to a recognition of the miraculous character of the event" (ibid., 24).

13 Ibid., 118.

14 Ibid., 54 (commenting on The Song of the Sea, Exod. 15:1–18).

15 Ibid., 53.

16 The psalm was given to me in a minor type of the larger type. My wife and I attended an Episcopal church service in Athens, Georgia. I was put to a small crisis by the first song, sung with gusto: "Onward Christian Soldiers." To sing this bathetic, triumphalist song strikes me as blasphemy in Athens, where, in my lifetime, crosses were paraded around and set ablaze as an act of terror and where there was some overlap be-

tween the leaders of the city's establishment and the Ku Klux Klan. Torn between marching out and standing silently, I looked down and my eye caught one of the texts for the day in the leaflet containing the liturgy. It was Psalm 114. At the time I had been working on this chapter with no thought for the Psalms but with Robert Alter's *Art of Biblical Poetry* freshly in mind. At that instant I began to work out the reading that I have just offered. I stayed in the church. The remaining liturgy, texts, and a redeeming sermon made me thankful that I had not departed. I was doubly relieved by the absorbing calm that the psalm and the interpretation of it afforded in the midst of the militaristic beat of the congregation's singing.

Some weeks later, as a guest teacher in one the church's classes, I offered my reading of Psalm 114 together with an explanation of the occasion that had directed me to it. I hoped that the congregation had surrendered its singing of that psalm. In due course my hope was dashed.

17 The image of the word as seminal rain is employed also as the opening for the song of Moses in Deuteronomy 32: "Give ear, O heavens, and I will speak; let the earth hear the words of my mouth. May my teaching drop like the rain, my speech condense like the dew; like gentle rain on grass, like showers on new growth. For I will proclaim the name of the Lord; ascribe greatness to our God!" (Deut. 32:1–3).

18 Alter, *Art of Biblical Poetry*, 210–12.

9. The Midwives

1 In these verses, the text uses "Pharaoh" and "king of Egypt" interchangeably.

2 Midwives' political role in the story may correspond with the political role they played in the society. Victor Matthews and Don Benjamin describe midwives of the time as performing legal as well as medical-clinical work: negotiating precoital covenants, supervising times for conception, certifying pregnancy, negotiating household adoption and naming of the baby, etc. (Matthews and Benjamin, *Social World of Ancient Israel, 1250–587* BCE [Peabody, Mass.: Hendrickson, 1993], 67–81.) See also Matthews and Benjamin, *Old Testament Parallels* (New York: Paulist Press, 1991), 17, 20, 86–88, 93, 154–55.

3 The appearance of the midwives and the ensuing byplay could be taken as a virtuosic flourish unnecessary to the development of the narrative action. The story could move sensibly from the exploding population of slaves directly to the general order to throw babies into the Nile without the intervention of the midwife scene.

4 Socrates' mother was a midwife, and it may have been that midwives

generally in Greece were past the age of childbearing. That the Hebrew midwives were given families may indicate that the same was not true in Israel and Egypt. However, if in those cultures midwives belonged to a separate, special community, Shiphrah's and Puah's families of their own would represent an extraordinary gift. See Victor Matthews and Don Benjamin, "The Midwife," in Matthews and Benjamin, *Social World of Ancient Israel*.

5   Textually, it is not clear whether they were Hebrew midwives or were midwives to the Hebrews. Extratextually, Josephus maintained that they were Egyptian. Also, "the fear of God" is employed elsewhere in the Bible as an explanatory description of gentiles' sympathy for the Hebrew cause. See Drorah O'Donnell Setel, "Exodus," in The Women's Bible Commentary, ed. Carol Newsom and Sharon Ringe (Louisville, Ky.: Westminster/John Knox Press, 1992), 30; Stalker, "Exodus," 208, 210.

6   See, e.g., *The New Oxford Annotated Bible*, 71 (note to Exod. 2:10); Nahum Sarna, *Exploring Exodus* (New York: Schocken Books, 1986), 32–33.

7   Setel, "Exodus," 29.

8   This is Phyllis Trible's translation, from *God and the Rhetoric of Sexuality* (Philadelphia: Fortress Press, 1978), 60. For other uses of the midwife image see Job 10:18–19, Jeremiah 1:5.

9   This translation follows that of Trible, *God and the Rhetoric of Sexuality*, 16. My comments here draw upon pages 14–21.

10   Ibid., 17.

11   Ibid., 21.

12   Ibid., 69.

13   "Correlative with the patriarchal co-optation and domestication of God's name have been the domestication and distortion of the covenantal story and its Scripture. The fatherhood of God became the principal warrant for the dehumanizing subordination, chiefly of women, but also of servants and calves, of the underprivileged and the untalented" (Lehmann, *Decalogue and a Human Future*, 130–31). "There is a radical and uncompromising contradiction and opposition between God the father—so understood and responded to—and the God of Adam and Eve, of Abraham and Sarah, of Isaac and Rebekah, of Jacob and Rachel, of Moses and Miriam" (ibid., 129).

14   Trible, *God and the Rhetoric of Sexuality*, 21.

15   Lehmann, *Decalogue and a Human Future*, 116.

16   Phyllis Trible, *Texts of Terror* (Philadelphia: Fortress Press, 1984), 16.

17   Dennis Curtis and Judith Resnik, *Images of Justice*, 96 Yale L. J. 1727, 1731 (1987).

10. Socratic Midwifery That Isn't

1 Moses and Socrates come from entirely different worlds, one from the discourse and experience of the *davar,* the powerful word of God, and the other from the discourse and experience of the *logos,* the word of rationality. However, so far as I have been able to determine, Greek midwifery did not differ substantially from the practice in Egypt. And, although I would not compose the differences between the two, the generosity of the biblical precedent encourages a positive reevaluation of Socrates as midwife.

   On ancient midwifery, see, e.g., Léonie Archer, "Notions of Community and the Exclusion of the Female in Jewish History and Historiography," in *Women in Ancient Societies,* ed. Léonie Archer, Susan Fischler, and Maria Wyke (New York: Routledge, 1994), 65–66; Nancy Demand, *Birth, Death, and Motherhood in Classical Greece* (Baltimore, Md.: Johns Hopkins University Press, 1994), 63–68, 130–33. Jean Towler and Joan Bramall comment that "the basic principles of Greek medicine and also of midwifery were derived from the Egyptian body of knowledge. However, even in this age in which the art of midwifery appeared highly developed, and midwives and doctors were clinically skilled practitioners, the Greeks made very little contribution to obstetrics" (Towler and Bramall, *Midwives in History and Society* [Dover, N.H.: Croom Helm, 1986], 12).

2 *Theaetetus,* in *The Dialogues of Plato,* trans. B. Jowett (New York: Random House, 1937), 2:150 [149], 151 [150].

3 *Theaetetus,* 151 [150]. The metaphor continues in the *Symposium* and the *Phaedrus.* See Demand, *Birth, Death, and Motherhood in Classical Greece,* 136–38, 225 n. 70.

4 See Gregory Vlastos, *Socrates, Ironist and Moral Philosopher* (Ithaca, N.Y.: Cornell University Press, 1991), 266. Of course, it could still be said that Plato, if not Socrates, is a midwife. Or so says Raphael Demos: "Plato is averse to providing the reader with answers to questions; since such generosity on his part would remove from the reader that very sense of wonder which is the stimulus to speculation. In one of the dialogues, Socrates explains his function as a teacher by comparing himself to a midwife. The midwife, usually old and sterile, bears no children of her own; she helps others to bring forth children. So Plato, in his dialogues, is not giving formed and finished ideas to the reader; he is assisting the reader to bear his own intellectual children" (introduction to *The Dialogues of Plato,* 1:viii).

   In helpful criticism of an early version of this book, a friend said that in the *Theaetetus* and elsewhere, Socrates "expects his interlocutors to

recognize and endorse the opinions he creates or expresses *as their own* —
if only they could express themselves as well as Socrates expresses himself." It seems to me that in these circumstances Socrates persuades the
interlocutors and leads them to views that they could not otherwise produce.

5 *Theaetetus,* 150 [148], 152 [151].

6 Ibid., 151 [150].

7 *Symposium,* in *The Dialogues of Plato,* 333 [209].

8 Nancy Demand comments that, in this way of thinking, women are
"considered capable only of giving birth to other females and to incomplete males" whose completion depends upon "a rebirthing process"
(*Birth, Death, and Motherhood in Classical Greece,* 139). Her remark is
made in the process of exploring the metaphor of male pregnancy (ibid.,
134–40). She proposes that in this devaluation of women, Plato's text reflects the prejudice of a society in which a boy must be born again "into
the symbolic order of 'masculinity' by men" (ibid., 139 [quoting David
Halperin]). M. F. Burnyeat notes about the *Symposium* that its "sexu-
alized view of teaching [is] devalued in that it has become separated
from the metaphor of mental conception and birth and is now associated
with sophistic education in pointed *contrast* to Socrates' own approach"
("Socratic Midwifery, Platonic Inspiration," *Bulletin of the Institute of
Classical Studies* 24 [1977]: 9).

9 Burnyeat, "Socratic Midwifery, Platonic Inspiration," 8.

10 John Osborne, *The Paper Chase* (New York: Houghton-Mifflin, 1971).

11 The *Harvard Law Review* published the outline for a lecture prepared
by Professor Areeda as a memorial to its author. I cite this piece from
among many others on the Socratic method in law school because it is
recent, because Areeda was "a master of the Socratic Method," and because it is suggested to "represent the most perceptive analysis of the
core of legal pedagogy available in the literature" (introductory note to
Areeda, *The Socratic Method (SM),* 109 Harv. L. Rev. 911 [1996] [report-
ing the comments of Clark Byse, who recommended the piece to the
editors]).

12 In this manner the student "becomes confident that he can discover answers that he didn't suspect he knew" (Areeda, *Socratic Method,* 922).

13 This eventual internalizing of the process, Areeda says, "is the essence
of legal reasoning and the prize of the" method (ibid.). I am not sure
why this is not an illusion. It may not be an illusion that the student
sooner or later internalizes the process. But what of the thing internal-
ized — the process of the teacher? According to Areeda, the test of the
teacher's skill lies in maintaining the illusion that the students have not
been led to the answers that the teacher could have given but did not

give in a lecture (ibid.). If that is true, doesn't the student who internalizes the process internalize the maintenance of illusion? Is that the nub of thinking like a lawyer?

14   Ibid., 915. In a large class, the teacher cross-examines some students, and their nonparticipating colleagues share the experience by silently going through the motions of giving answers to the questions. "The risk of being questioned induces this vicarious participation" (ibid., 916).

If students are more likely to stay awake and to learn better when they actually practice thinking like lawyers and actually use the peculiar logic of law to solve real problems, the Socratic method is not so good for the purpose as that other method known as the law school clinic. There the clients as well as the problems are assuredly real, and students really do have to use legal materials like lawyers. In my experience, by exposing students to real people with real problems, clinics expose students' own real need for knowledge and methodology in a way that excites their attentive appetites for other classes taught by either lecture or question-and-answer. The point has been well and repeatedly made to me by Steve Wizner of Yale's Legal Services Organization.

15   Some of the abuses, shortfalls, and inefficiencies of the Socratic method, especially as practiced by those less able than Areeda, could be overcome by translating it effectively into interactive electronic media. A one-on-one virtual encounter between student and program at home or in a school lab might be educationally and economically better than a real or vicarious encounter between student and teacher in a large class. Suitably humiliating comments by a virtual teacher could be individualized and preselected by the student. Of course, if the Socratic method has no essential need for a real teacher, it is not essentially Socratic.

To repair the weaknesses of the Socratic method and to rehearse its advantages in comparison to lecturing does not establish its relation to Socrates. Areeda does not intend it to. He does not address the issue.

The absence of a Socratic connection can be read into Areeda's careful observation that the law school method is "most useful in highly analytical (and somewhat less ideological) subjects, such as contracts" (ibid., 916), but unsuitable in ventilating "mega-level questions" like "What is justice?" (ibid., 913).

16   For comment that the method is not midwifery, see Barbara Woodhouse, *Mad Midwifery: Bringing Theory, Doctrine, and Practice to Life*, 91 Mich. L. Rev. 1977, 1994 (1993) ("Socratic master commands the podium as the high class surgeon commands the operating theater").

17   That the method is a generally oppressive form of control is the point of Duncan Kennedy's send-up of law school in *Legal Education and the Reproduction of Hierarchy: A Polemic against the System* (Cambridge, Mass.: Afar, 1983). I find that this work still provokes students to wonderful re-

sponses of all kinds. See also Karl Klare, *The Law School Curriculum in the 1980's: What's Left?* 32 J. Leg. Ed. 336 (1982).

18 For example, Jenny Morgan suggests that the method is "a powerful model of a male-preferred style of interaction" that silences cooperation and "may work differentially to silence women in the classroom" (*The Socratic Method: Silencing Cooperation*, 1 Leg. Ed. Rev. 151, 161, 164 [1989]). Deborah Rhode notes that feminists' perspectives "highlight some of the most problematic aspects of law school pedagogy: the hierarchical, authoritarian relationship between students and professors; the competitive ethos of class participation and evaluation; and the effects of these dynamics when other status inequalities such as race and gender are also present" (*Missing Questions: Feminist Perspectives on Legal Education*, 45 Stan. L. Rev. 1547, 1555 [1993]). (Margaret Jane Radin points out the risk of reinforcing stereotypes in Rhode's approach. See *Reply: Please Be Careful with Cultural Feminism*, 45 Stan. L. Rev. 1567 [1993].) See also Judith Resnik, *Ambivalence: The Resiliency of Legal Culture in the United States*, 45 Stan. L. Rev. 1525 (1993).

Others have noted the identification of legal education with maleness and masculine qualities. See, e.g., Carrie Menkel-Meadow, "Women as Law Teachers: Toward the 'Feminization' of Legal Education," in *Humanistic Education in Law, Monograph III* (New York: Project for the Study and Application of Humanistic Education in Law, Columbia University School of Law, 1981), 16, 18. Susan Williams finds that the method rests upon a mainstream epistemology that feminists challenge (*Legal Education, Feminist Epistemology, and the Socratic Method*, 45 Stan. L. Rev. 1571 [1993]). For a study of how law school coursebooks and courses can disenfranchise women, see Mary Jo Frug, *Re-Reading Contracts: A Feminist Analysis of a Contracts Casebook*, 34 Am. U. L. Rev. 1065 (1985).

19 Plato did achieve a view of women as equals in the *Republic*, in *Dialogues of Plato*, 1:710 [449]. But see Julia Annas, "Plato's *Republic* and Feminism," *Philosophy* 51 (1976): 307; Sabina Lovibond, "An Ancient Theory of Gender: Plato and the Pythagorean Table," in Archer, Fischler, and Wyke, *Women in Ancient Societies*, 88.

11. Socratic Midwifery That Is

1 Vlastos's reading of Plato in general and in its specifics is controversial. A friend who is a Plato scholar offered helpful criticism of a manuscript for this book. He warned about the hazards of employing Vlastos's approach. He noted that "the order of the dialogues itself is contentious, and . . . most dialogues have at one time or another been assigned to almost every period." He also warned against constructing biographical narratives of either Socrates or Plato out of the order of the dialogues.

There is no cause—and Vlastos has no need—for me to defend his interpretation. I find his position useful for present purposes and plausible if not exclusively right. My friend asked: "Can't you just argue that maieutics, ironically unproductive in the *Theaetetus,* where the art is expounded, are productive elsewhere in the corpus?" That is more or less what I argue, but I find it convenient and valid to follow Vlastos here in identifying the "elsewhere" as the material he refers to as "earlier." I do not mean to endorse attempts to derive a biography of either Socrates or Plato from the order of the dialogues.

2 Vlastos, *Socrates, Ironist and Moral Philosopher,* 46–47, 49.

3 Ibid., 155. See also pp. 46–53, 85, and the notes thereto. Vlastos describes the earlier Socrates as "complicated, devious, cunning" (ibid., 133).

4 Ibid., 49.

5 *Gorgias,* 467. The translation is that of Vlastos (*Socrates, Ironist and Moral Philosopher,* 156). (Jowett: "Either prove that I am in error or give the answer yourself" [*Dialogues of Plato,* 1:525].)

6 He employs the *elenchos* as his method of philosophical investigation. In Vlastos's description: "Socrates refutes a thesis p, defended by the interlocutor as his personal belief, by eliciting from him additional premises, say {q,r}, whose conjunction entails the negation of p. The refutation is accomplished by 'peirastic' argument: the refutand p, proposed and defended by the interlocutor, is refuted out of his own mouth: p is shown to be inconsistent with propositions in his own belief-system" (Vlastos, *Socrates, Ironist and Moral Philosopher,* 266). It is a matter of "making *trial* of one another in give-and-take argument," 94 n. 53. James Boyd White notes that in the dialectical conversation, "there are only two parties to the conversation; they proceed by question and answer, not making speeches; each promises to tell the truth as he sees it; each, knowing that his own knowledge is defective, actively seeks refutation from the other; and each, for the moment, is loyal only to that relation, calling in no others as witnesses, asking what they think, but calling only on the other party to the dialectic as his witness" (*Acts of Hope* [Chicago: University of Chicago, 1994], 37). Clark Cunningham notes that the *Crito* itself is not a good example of the kind of dialectic White describes (*Learning from Law Students: A Socratic Approach to Law and Literature,* 63 U. Cinn. L. Rev. 195 [1994]).

7 I. F. Stone, *The Trial of Socrates* (Boston: Little, Brown, 1988), 55. (Stone takes note of the complaints about Socrates' "negative dialectic" registered by both Cicero and Augustine, neither of whom was a hostile critic [ibid., 60–61].)

8 Vlastos contrasts the elenctic approach to the maieutic and so rejects the midwife metaphor as appropriate to the early Socrates. See, e.g., Vlastos, *Socrates, Ironist and Moral Philosopher,* 49, 85, and notes thereto. I

think this is to throw the midwife out with the bathwater. The problem, as I see it, is that the use of the midwife metaphor in the *Theaetetus* is inconsistent with the performance in that dialogue. I think it is consistent with what Socrates does in the earlier dialogues. I thus take the metaphor as a valid figure for what Socrates has been but will not always be. I think that elenctics is maeiutics properly understood and practiced. Burnyeat effectively takes the same position. See Burnyeat, "Socratic Midwifery, Platonic Inspiration," 9. See also Thomas Brickhouse and Nicholas Smith, *Plato's Socrates* (New York: Oxford University Press, 1994), 3–5. Following the narrator of the exodus, I take a robust view of maieutics.

9 A Socratic encounter, when it works, leads to an ongoing examination of the person, the person's life and beliefs, the discrepancies between the beliefs, and the discrepancies between the beliefs and the way one lives. The movement is toward a coherent set of justifiable beliefs, a life's journey on the way to truth and virtue. It is a journey and it is lifelong because truth seeking never settles into certainty. See Vlastos, *Socrates, Ironist and Moral Philosopher,* 15, 113–15; and see generally Brickhouse and Smith, *Plato's Socrates.*

10 In this interpretation I depend upon not only Vlastos but also Thomas Brickhouse and Nicholas Smith (*Plato's Socrates,* 10–29).

11 *Charmides,* in *Dialogues of Plato,* 1:15 [165]. Socrates says he has the mission of searching into himself as well as other men (*Apology,* in *Dialogues of Plato,* 412 [29]). The dialogues seldom present him subjected to Socratic examination by others. See *Protagoras,* in *Dialogues of Plato,* 1:108–9 [338–339]; *Gorgias,* 520–25 [462–467]. But they do portray him examining himself in examining others. See Brickhouse and Smith, *Plato's Socrates,* 16.

12 *Republic,* 1:618 [352].

13 What he brings to his encounters are himself and his beliefs, and he puts both to the test in testing others. And when he must finally appear in court he offers himself and his beliefs once more as he always has. Even in court in his own defense he has no prepared remarks. He uses, he says, "the words and arguments which occur to [him] at the moment" (*Apology,* 401 [17]).

He brings only himself and defends himself in his accustomed manner of speaking and arguing and being. He explains that he cannot go about in Athens without inquiring and speculating in his troubling manner and that life in exile would be no different (ibid., 412 [29], 419 [37]). He can no more hold his tongue abroad than he can in Athens. "Now I have great difficulty in making you understand . . . this," he says. "For if I tell you that to [remain silent] would be a disobedience to the God, and therefore that I cannot hold my tongue, you will not believe that I am serious; and if I say again that daily to discourse about virtue, and of those other things about which you hear me examining myself and others, is the greatest good of man, and that the unexamined life is not worth living, you are still less likely to believe me" (ibid., 419–20 [37–38]).

14 *Crito,* in *Dialogues of Plato,* 437 [53].

15 White, *Acts of Hope,* 35. I have been well educated by White's readings of Plato, and I have been much influenced by his interpretation of Socrates.

16 In comparison to being not Socrates, death appears to be not so bad. Either it is an undisturbed, welcome sleep, or it is a journey to another world in which he can continue to be Socrates, only infinitely so and at a higher level: "What would not a man give, O judges," he says, "to be able to examine the leader of the great Trojan expedition; or Odysseus or Sisyphus, or numberless others, men and women too! What infinite delight would there be in conversing with them and asking them questions! In another world they do not put a man to death for asking questions" (*Apology,* 422 [41]).

17 Ibid., 417 [35].

18 Ibid.

19 Brickhouse and Smith, *Socrates on Trial* (Princeton, N.J.: Princeton University Press, 1988), 199.

20 Gregory Vlastos's description is "conduct which falls entirely within the limits of the habitual expectations sustained by the institutional framework" (*Socrates, Ironist and Moral Philosopher,* 180).

21 Vlastos says that Socrates "finds reason to stigmatize as unjust one of its most venerable, best established, rules of justice" (ibid., 179).

22 *Crito,* 433 [49]. Vlastos's translation: "We should never return a wrong or do an evil to a single human being no matter what we may have suffered at his hands. And watch out Crito, lest in agreeing with this you do so contrary to your real opinion. For few are those who believe or will believe this. And between those who do and those who don't there can be no common counsel. Of necessity they must feel contempt for one another when viewing each other's deliberations" (*Socrates, Ironist and Moral Philosopher,* 194–95).

23 George Steiner holds that Socrates' argument "contradicts not only natural instinct, but the entirety of the heroic, masculine traditions of the ancient Mediterranean world" (*No Passion Spent* [New Haven, Conn.: Yale University Press, 1996], 381). A friend who offered good criticism of an earlier version of this book noted that, in comparison to its treatment of the midwives, the biblical texts generally treat women dreadfully. He advised me to credit Plato for proposing that "women could be guardians in his ideal state" and to credit "the Greek culture more generally, which, while practicing nearly every unimaginable op-

pression of women in almost every way, managed at the same time to present women in their theater in a more accurate and respectful way, more acknowledging of their individuality and importance, than perhaps any other literature in the Western tradition." I am glad to take his advice. I do credit Plato's achievement in the *Republic* and much admire the dramatic achievements of Athena, Clytemnestra, Antigone, Medea, and other powerfully memorable women.

24 Martha Nussbaum, *The Use and Abuse of Philosophy in Legal Education*, 45 Stan. L. Rev. 1627, 1630 n. 13 (1993).

25 *Apology*, 1:422 [41].

26 "Socrates has no method, if by 'method' we mean an orderly procedure which follows patterns that must be learned and mastered before one is able to achieve effective results. There is no 'cookbook' for the Socratic *elenchos*, nor could a step-by-step procedure ever be set forth. Any of us *could* do what Socrates does, although, of course, not as well; and according to Socrates, *all* of us *should* do what he does. The fact that we would get better at it with practice should be no impediment to our undertaking Socratic examinations right away and for the rest of our lives. Accordingly, we have nothing to learn before we employ Socrates' method. It follows from these considerations that Socrates thinks there is no method to learn" (Brickhouse and Smith, *Plato's Socrates*, 10).

27 Brickhouse and Smith begin with a description of the Socratic method —as it is used generally and not only in law schools—that is very like Areeda's, but they resist seeing Socrates as a teacher of the sort we call "Socratic." They detect three primary distinctions: Socrates claims not to know the subjects about which he asks questions; he denies that he is a teacher (we never see his students master a lesson); and Socrates' mission is destructive, not constructive (*Plato's Socrates*, 3–4). Instead of instructing students, Socrates invites others to join him in the search for wisdom.

For comment that the Socratic method employed in law schools is not Socratic, see, e.g., Thomas Shaffer and Robert Redmount, *Lawyers, Law Students, and People* 8 (Colorado Springs: Shepards, 1977) (a "method of intimidation" that "Socrates would decline the honor of being identified with"); Harris Wofford, *On the Teaching of Law and Justice*, 53 N.Y.U. L. Rev. 612, 614 (1978) ("usually not Socratic . . . what Socrates called eristic"); William C. Heffernan, *Not Socrates, But Protagoras: The Sophist Basis of Legal Education*, 29 Buffalo L. Rev. 399, 407 (1980) ("Protagoras foreshadow[s] modern legal education and Socrates creat[es] a system of moral education peculiarly his own"); James R. Elkins, *Thinking Like a Lawyer: Second Thoughts*, 47 Mercer L. Rev. 511, 524 (1996) ("a perverted version of the Socratic dialogue"); Richard K. Neumann, *A Preliminary Inquiry into the Art of Critique*, 40 Hastings L. J. 725, 728 (1989) ("not Socratic at all: the accurate term would be 'Langdellian' or even 'Protagorean' ").

"If law professors were to employ the educational methods of Socrates, then they would violate the fundamental norms of their profession. However strong the current interest in moral issues surrounding professional responsibility may be, law professors are not permitted to use their classrooms to carry out direct moral instructions of their students" (Heffernan, *Not Socrates, but Protagoras,* 412). See also sources in Neumann, *Preliminary Inquiry into the Art of Critique,* 729 n. 18.

In correspondence with me, Thomas Eisele, whose Socratic life and teaching are exemplary, says that he tends to speak of the differences between Socrates and the teaching that takes place in law schools in terms of "the reality of the classroom," a phrase which suggests the following differences to him: "1. Our students are not met accidentally or occasionally in the marketplace, but rather attend scheduled classes. . . . 2. The enrollment in the class is settled and definite, not the ebb-and-flow of a gathering or crowd where speakers and participants come and go. 3. The object of our classroom presentations are 'the class' as a group, in general, not individual law students or interlocutor. (These are just a few of the separate conditions that define us differently from Socrates)."

28 Thomas Eisele's series of fine essays on Socratic teaching contain worthy suggestions for opening the classroom to the possibilities for self-discovery, disillusionment, and appropriate teacher humiliation of a student humanely contextualized by continuing friendship between teacher and student outside class: *Must Virtue Be Taught?* 37 J. Legal Ed. 495 (1987); *Never Mind the Manner of My Speech,* 14 Legal Stud. F. 253 (1990); *Bitter Knowledge: Socrates and Teaching by Disillusionment,* 45 Mercer L. Rev. 587 (1994); and *The Poverty of Socratic Questioning: Asking and Answering in the Meno,* 63 U. Cinn. L. Rev. 221 (1994).

James R. Elkins helpfully and affectingly notes how teachers may follow Socrates' example to more acute classroom questioning, listening, and seeing: *Socrates and the Pedagogy of Critique,* 14 Legal Studies Forum 231, 243 (1990). See also James Elkins, *Reflections on the Religion Called Legal Education,* 37 J. of Leg. Ed. 522 (1987); *Thinking Like a Lawyer: Second Thoughts,* 47 Mercer L. Rev. 511 (1996).

And John Cole thoughtfully argues that, if it is to be Socratic, the law school method must help students understand that every position they argue can be assailed and that they must therefore take responsibility for ordering in a coherent, defensible way the values they do advocate and hold (*The Socratic Method in Legal Education: Moral Discourse and Accommodation,* 35 Mercer L. Rev. 867, 869 [1984]).

Amy Gutman is not a teacher of law, but she makes the fruitful suggestion that law and the teaching of law could be rendered more Socratic by becoming more deliberative (*Can Virtue Be Taught to Lawyers?* 45 Stan. L. Rev. 1759 [1993]).

Although she does not mention Socrates, Barbara Woodhouse does propose that teachers take the midwife image seriously and make of classes "a collaborative experience, calling for encouragement, structure, and support, but most productive when students push themselves, investing their own creative energy and sweat" (*Mad Midwifery,* 1981). She does not specifically ground the metaphor but seems to have in mind modern practices of midwifery.

Deborah Rhode suggests that the method could be improved by taking feminist (if not midwific) perspectives seriously: more focus on social contexts, more room for narrative, as well as interdisciplinary and ethical materials and acknowledgment of differences (*Missing Questions,* 1563–64).

Students' prior experience and their writing can be Socratically made subjects in ways that allow the teacher to learn from the student. See Cunningham, *Learning from Law Students;* Frances Ansley, *Starting with the Students: Lessons from Popular Education,* 4 Rev. of L. & Women's Studies 7 (1994). John Denvir suggests that discussion of films has a democratic effect because students are more visually adept at absorbing a film than their older, print-bound teachers (introduction to *Legal Reelism* [Urbana: University of Illinois, 1996], xii).

Martha Nussbaum proposes that Socrates' foundational questioning could be advanced in legal education by adding professional philosophers to law school faculties (*Use and Abuse of Philosophy,* 45 Stan. L. Rev. 1627 [1993]). But see Richard Posner, *Overcoming Law* (Cambridge, Mass.: Harvard University Press, 1995), 463–67.

29 Socrates is never far below the surface of James Boyd White's reflections on and engagement in legal education, and, beginning with his first book, *The Legal Imagination,* he has pursued the question of how one constitutes a life in law. I mark as centrally Socratic not only his pursuit of the question in his writing but also his own, ongoing constitution of such a life. See his reading of the *Gorgias* in *When Words Lose Their Meaning* (Chicago: University of Chicago Press, 1984), 110, and his imaginative re-creation of that dialogue in specific relation to lawyers in *Heracles' Bow* (Madison: University of Wisconsin Press, 1985). See also his reading of the *Crito* in *Acts of Hope,* 2–44, and its placement as the orienting first chapter of that book.

His notion of the relation between the text of the *Gorgias* and its reader, of educative friendship and community, animates his approach to the relation between teacher and student. So, for example, he says that "law should be taught as a discipline of thought and argument with its own structure, its own elements, at the center of which is the activity of claiming meaning for human experience, at the individual and collective level, and doing so in a language that is at once a source of authority and itself subject to perpetual revision" (White, *Meaning in the Life of the Lawyer*, 25 Cumberland L. Rev. 763, 767 [1996]). See also White, *Doctrine in a Vacuum: Reflections on What a Law School Ought (and Ought Not) To Be*, 18 J. L. Reform 251 (1985), and White, *Law Teachers Writing*, 91 Mich. L. Rev. 1970, 1972 (1993).

12. Are You the Lawyers?

1 Howard Lesnick's goal is to have students ask themselves: "Who am I? In my work as a lawyer, what will I be doing in the world? What do I want to be doing in the world?" (*Being a Teacher of Lawyers: Discerning the Theory of My Practice*, 43 Hastings L. J. 1095, 1097 [1992]).

2 I often started with James Boyd White's *Legal Imagination*. We did continue to read such authors as Ronald Dworkin, H. L. A. Hart, and Richard Posner.

3 The encouraging examples included Howard Lesnick's way of putting himself into the subject matter of his teaching (*Being a Teacher of Lawyers*), Thomas Shaffer's and Andrew W. McThenia's lawyering from, in, and for communities (Shaffer, *American Lawyers and Their Communities* [Notre Dame, Ind.: Notre Dame University Press, 1991]; McThenia, *Civil Resistance or Holy Obedience? Reflections from within a Community of Resistance*, 48 Wash. & Lee L. Rev. 15 [1991]); and Clark Cunningham's way of working on cases with students and reflecting with them, and with a client, on their performance (*A Tale of Two Clients: Thinking about Law as Language*, 87 Mich. L. Rev. 2459 [1989]; *The Lawyer as Translator, Representation as Text: Towards an Ethnography of Legal Discourse*, 77 Cornell L. Rev. 1298 [1992]).

Also, in the process of writing my last book I had observed and interviewed lawyers and judges for whom the practice of law is in fact a medium of community. I was moved by them and wondered how their example could be translated actively into forms of legal education. I had been particularly well instructed by Steve Wizner at Yale and his clinical work with students.

4 Gutman, *Can Virtue Be Taught to Lawyers?* 1770. But see Robert Condlin, *"Tastes Great, Less Filling": The Law School Clinic and Political Critique*, 36 Legal Educ. 45 (1986).

5 This is not an argument against the traditional law school classroom. In my experience, by exposing students to real people with real problems, clinics expose students' real need for knowledge and methodology. The exposure excites their attentive appetites for other classes taught by lecture, question-and-answer, or some other method.

Howard Lesnick correctly maintains that "all teaching is clinical teaching" (*Infinity in a Grain of Sand: The World of Law and Lawyering as Portrayed in the Clinical Teaching Implicit in the Law School Curriculum,* 37 UCLA L. Rev. 1157, 1158 [1990]).

6 On the history of Yale's pioneering clinic and of clinics in general, see Ball, *The Word and the Law* (Chicago: University of Chicago Press, 1993), 62–65. On the literature and approach of lawyering theory, see Ball, *Power from the People,* 92 Mich. L. Rev. 1725 (1994) (review of Gerald Lopez, *Rebellious Lawyering*); Ball, *Jurisprudence from Below,* 61 Tenn. L. Rev. 747, 759–62 (1994).

7 See Ball, *Power from the People; Jurisprudence from Below.*

8 William Stringfellow, *A Private and Public Faith* (Grand Rapids, Mich.: Eerdmans, 1962), 69.

9 Ibid.

10 The statement comes from comments made by Hartigan on an early version of this book. See Ball, *Jurisprudence from Below,* 764 and n. 74.

11 The connections continued outside class. I remember one hasty courthouse conversation with an embattled student who was attempting to mediate a dispute between a landlord and a tenant. In the course of describing the problem and her mediation to me in a few sentences, she twice drew comparisons to episodes in recent reading the class had discussed. One involved *Huck Finn;* the other *Antigone.* They had become part of her working vocabulary of explanation.

12 Steve Wizner reports that students in the Yale Law School clinic sometimes complain: " 'This isn't law, it's social work!' One flip response I sometimes give is, 'Don't flatter yourself.' More often I will ask: 'What do you think rich people's lawyers do? Is there any real difference between our helping a client to apply for welfare or Social Security or public housing, and a rich person's lawyer accompanying a client to a government agency to apply for a license, or negotiating on his behalf the purchase of a condominium?' " (Wizner, "Beyond Skills Training: Some Reflections upon Approaching My First Quarter Century as a Clinical Teacher" [paper presented at the Association of American Law Schools Section on Clinical Legal Education, Orlando, Fla., January 6, 1994]).

13 In the desert following the exodus, the Israelites called the flakelike thing they gathered for food "manna." This descriptive label may be read as the question they kept asking: "Man hu? Man hu?" (What's this? What's this?).

14 Of course, in order to become a law school student a person will have acquired considerable experience in the successful navigation of institutions, bureaucracies, and funding sources. Accordingly, before they are licensed to practice, my students already possess well-developed, result-oriented skills in advocacy that they can put to good use on be-

half of clients. The students are usually slow to recognize this acquired usefulness and to recognize it as distinctive.

15 "Clients need lawyers not only to hear their stories," Robert Dinerstein notes, "but also to help them shape those stories to make them as effective as possible within the existing legal milieu, or to collaborate with them to devise the best means to transform it" (*A Meditation on the Theoretics of Practice,* 43 Hastings L. J. 971, 985 [1992]).

16 "Katie Davis Visits with Poet Jimmy Santiago Baca," *All Things Considered,* National Public Radio, June 5, 1993 (available from Lexis, New Library, Script File at *2).

17 Ibid., *8.

18 For an imaginative reflection on Bartleby, the lawyer's scrivener, see Robin West, *Invisible Victims: A Comparison of Susan Glaspell's "Jury of Her Peers," and Herman Melville's "Bartleby the Scrivener,"* 8 Cardozo *Studies in Law and Literature* (1996): 203.

13. Miriam

1 Trible, *God and the Rhetoric of Sexuality,* 69.

2 Biblical scholars identify this song at the sea as one of the oldest extant writings in the Bible. See, e.g., Stalker, "Exodus," 222–23.

3 On biblical women and war songs, see Setel, "Exodus," 31–32.

4 Katherine Doob Sakenfeld, "Numbers," in Newsom and Ringe, *Women's Bible Commentary,* 45, 48.

5 See Setel, "Exodus," 29.

6 Aaron's death is more elaborately reported at the end of the same chapter (Num. 20:22–29). Sakenfeld: "That her death is reported at all suggests her importance, and the location of her death geographically and narratively functions to raise her status closer to that of her brothers" ("Numbers," 48).

14. Rachel

1 Rachel sent her maid Bilhah to Jacob to bear children in her stead. Leah's maid Zilpah also bore children to Jacob (Gen. 30:1–13).

2 "When she was in her hard labor, the midwife said to her, 'Do not be afraid; for now you will have another son' " (Gen. 35:17). This is the first mention of midwives in the Bible.

3 One tradition places Rachel's tomb in the territory of Benjamin, north of Jerusalem (see I Sam. 10:2, Jer. 31:15); another south of Jerusalem (Gen. 35:16, 48:7; Matt. 2:16–18). The latter site is the one "shown to tourists today" (*New Oxford Annotated Bible,* 353 [note to I Sam. 10:2]).

4 Gen. 49:29–33. In one tradition, Jacob's tomb is east of the Jordan (Gen.

50:5, 10). In another it is at Machpelah, near Mamre, Abraham's burial site (Gen. 50:13).

5 Genesis Rabbah, vol. 3 trans. Jacob Neusner (Atlanta: Scholar's Press, 1985), 82:10 trans. Rashi quotes a midrash elaborating Jacob's deathbed words to Joseph: "I did not even take her to Bethlehem, bring her into the Holy Land, proper. I know you resent this. But you know that it was at the command of God that I buried her there, so that she might be a help to her children. When Nebuchadnezzar will send them into exile, and they pass her grave, 'there on the road,' Rachel will come out of her grave and cry and ask mercy for them" (Rashi, Gen. 48:7. See Pesikta Rabbati 3). See Avivah Gottlieb Zornberg, *Genesis: The Beginning of Desire* (Philadelphia: Jewish Publication Society, 1995), 213, 305. I am indebted to Rachel Wizner for the gift of this book, one of many and various, much-needed gifts that she and Steve have bestowed on my family.

See also Suzanne Last Stone, "Justice, Mercy, and Gender in Rabbinic Thought," 8 *Cardozo Studies in Law and Literature* (spring–summer 1996): 156–57.

6 They will return by the road on which they were driven out (Jer. 31:21). In line with the rabbinic commentary, this would presumably be the road by which Rachel is buried.

7 Robert Alter observes that there is "no absolute fit between the nature of reality and the human mind. The biblical tale is fashioned in ways that repeatedly remind us of that ontological discrepancy" (*The World of Biblical Literature* [New York: Basic Books, 1992], 22).

15. Jeremiah's Rachel Poem

1 Trible, *God and the Rhetoric of Sexuality*, 40–50.

2 In the same verse, instead of having Rachel inconsolable because her sons "are no more," Trible has Rachel say: "Oh, not one here." The effect is to give Rachel voice in words that fade "into the silence of desolation" (ibid., 40). In verses 15–16, Trible also employs the repeated phrase "oracle of Yahweh" instead of John Bright's "Yahweh's word" (Bright, "Jeremiah," in The Anchor Bible [New York: Doubleday, 1965], 275) or "says the Lord" in the New Revised Standard Version. However rendered, the formula underwrites God's promise.

3 Bright, "Jeremiah," 275. Trible extends the female imagery with "I will truly show motherly compassion upon him." Her translation suits the parental, motherlike voice of the strophe. I have taken verse 21 from the NRSV and 22a from Bright, "Jeremiah."

4 Bright, "Jeremiah," 276, 282.

5 Trible, *God and the Rhetoric of Sexuality*, 45.

6 Ibid., 46.

7 Ibid., 48.

8 Ibid., 50.

9 Ibid., 40, 50.

10 Ibid., 50.

11 Jonathan Kozol, for example, gave "Rachel" as the pseudonym for a lead figure in his book on homeless families in America and titled the volume *Rachel and Her Children* (New York: Crown Publishers, 1998). It is to be remembered, too, that at the end of Herman Melville's *Moby-Dick*, the Rachel was the ship in distress searching for her captain's child.

12 Trible, *God and the Rhetoric of Sexuality*, 48.

13 Moses is remembered this way in Psalms as well: "Therefore [God] said he would destroy [the people]—had not Moses, his chosen one, stood in the breach before him, to turn away his wrath from destroying them" (Ps. 106:23).

14 Rabbinic literature envisions a trial scene: Moses and the patriarchs appeal to God on behalf of Israel, but it is Rachel who moves God to mercy (Lamentations Rabbah, trans. Jacob Neusner [Atlanta: Scholars Press, 1989], 24, 72–79). On this interpretation, Rachel's story clearly surpasses Moses' arguments.

In the midrash Moses and the patriarchs make unsuccessful legal arguments. Rachel appears and instead of making an argument tells a story about having to share her husband with Leah, about her jealousy, and about conquering that jealousy. If she, a mere mortal, has overcome jealousy, she asks, how can God be jealous of idols and allow her children to be killed for worshiping them? God's pity is stirred, and for Rachel's sake he agrees to restore Israel. For suggestive reflections on the midrash, see Zornberg, *Genesis*, 374–81; and Stone, "Justice, Mercy, and Gender in Rabbinic Thought."

Stone treats the anthropomorphisms as personifications of concepts. The narrative depictions of tension in the person of God are a form for affirming both God's transcendence and His relationship with humanity, and "this tension is played out in literary terms to such an extent that at times God appears as two separate, contrasting 'characters'" ("Justice, Mercy, and Gender in Rabbinic Thought," 147). One is aligned with justice, the other with mercy.

16. Law and Tears

1 The judge's "duty is, not to make a present of justice, but to give judgment; and he has sworn that he will judge according to the laws, and not according to his own good pleasure" (*Apology*, 417 [35]).

2 *State v. Post*, 20 N.J.L. 368 (1845).

3 Ball, *The Play's the Thing: An Unscientific Reflection of Courts under the Rubric of Theater,* 28 Stan. L. Rev. 81 (1975); *Promise of American Law,* 42–94.

4 Herman Melville, *Billy Budd, Sailor,* in *Billy Budd, Sailor and Other Stories,* ed. H. Beaver (Harmondsworth, U.K.: Penguin, 1981), 317, 388. Aviam Soifer draws attention to the figure of the ship's surgeon in *Billy Budd:* "The surgeon, like us, knows that much is unknowable and more is 'not susceptible to proof.' His plight and his retreat into formalism and duty speak to us, and to our possibilities and limitations in thinking with skeptical realism about law" (*Status, Contract, and Promises Unkept,* 96 Yale L. J. 1916, 1957 [1987]). Soifer notes Melville's double pun in concluding a chapter with this narrative comment about the surgeon: "And rising from the mess he formally withdrew" (ibid.).

5 In Sophocles' *Antigone,* for example, Creon's struggle to uphold the law of the state meant for him struggling to be not womanly, and the consequence was that he became the cursed killer of his children (*Antigone,* trans. Elizabeth Wyckoff, in *Greek Tragedies,* ed. David Grene and Richard Lattimore [Chicago: University of Chicago Press, 1968], 1:224. 1305–6).

6 Jeremy Bentham, *Rationale of Judicial Evidence,* in *Works of Jeremy Bentham,* ed. J. Bowring (New York: Russell and Russell, 1838–1843), 6:353, 354 passim.

7 Hannah Arendt, *On Revolution* (New York: Viking, 1965), 78.

8 Ibid., 82.

9 Ball, *Promise of American Law.*

10 I explored this subject in *Lying Down Together* (Madison: University of Wisconsin Press, 1985).

11 *McCulloch v. Maryland,* 17 U.S. (4 Wheat.) 316, 431 (1819).

12 *The Federalist,* no. 51, ed. Jacob Cooke (Middletown, Conn.: Wesleyan University Press, 1961), 352. (Madison).

13 *The Antelope,* 23 U.S. (10 Wheat.) 66, 116–20 (1825).

14 Ibid., 121.

15 *Johnson v. M'Intosh,* 21 U.S. (8 Wheat.) 543, 591–92 (1823).

16 388 U.S. 307 (1967).

17 See ibid., 217; *Shuttlesworth v. City of Birmingham,* 394 U.S. 147 (1969).

18 388 U.S. 321.

19 481 U.S. 279 (1987).

20 Ibid., 314–15.

21 *The Federalist,* no. 1, 3 (Hamilton).

22 Arendt, *On Revolution,* 79.

23 Ibid., 81.

24 H. L. A. Hart, *The Concept of Law* (Oxford: Oxford University Press, 1961), 206.

25 See Ball, *Stories of Origin and Constitutional Possibilities*, 87 Mich. L. Review 2280, 2304–9 (1989). For an extended examination of the phenomenon, see Ball, *Constitution, Court, Indian Tribes*, 1987 A.B.F. Res. J.1.

26 Mark Twain, *The Adventures of Huckleberry Finn*, in *Mark Twain: Mississippi Writings*, ed. Guy Cardwell (Library of America, 1982), 714.

27 Paul Valliere, quoted in Paul Lehmann, *Transfiguration of Politics*, 286 (italics omitted). See Ball, *Word and the Law*, 134.

28 It is no part of self-transcendence for a court simply to point to or defer to a legislature beyond itself. That is a fundamentally self-referential gesture and a technique for avoiding responsibility. See Ball, *Word and the Law*, 145–46.

29 See, e.g., Frances Ansley, *Standing Rusty and Rolling Empty: Law, Poverty, and America's Eroding Industrial Base*, 81 Georgetown L. Rev. 1757, 1758 (1993). "For instance, criticisms of the human suffering and social chaos engendered by sudden capital flight from the U.S. or by sudden capital infusion into Mexico are repeatedly met with a nested set of economic arguments," which have to be understood and met (Ansley, *The Gulf of Mexico, the Academy and Me: Hazards of Boundary Crossing*, 78 *Soundings* [1995]: 92). She recognized that travel across borders risks incompetence in new territory, and she did not minimize the danger (ibid., 94). She would face academic border guards quick to repel and punish disciplinary intrusions (ibid., 96–97). But she also held the conviction that uncrossed boundaries may restrict vision, sever what should be joined, monopolize information, and prevent challenges to existing arrangements (ibid., 95). She therefore aimed not at some defensive "performance before an elite circle of highly trained specialists, but rather at an inclusive and expanding conversation carried on among a diverse group of people," some of whom represent different disciplines and some of whom did not complete high school (ibid., 98).

30 She recounts the odyssey affectingly in *The Gulf of Mexico*. Along the way she engaged in collaborative research with two "articulate, brave, and seasoned organizers for the rights of working people, Luvernel Clark and Shirley Reinhardt" (ibid., 69).

31 " 'Maquiladoras' are foreign-owned factories that produce or partially produce goods in Mexico for export back into the United States, using low-wage Mexican labor. They are mostly U.S.-owned and mostly located along the U.S.-Mexican border" (*Gulf of Mexico*, 79).

32 Ibid., 82.

33 Ansley, *North American Free Trade Agreement: The Public Debate*, 22 Ga. J. Int'l & Comp. L. 329, 398 (1992).

34 Ansley, *Gulf of Mexico*, 84.

35   Ibid., 85. See also accounts in *North American Free Trade Agreement*, 392–403.

36   Ibid., 85.

37   Ansley, *North American Free Trade Agreement*, 391.

38   Ansley, *Gulf of Mexico*, 87–88.

39   Ansley, *North American Free Trade Agreement*, 399.

40   Luvernel Clark, cited in ibid., 394.

41   Ansley, *Standing Rusty and Rolling Empty*, 1758 (quoting "Elena," a pseudonym for an interviewed worker).

42   Ansley, *Gulf of Mexico*, 101–2.

43   Ibid., 89, 102.

44   See, e.g., Ansley, *Standing Rusty and Rolling Empty*.

45   Ibid.

46   See Ibid., 1762–63.

47   Ibid., 401.

48   Ibid.

49   Ibid., 330–31.

50   Ibid., 332.

51   Ibid., 1890.

52   Ibid., 1785.

53   Aeschylus, *The Choephori*, trans. Philip Vellacott (London: Penguin, 1956), 106, l. 82.

54   See Telford Taylor, *Nuremberg and Vietnam: An American Tragedy* (Chicago: Quadrangle Press, 1970); Richard Falk, *The Vietnam War and International Law* (Princeton, N.J.: Princeton University Press, 1968); Robert Cover, *The Folktales of Justice: Tales of Jurisdiction*, 14 Capital U. L. Rev. 179, 197–203 (1985).

55   John Duffett, ed., *Against the Crime of Silence, Proceedings of the International War Crimes Tribunal* (New York: Bertrand Russell Peace Foundation, 1968).

56   Cover, *Folktales of Justice*, 202.

57   On the recent history and theory of supranational courts, not people's tribunals, see Laurence Helfer and Anne-Marie Slaughter, *Toward a Theory of Effective Supranational Adjudication*, 107 Yale L. J. 273 (1997).

58   S. J. Res. 19, 103d Cong., 1st Sess., 107 Stat. 1519 (1993).

59   See James Anaya, *The Native Hawaiian People and International Human Rights Law: Toward a Remedy for Past and Continuing Wrongs*, 28 Ga. L. Rev. 309 (1994).

60   Nā Maka o ka 'Āina, Peoples' International Tribunal Hawai'i 1993 (1994) (3020 Kahaloa Drive, Honolulu, Hawai'i 96822).

61   1891 Commissioner of Indian Affairs Annual Report 412 (report of J. George Wright, Rosebud Agency, Aug. 27, 1891), quoted in Allison

Dussias, *Ghost Dance and Holy Ghost: The Echoes of Nineteenth-Century Christianization Policy in Twentieth-Century Native American Free Exercise Cases*, 49 Stan. L. Rev. 773, 799 (1997).

62 Black Elk, *Black Elk Speaks*, ed. John Neihardt (Lincoln: University of Nebraska Press, 1979), 270.

63 Ibid., 274.

64 For comments on the subsequent failures of NAFTA, see Lori Wallach and Michelle Sforza, "NAFTA at 5," *The Nation*, January 25, 1999, 7.

In Hawai'i, the tribunal has subsequently drawn no notice, but the role of the native peoples has figured in three prominent controversies. One was set in motion in 1993 by the Hawai'i state legislature ostensibly to ascertain the opinion of the Kanaka Maoli on their governmental future as a distinct people. A plebiscite was held in 1996. More than eighty thousand ballots were mailed, and less than thirty-one thousand were cast. Most of those who voted favored electing delegates to a kind of constitutional convention. That election took place in 1999. A convention was slated for 1999. The leading native sovereignty groups opposed the plebiscite and the election, and they oppose the convention. They have urged boycotts. (Opponents have included Kekuni Blaisdell and Mililani Trask, prime minister of the native Ka Lahui.) They have done so because it is a state-managed process instead of being internationally supervised, there was insufficient education of the electorate, most ballots were not returned, and all the alternatives were never presented. For example, in confirmation of the limited options presented to the Kanaka Maoli, both Hawai'i's governor Ben Cayetano and senator Daniel Inouye reportedly said they would never permit an independent Hawaiian nation. See Mindy Pennybacker, "Should the Aloha State Say Goodbye? Natives Wonder," *The Nation*, August 12, 1996 (1996 WL 9220584).

Another controversy swirls around the Bishop Estate, a charitable trust created in the nineteenth century by Princess Bernice Pauahi Bishop, the last direct descendant of King Kamehameha. The trust holds the largest private tract of land in the islands, 8 percent of Hawai'i, and worldwide investments valued in the billions of dollars. The income is used to fund private schools for children of Hawaiian ancestry, the Kamehameha Schools. Of fifty-five thousand Hawaiian children, only three thousand are educated in these schools. The five trustees of the estate have been closely aligned with the political establishment. A probate judge removed four of them from office after a lengthy struggle that featured charges of mismanagement, conflicts of interest, self-dealing, and lavish trustee compensation. Sovereignty groups have been sharply critical of the way the trustees performed. See Todd S. Purdum, "For $6

Billion Hawaii Legacy, a New Day," *New York Times*, May 15, 1999, p. 1, col. 4, national edition.

The third controversy revolved around the election of a different set of trustees, the trustees of a state agency, the Office of Hawaiian Affairs. The OHA was created in 1959 upon Hawai'i's admission to the union as the fiftieth state. As part of that admission, the United States granted Hawai'i title to 1.8 million acres of public lands to be held as a trust for purposes that include support of public education and the benefit of native Hawaiians. The OHA was established to address the needs of native Hawaiians and to utilize the public land trust for their betterment. (The two hundred thousand acres of Hawai'i Homelands set aside in 1920 are separately managed by the Department of Hawaiian Homelands.) The OHA trustees and their electors must be of aboriginal Hawaiian descent. Harold Rice, a Caucasian resident of Hawai'i, brought suit in federal court challenging his exclusion from voting for OHA trustees. Both the District Court and the Ninth Circuit Court of Appeals upheld the limitation to Hawaiians, but the Supreme Court has accepted the case for review. See *Rice v. Cayetano,* 146 F3d 1075 (9th Cir. 1998), U.S. Supr. Ct. No. 98-818; Linda Greenhouse, "Justices to Weigh Race Barrier in Hawaiian Voting," *New York Times*, March 23, 1999, p. A18, col. 1, national edition.

17. The Womb of God and Tears

1 John Calvin, *Institutes of the Christian Religion,* trans. John Allen (Grand Rapids, Mich.: Eerdmans, 1949), 47.

2 Alter, *Art of Biblical Poetry*, 212.

3 E.g., 6:24, 22:23. The conclusion of one poem is particularly and starkly affecting—a woman in labor attended by murderers rather than midwives: "For I heard a cry as of a woman in labor, anguish as of one bringing forth her first child, the cry of daughter Zion gasping for breath, stretching out her hands, 'Woe is me! I am fainting before killers!'" (4:31).

4 Trible, *God and the Rhetoric of Sexuality,* 41, 42, 46–47.

5 See ibid., 48.

6 Ibid., 50. The same sense of protectively surrounding is present in Psalm 32:7, 10 and, notably, in the song Moses recites near the end of Deuteronomy (32:10).

7 The image of the word as fructifying rain is employed in Moses' song (Deut. 32:1–3). In the vocabulary of native Hawaiians, rain is semen.

8 "At the very beginning of the poem stands the prophetic formula 'thus

says the Lord, so that even the voice of Rachel comes under its rubric' "
(Trible, *God and the Rhetoric of Sexuality,* 47).

9 Ibid., 42.

10 Robert Jenson observes: "God . . . is *identified* by the narrative of which
his word by his prophets and our answering prayer make the dialogue.
Therefore also the conversational form of his word cannot be regarded
as a contingent adaptation to the existence or need of creatures. 'In the
beginning,' the Word 'is' not only God, but also 'with' God" (*Systematic
Theology,* 80).

11 Sakenfeld, "Numbers," 48.

III. The Gospel According to John

1 See, e.g., Raymond E. Brown, *The Gospel According to John I–XII,*
vol. 29 of The Anchor Bible (New York: Doubleday, 1966), lx; Brown,
The Gospel According to John XIII–XXI, vol. 29A of The Anchor Bible
(New York: Doubleday, 1970), 949–52; Wayne A. Meeks, *The Prophet-
King: Moses Traditions and the Johannine Christology,* XIV Supplements
to Novum Testamentum (Leiden: Brill, 1967); Severino Pancaro, *The
Law in the Fourth Gospel,* XLII Supplements to Novum Testamentum
(Leiden: Brill, 1975); D. Moody Smith, *The Theology of the Gospel of John*
(Cambridge: Cambridge University Press, 1995); Smith, *John* (Philadel-
phia: Fortress, 1986). Throughout I have relied upon Brown and been
well instructed by Smith.

I shall have occasion to take up only some of the details of Moses'
presence in the Gospel of John. Included in the omitted material are
resonances of his pharaonic temptation (6:15) and his bringing water
from the rock (7:37–38).

18. The Jerusalem Trial

1 Whether this prologue is an adaptation of a preexisting pre-Christian or
early church hymn is a subject for discussion among biblical scholars.
So is the question of which lines may be read as the poem — whether,
for example, the lines incorporating John the Baptist are prose interrup-
tions of the poetry. A judicious summary of the scholarly discussion, the
translation choices, and the interpretation of the prologue is provided
in Brown, *John,* 29:1–37.

Brown's translation of the prologue presents as prose intercalations
verses 6–9, 12a–13, 15, and 17–18 (see ibid., 3–4) and thereby helpfully
emphasizes the lines on John the Baptist as openings in the christological
hymn.

I have not separated these lines — set them off as prose — both because I lack the competence to make judgments about sources and because I am primarily concerned with the text as we now have it and with how we now may read it. In this I join Frank Kermode's approach to John in *The Literary Guide to the Bible* (440–66).

In translating the first eighteen verses, I bore in mind the King James Version, the Revised Standard Version, and the New Revised Standard Version, as well as Brown's translation, and employed the Greek text in the twenty-third edition of Eberhard Nestle, *Novum Testamentum Graece*, ed. Erwin Nestle and Kurt Aland (Stuttgart: Privilegierte Wurtemburgische Bibel Anstalt, 1957).

2 To say that the Word was God does not imply that He has ceased to be God. "Was" also carries the sense of "is."

3 After the prologue, there are other ties between John the Baptist and Jesus and the disciples of each in 1:19–42, 3:22–30, 5:33–36, and 10:40–42. (Compare the treatment of John the Baptist in the Synoptic Gospels. According to Luke 1, John the Baptist was a kinsman of Jesus.) From these textual relations between the two, it is possible to conclude that former disciples of John the Baptist played a continuing role in the Church that was the matrix of the gospel.

Rudolph Bultmann theorized that the prologue was based on a hymn of the Baptist community (Das Evangelium des Johannes [Gottingen, 1941], translated as *The Gospel of John: A Commentary*, trans. G.R. Beasley-Murray et al. [Philadelphia: Westminster, 1971], 18. See also ibid., 84–97, 108, 174). J. Massingberde Ford argued that the bulk of Revelation originated in the visions and message of John the Baptist (*Revelation*, vol. 38 of The Anchor Bible [New York: Doubleday, 1975], 28–40, 50–56).

The Gospel of John, the three Epistles of John, and Revelation may have arisen out of a particular circle of early Christians. It has been argued that there was a Johannine community. See generally Raymond E. Brown, *The Community of the Beloved Disciple* (New York: Paulist Press, 1979); Oscar Cullmann, *The Johannine Circle* (Philadelphia: Westminster, 1976). Such a community or movement may have arisen in Palestine and removed to Ephesus; may have arisen among Jews, including followers of John the Baptist; and may have had close ties to Jesus through one or more of his disciples.

There are several Johns to be sorted out here. Besides John the Baptist there are four other Johns. Each of these four has been considered as the John who authored the gospel: (1) John the son of Zebedee and one of the Twelve Apostles of Jesus; (2) the "beloved disciple" (John 13:23–26, 19:25–27, 20:2–10, 21:7, 21:20–23, 21–24) who may have played a central role in the Johannine community and who may or may not have been John the son of Zebedee or some other John; (3) John Mark, a part-time companion of Paul; and (4) John the Presbyter, who may have been among Jesus' followers and/or a leader of a Christian community in Ephesus. The evidence and arguments about authorship are presented and evaluated in Brown, *John*, 29:lxxxvii–cii.

Brown himself tended to the hypothesis that John the son of Zebedee was the "beloved disciple" and that the "beloved disciple" was the origin of the Johannine tradition (ibid., xcviii–cii). Later, by the time he wrote *The Community of the Beloved Disciple* in 1979, Brown had changed his mind about identifying the "beloved disciple" as John the son of Zebedee and tended to Cullmann's theory that the name of this disciple cannot be known, although he may have been a disciple of John the Baptist, and then a follower of Jesus when Jesus was close to the Baptist, and then a companion of Jesus in the last days. See Brown, *Community of the Beloved Disciple*, 33–34, 176–78 (discussing Cullmann's *Johannine Circle*).

That the "beloved disciple," whoever he was, was the source for the gospel is the statement of the text itself: "This is the disciple who is testifying to these things and has written them, and we know that his testimony is true" (21:24). It is tradition and not the text that identifies the gospel as "according to John."

The textual statement about the disciple "whom Jesus loved" appears to be made by another or others not that disciple ("*we* know that *his* testimony is true"). If so, the reader could conclude that more than one hand had been at work in what we now have as the gospel. Brown's review leads him to the supposition that the gospel reached its final form between A.D. 90 and 100 in Ephesus within the Johannine community (Brown, *John*, 29:lxxx–lxxxvi, ciii–civ), and he hypothesizes — an "ad hoc theory" (idid., cii) — five stages of composition: (1) a body of material from the beloved disciple similar to but independent of that in the other gospels; (2) its development in preaching and teaching; (3) its organization into a consecutive gospel in Greek by the evangelist; (4) a second edition by the evangelist; and (5) a final edition by a redactor (ibid., xxxiv–xxxix). The author of the Epistles of John identifies himself as "the Presbyter." Brown offers no name for him either.

With respect to the Johannine corpus, Brown thus posits four figures: the beloved disciple who was the source of the Johannine tradition about Jesus, the evangelist, the final redactor of the gospel, and the Presbyter who authored the Epistles (*The Epistles of John*, vol. 30 of The Anchor Bible [New York: Doubleday, 1982]). The author of Revelation may now constitute a fifth figure for Brown. Brown had agreed with the view that Revelation was authored by John, son of Zebedee (Brown, *John*, 29:cii) but was subsequently persuaded otherwise. "All that can be said is that the author was an unknown Christian prophet named John" (Brown, *Epistles of John*, 57 n. 131).

Rudolf Bultmann's theory of composition assumed three principal sources — a Sign Source, a Revelatory Discourse Source, and a Passion and Resurrection Source — that were woven together by a creative evangelist who had previously been a Gnostic and follower of John the Baptist. After this evangelist's work became disordered, a final ecclesiastical redactor both reordered the material and rendered it theologically orthodox. Bultmann then undertook rearrangement of the present text to reestablish the underlying "original" gospel. See Bultmann, *Gospel of John*.

4 Oscar Cullmann focused on what he regarded as the main theological point of the prologue: "It is expressed in the alternating juxtaposition of the assertions about John the Baptist as the historical 'beginning' . . . and about the absolute 'Beginning' " ("The Theological Content of the Prologue to John in Its Present Form," in *The Conversation Continues: Studies in Paul and John in Honor of J. Louis Martyn*, ed. Robert Fortna and Beverly Gaventa [Nashville: Abingdon Press, 1990], 296). Cullmann also observed that the prologue, "closely dependent on Genesis 1, . . . begins exactly like the First Book of Moses" and constitutes a kind of retelling anew of the creation story (ibid., 297).

5 "One historical fact is lucidly clear: Jesus of Nazareth was sentenced by a Roman prefect to be crucified on the political charge that he claimed to be 'the King of the Jews.' On this Christian, Jewish, and Roman sources agree" (Brown, *John*, 29A:792).

6 Rudolf Bultmann first identified the words "witness" and "testimony" employed in the portrayal of John the Baptist as legal terms (*Gospel of John*, 50–51 n. 5). See also ibid., 86. Theo Preiss noted the gospel's juridical aspect ("La justification dans la pensee johnaique," in *Hommage de Reconnaissance K. Barth* [Neuchatel, 1946]). And then Charles Masson detected the fact that John uses juridical terms repeatedly where the other gospels employ the language of evangelizing, announcement, and preaching. Masson suggested that the difference arose from a difference in the Church's situation ("Le Temoignange de Jean," *Revue de Theologie et de Philosophie* 28 [1950]: 120–27). In its earliest days, the Church addressed an audience who had not heard of Jesus, and missionary preaching was in order. Later the Church found itself addressing people who had heard the message but challenged it. Proclamation was no longer sufficient. Defense — testimony and substantiating witnesses — became necessary as well. John was written in this period and, Masson argued, took up the vocabulary of trial from the testing that the story was undergoing in the life of the Church.

Raymond Brown notes that the verb *martyrein*, "to bear witness" or "testify," occurs thirty-three times in the Fourth Gospel as compared to a total of two uses in the other three, "a contrast that indicates the extent to which the legal and trial atmosphere dominates Johannine thought" (*Epistles of John*, 167).

7 On my own layered approach to reading biblical texts, see chapter 1, note 1.

8 In discussion of the texts of the Hebrew Bible, I referred to "narrator" and "writer." See chapter 6, notes 6 and 9. My approach is similar when I speak of a "John" and refer to him as the "author" or "writer."

Chapters 20 and 21 may be read as two conclusions to the Fourth Gospel and as the product of two hands. In addition, throughout the gospel there are differences in style, difficulties in sequence, repetitions, and seeming dislocations. Biblical scholars have been led thereby to investigate possible underlying sources and may conclude that there were many composers or that there was one composer or final editor. They may also conclude, after the fashion of Bultmann, that an original text for the gospel somehow fell out of order and that the present text requires rearranging in order to establish an underlying original.

Brown says that "we can reasonably assume that this form of the Gospel made sense to the one who had the final responsibility for the Gospel's appearance" (Brown, *John*, 29:xxvii). I proceed on that assumption and another: "Long continuance has endowed the book as it stands with a certain unchallengeable integrity" (Kermode, "John," in Alter and Kermode, *Literary Guide to the Bible*, 441).

9 In John Berger's story, "The Three Lives of Lucie Cabrol," Lucie Cabrol is murdered at the age of sixty-seven. She returns to speak with her sometime lover, Jean, the narrator, and begins to recount to him her life, beginning with her birth: " 'You know everything about your life now,' I said. 'If I told you all that I know it would take sixty-seven years' " ("The Three Lives of Lucie Cabrol," in *Pig Earth* [New York: Pantheon, 1979], 173).

10 The authoritative manuscripts and interpreters divide on whether John 21:30 should read "these are written so that you may come to believe" or "these are written so that you may keep believing." This distinction is thought to reflect a distinction in intended primary audience, either nonbelievers or already believing Christians. This may be a distinction without a difference. I am unconvinced that two such audiences would entail two different messages. I should think that the same story would be properly and honestly told either way, for both the engendering and the sustenance of belief. The fact that ancient, authoritative sources yield both possibilities may reflect a judgment that the message would be, should be the same. Either way the question of how to tell it is com-

plex and pressing. In the text, I approach the issue as one of engendering belief.

11 Karl Mannheim, *Ideology and Utopia* (New York: Harcourt, Brace and World, 1936), 36.

12 Thomas Kuhn, *The Structure of Scientific Revolutions*, 2d ed. (Chicago: University of Chicago Press, 1970), 56.

13 The author would have had examples to consult, including Hellenic as well as Jewish ways of writing about mythological or real people and also perhaps one or more earlier Christian gospels. See Frank Kermode, introduction to the New Testament, in Alter and Kermode, *Literary Guide to the Bible*, 375, 376; Charles Talbert, *What Is a Gospel? The Genre of the Canonical Gospels* (Philadelphia: Fortress Press, 1977). See generally, D. Moody Smith, *John among the Gospels: The Relationship in Twentieth-Century Research* (Minneapolis, Minn.: Fortress Press, 1992); John Ashton, *Understanding the Fourth Gospel* (Clarendon: Oxford University Press, 1991).

14 The Gospel of John does employ an assortment of writers' tools, including poetry, narrative, discourse, and drama; prophecy and history; metaphor, ambiguity, and irony, especially irony; and the development of themes of contrasting pairs (light/darkness, day/night, being/becoming, revealing/hiding, life/death, Word/world).

Some repetitions, like chronological and geographic inconsistencies, appear to be nonpurposive. If they are, then the text may be said to suffer lapses of economy and discipline. As Brown notes, what is said and happens in 6:35–50, when Jesus refers to his revelation as the bread of life, is virtually repeated in 6:51–58, when he presents his body as the bread of life (Brown, *John,* 29:xxv). In the context of the last supper, Peter asks Jesus where he is going (13:36), but later Jesus says no one has asked him where he is going (16:5). It is said in chapter 7:3–5 that Jesus had worked no miracles in Judea, but Jerusalem is in Judea and according to 2:23 and 5:1–9 he had worked miracles there. Scholars have taken such repetitions and inconsistencies as occasion for apology, amendment, and rewriting, as well as conjecture about possible underlying sources.

I think that readers who concede the integrity of the text may more fruitfully take these instances as occasion for instruction. The contradictions may be an example. Perhaps the writer found contradiction more adequate than consistency for addressing the transcendent.

15 See Brown, *John,* 29:914.

16 Kermode, "John," 455. Just so, John 1:15 releases Genesis 1:15 into the prologue. (The prologue's "In the beginning. . . . All things came into being. . . . The light shines in the darkness" track the Bible's opening, "In the beginning God created the heavens and the earth. . . . Then God

said, 'Let there be light'; . . . and God separated the light from the darkness.")

17 Aileen Guilding even proposes that the motifs of the material that the Gospel of John associates with each festival are related to specific motifs of the synagogue readings for the season (*The Fourth Gospel and Jewish Worship* [Clarendon: Oxford University Press, 1956]). See generally Brown, *John*, 29:cxxxviii–cxliv.

18 Chapter 13 opens with statement of Jesus' knowledge of the coming end and his washing of the disciples' feet. The foot washing prefigures the sacrificially cleansing events about to take place and lays down an interpretive ground for later use ("You do not know now what I am doing, but later you will understand" [13:7]). Brown observes: "The footwashing . . . dramatically acts out the significance of Jesus' death — it is a death that cleanses the disciples and gives them a heritage with him. The majestic Last Discourse reassures the disciples that Jesus' death is not the end" (*John*, 29A:542).

The Last Discourse is also aimed at subsequent members of the community of faith and is undoubtedly meant to help them understand the meaning of Jesus' trial for their own, later testing.

19 He also dines with Lazarus, whom "the chief priests planned to put . . . to death as well" (12:10), and with Judas, "who was about to betray him" (12:4) (see also 6:71).

20 See also 8:20 (a confrontation ends: "No one arrested him, because his hour had not yet come").

21 Jesus' radical demonstration in the temple (2:13) is provocative. Although it is not expressly linked to the trial series of confrontations, it may signal the onset of the conflict between Jesus and the Jews. See Alan Watson, *The Trial of Jesus* (Athens: University of Georgia Press, 1995), 44–45.

22 A. E. Harvey, *Jesus on Trial* (Atlanta, Ga.: John Knox Press, 1977), 50.

23 Ibid., 127.

24 Brueggemann, *Theology of the Old Testament*, xvi passim.

19. The Gospel Trial: A Divine Lawsuit

1 Brown explains "that John presents the Paraclete as the Holy Spirit in a special role, namely, as the personal presence of Jesus in the Christian while Jesus is with the Father. This means, first of all, that the Johannine picture of the Paraclete is not inconsistent with what is said in the Gospel itself and in the other NT books about the Holy Spirit. . . . The peculiarity of the Johannine portrait of the Paraclete/Spirit, and this is our second point, centers around the resemblance of the Spirit to Jesus.

Virtually everything that has been said about the Paraclete has been said elsewhere in the Gospel about Jesus" (*John*, 29A:1139–40).

Brown has a compact but comprehensive appendix on the background and Johannine meaning of the Paraclete (ibid., 1135–43). Compare Brown, *Epistles of John*, 215–17. See also Ashton, *Understanding the Fourth Gospel*, 420–25; D. Moody Smith, *The Theology of the Gospel of John* (Cambridge: Cambridge University Press, 1995), 139–44; Stephen Smalley, "The Paraclete": Pneumatology in the Johannine Gospel and Apocalypse, in *Exploring the Gospel of John*, ed. R. Alan Culpepper and C. Clifton Black (Louisville, Ky.: Westminster John Knox, 1996), 289.

2 On "abiding with (or in)" see Brown, *John*, 29:510–12. See also Brown, *John*, 29A:711–17. The Paraclete (the Spirit, the presence of Jesus) empowers believers: "Very truly, I tell you, the one who believes in me will also do the works that I do and, in fact, will do greater works than these, because I am going to the Father" (14:12).

3 On a related trial-like advocate in Job, see chapter 2, note 1.

4 See 2:22, 12:16, 14:9.

5 Brown, *John*, 29A:712. Of course, there is no scene in the gospel in which we see this take place. The point arises from what Jesus says will happen after his death. See 14:26, 16:13–15. As I shall suggest, the text's replay of the trial is the written embodiment of the Paraclete's education of the disciples.

6 See Brown, *John*, 29A:689, 699; Ashton, *Understanding the Fourth Gospel*, 526–27.

7 "The Paraclete will focus on the expression of disbelief that culminated in putting Jesus to death, but those who are guilty are a much wider group than the participants in the historical trial of Jesus. Those participants are only the forebears of men in every generation who will be hostile to Jesus" (Brown, *John*, 29A:712).

These processes may actually resemble the one in Jerusalem to which Jesus was subjected; the last chapter makes reference to the kind of death Peter would suffer, and it is very like the crucifixion of Jesus (21:18–19).

8 The Paraclete is "a prosecuting attorney" (Wayne A. Meeks, "The Ethics of the Fourth Gospel," in Culpepper and Black, *Exploring the Gospel of John*, 317, 323). See Brown, *John*, 29A:710–17, 1135–43; Ashton, *Understanding the Fourth Gospel*, 526.

Statements of the prosecuting role can be read as simple repetitions in other terms of the Paraclete's role as a posttrial commentator and as the source of the disciples' testimony in the ongoing trials. That this is an additional, new role seems to me clear from the text. The Paraclete neither testifies on Jesus' behalf in the Jerusalem trial nor plays the role of prosecutor in the ongoing trials of the faithful who are defendants.

9 Brown, *John*, 29:45.

10 The crucifixion scene of the Isenheim altarpiece depicts John pointing with a long, bony finger to Jesus on the cross. It is theologically truthful if chronologically incongruous. It may be that Brown intends his comment in the theological sense.

11 3:36–4:1. Jesus cites the Baptist's testimony at one point later (5:32–36) and followers of Jesus remember him once (10:41), but he has no textual function in the legal process that begins in chapter 5 and culminates in chapter 19.

A. E. Harvey does not cite either Brown or Masson, but he, too, emphasizes the trial-like character of the gospel. In fact he sees the gospel as actually reflecting Jewish legal procedure and as based upon a pattern of two parties in dispute in a Jewish trial (Harvey, *Jesus on Trial*, 15). (He does not devote attention to Roman law.) He finds a series of legal encounters between Jesus and "Jewish lawyers" which forms a drawn-out, specifically legal proceeding in which "the normal procedures for pronouncing the verdict and carrying out the sentence were frustrated again and again" until the matter could finally be brought to a conclusion in Jerusalem (ibid., 127).

Harvey would have the whole gospel read as a specifically legal, two-party process (Jesus vs. Jews). However, he does not find the formal complaint initiated until chapter 5 of the gospel, with the healing of the cripple. His work is helpful, and I shall return to parts of it. However, I do not find it necessary to read John as a reflection of a specific legal proceeding, and I believe that it may misdirect interpreters to take the gospel as a kind of appellate brief challenging readers "to reach their own verdict" (ibid., 17) or to find "that the Jewish judges who condemned [Jesus] were wrong" (ibid., 103).

John Ashton's view of the text is closer to my own: "Jesus' public career takes the form of a prolonged and bitter dispute with the Jews. From one perspective this may be seen as a *trial*—a trial whose eventual outcome, never really in doubt, is the sentence of crucifixion passed by Pilate. But the trial motif in the Fourth Gospel is not just another theological theme, distinct and separable from that of judgement. It is judgement in action, judgement *as story* or *drama*. . . . Judgement . . . is embodied in a narrative" (*Understanding the Fourth Gospel*, 226).

12 Perhaps the legal descriptions of the Baptist and his encounter with the authorities are meant to have no independent significance. They may simply set the scene for the ensuing trial of Jesus. Bultmann says that the initial confrontation between John the Baptist and the Jews is "the prelude to the struggle which runs through the whole of the life of Jesus: it is a struggle between the Christian faith and the world, represented by Judaism, a struggle which is continually portrayed as a trial" (*Gospel of John*, 86).

13 Ibid., 553 n. 5. See also Harvey, *Jesus on Trial*, 15–16, 126–27.

14 On the *riv* see Ball, *Word and the Law*, 110–13, 117, 188–90 nn. 10–17.

15 Opening the prologue to include him is the textual equivalent to interrupting the heavenly assembly to admit a prophet.

The Baptist's second interruption of the text is grammatically noteworthy: "John testified and cried out: 'This is he of whom I said: "The one who comes after me ranks ahead of me, for he was before me" ' " (1:15). The quote within a quote is repeated in 1:30; the text never presents him saying what he said he said. This may be a way of calling attention to the Baptist—his function in the text—as only a message bearer.

16 The gospel quotes from Isaiah four times (1:23, 6:45, 12:38, 40) or arguably five (12:13). Ashton observes that the Isaiah verses are "drawn from the common stock of the gospel tradition" (*Understanding the Fourth Gospel*, 543). However, as is true of other material from the common stock, it is important to discern how John employs it.

17 Ashton, *Understanding the Fourth Gospel*, 220–26; Brown, *John*, 29: cxvii, 134, 219, 345.

The influential source for my understanding of *krisis* is Karl Barth, whose theology early and late flowed from the crisis: "If I have a system, it is limited to a recognition of what Kierkegaard called the 'infinite qualitative distinction' between time and eternity, and to my regarding this as possessing negative as well as positive significance: 'God is in heaven, and thou art on earth.' The relation between such a God and such a man, and the relation between such a man and such a God, is for me the theme of the Bible and the essence of philosophy. Philosophy names this KRISIS of human perception—the Prime Cause; the Bible beholds at the same cross-roads—the figure of Jesus Christ" (*The Epistle to the Romans*, 6th ed., trans. Edwyn Hoskyns [London: Oxford University Press, 1933], 10).

18 This is the Cana to Cana unit. In a first sign performed at Cana, water is changed to wine, and "his disciples believed in him" (2:11). A Passover visit to Jerusalem follows. During it Jesus drives merchants from the temple and performs signs, "and many believed in his name" (2:23).

Chapter 3, too, is permeated with the language and setting of law. It features the taking and testing of testimony. In this chapter Nicodemus enters the text and John the Baptist departs it. Nicodemus is a Pharisee well if tentatively disposed toward Jesus, whom he seeks out in the night. The encounter takes juridical character when Jesus describes himself as testifying (3:11). Nicodemus fades from the scene as Jesus attests that he is the Son of God (3:11–18), and the discourse revisits the dynamic setting of the prologue: "this is the *krisis*, that the light has come into the world, and people loved darkness rather than light" (3:18–19).

In the second episode of chapter 3, John the Baptist makes his last appearance. He repeats his testimony that he has been sent ahead of the Messiah and that he must decrease as the Messiah increases (3:25–30). With his testimony concluded and corroborated and with Jesus' own testimony having begun, the Baptist is dismissed from the text. Another section of discourse follows. It revives the crisis themes and introduces yet another legal term: certify or confirm or set one's seal to. "Whoever accepts Jesus' testimony has certified this, that God is true" (3:33).

The circle of certifying believers expands twice more in chapter 4 to include, surprisingly, Samaritans and a government official. In the beautifully worked story of Jesus and a Samaritan woman, "many Samaritans" become believers and "know that this is truly the Savior of the world" (4:7–42). In the concluding story, Jesus returns to Cana and in a second sign there heals the son of a royal official who then becomes a believer "along with his whole household" (4:46–54). A welcome by Galileans is added toward the end of the section as a grace note to highlight the accumulation of affirmation (4:45).

19 The pointed question of 2:18–21 could be taken as an expression of opposition but certainly does not have to be so read. Narrated, active opposition does not start until chapter 5, when the trial of Jesus is set in motion. Until then, with the qualified exception of the meeting with Nicodemus, all the episodes feature belief. And even Nicodemus is present to prompt an examination of believing.

20 The believing that serves as corroborating evidence in the affirmative part of the case continues to appear from time to time in chapters 5–19. See, e.g., 6:69 (the twelve), 7:31 and 8:30 (many), and 12:42 (authorities). It is concentrated in the text around the raising of Lazarus toward the close of Jesus' public ministry. First John the Baptist is remembered, and many believe (10:42). Then before Lazarus is raised, in terms that recall the prologue and the Baptist's testimony, Martha, the sister of Lazarus, responds to Jesus: "I believe that you are the Messiah, the Son of God, the one coming into the world" (11:27). After the raising of Lazarus, "many of the Jews" believe (11:45).

The "belief" attributed to crowds in chapters 5–19 may even perform a negative function. For example, "many of the Jews" believe in Jesus after the raising of Lazarus, "but some of them went to the Pharisees and told them what he had done" (11:45–46), and the belief is a prompt to the authorities to act: "If we let him go on like this, everyone will believe in him, and the Romans will come and destroy both our holy place and our nation" (11:48).

Similarly, belief among the authorities bears negative connotations: "Many, even of the authorities, believed in him. But because of the Pharisees they did not confess it, for fear that they would be put out of the synagogue; for they loved human glory more than the glory that comes from God" (12:42–43).

21 Bultmann says that "the 'Jews' are under the illusion that they are the judges, whereas in fact they are the accused before the forum of God" (*Gospel of John*, 86). His later comments on the account of one discussion between Jesus and the people of Jerusalem (7:28ff.) are characteristic of his reading of John as a whole: "The historical scenery is only a disguise for the real event, which is the conflict between the world and the Revealer before the tribunal of God" (ibid., 297). I am wary of embracing Bultmann's description because the trial—like history in the Gospel—is not a question of "illusion" and "disguise." It is ironic, and there is all the difference in the world between irony and illusion or put-on.

For a summary of scholarship on irony in the gospel, see, e.g., R. Alan Culpepper, "Reading Johannine Irony," in Culpepper and Black, *Exploring the Gospel of John*, 193. See also George Macrae, "Theology and Irony in the Fourth Gospel," in *The Gospel of John as Literature*, ed. Mark Stibbe (Leiden: Brill, 1993), 103–13. Stibbe's selection of material for this small, interesting book demonstrates that literary approaches to John are not new, as has been commonly assumed, and that such approaches have been plural as well as long-standing.

Brown notes that the Gospel of John makes two different kinds of statements about Jesus and judging (*John*, 29:345). According to some passages Jesus did not come to judge (3:17, 12:47). The idea in such verses is that he is not the apocalyptic judge of the last day. Instead, his presence causes people to judge themselves.

According to other statements, he did come to judge (9:39, 4:22). This is not a contradiction but an expansion of the first idea. So in 8:15–16 both kinds of statements are made: "You pass judgment according to human standards, but I pass judgment on no one. Yet even if I do judge, that judgment of mine is valid because I am not alone—I have at my side the One who sent me [the Father]." The second sentence means, Brown suggests, that the judgment Jesus' presence provokes will be accepted by the Father. That is, the self-judgment has an eternal dimension.

22 Bultmann, *Gospel of John*, 86. See also on irony Macrae, "Theology and Irony in the Fourth Gospel," 103.

23 John Ashton points out that, at the time of Jesus, Judaism was composed of a rich variety of sects and philosophies and that Johannine Christians may have been a dissenting group among them (*Understanding the Fourth Gospel*, 156, 159). He suggests that the hostility to "the Jews" in the gospel had a contemporaneous, external referent: "the powerful party" that assumed authority and gave founding shape to what we now know as Judaism succeeded in expelling the Johannine community from

the synagogue (ibid., 152, 158). In this view, the acrimony in the gospel is then to be read as reflecting religious antagonism present at the time the text was composed. It would have been "the type of family row in which the participants face one another across the room of a house which all have shared and all call home" (ibid., 151; see generally 131–59).

24 For summary, discussion, and response to the issue of anti-Semitism and the Gospel of John, see D. Moody Smith, "Judaism and the Gospel of John," in *Jews and Christians: Exploring the Past, Present, and Future*, ed. James Charlesworth (New York: Crossroad, 1990), 76; Smith, *Theology of the Gospel of John*, 169–73; Smith, "John," in *Early Christian Thought in Its Jewish Context*, ed. Barclay and Sweet (Cambridge: Cambridge University Press, 1996).

In the text, "the Jews" and Jews who are followers of Jesus are linked not only negatively (Jews, disciples, and Romans compose the world who judge Jesus) but also positively: The story of the gospel cannot be told except in reliance upon the language of Jewish liturgy and stories. There is a further issue here that has to do with a certain kind of scholarship that focuses on a hypothesized reflection of synagogue-church hostility. See chapter 22, note 15; chapter 23, note 2.

25 The world is all "creation capable of response" (Brown, *John*, 29:508, 10).

26 See 1:35–51. There is in John no list of the Twelve Disciples of the other gospels, and he does not say that there are twelve of them.

27 The reader has been prepared to reach this unstated conclusion by chapter 3: Those "who do not believe are condemned already" (3:18), and "whoever believes in the Son has eternal life; whoever disobeys the Son will not see life, but must endure God's wrath" (3:36). Karl Barth observed that the "wrath of God is the righteousness of God — apart from and without Christ" (*Epistle to the Romans*, 43). To judge Jesus is an act of separation that is self-condemning. It is to remain apart from him and therefore to continue in existing darkness. It is to refuse to be liberated.

On the issue of Jesus and judging — *krinein*, which can mean either "judge" or "condemn" — see Brown, *John*, 29:345. The gospel at various points says that Jesus did not come to judge/condemn and at others that he did. Brown observes that "the statement that Jesus did not come to condemn does not exclude the very real judgment that Jesus provokes. . . . The idea . . . seems to be that during his ministry Jesus is no apocalyptic judge like the one expected at the end of time; yet his presence does cause men to judge themselves" (ibid., 345).

20. A Reversal and Appeal

1 In proving Jesus to be right and the world wrong (16:8–11), the Paraclete prosecutes the world. But this is also a saving action that is to the world's advantage. If the world were right, it would have no hope.

2 Brown comments on the drama of the moment: "Throughout the Gospel . . . on the stage of 1st-century Palestine, [the author] has in mind an audience seated in a darkened theater of the future, silently viewing what Jesus was saying and doing. . . . now, as the curtain is about to fall on the stage drama, the lights in the theater are suddenly turned on. Jesus shifts his attention from the disciples on stage to the audience . . . and makes clear that his ultimate concern is for them" (*John*, 29A:1049).

  I would describe the circumstance as a courtroom rather than a theater—to the extent that there is a difference. The point is that the text may here be making appeal to the reader as either judge/jury or as playgoer.

3 Macrae observes that "where the distance of tragedy is meant to bring about catharsis without actual terror, in the Fourth Gospel this distance has the effect of involving the spectator in the challenge of faith" ("Theology and Irony in the Fourth Gospel," 108).

21. The Power of the Word: Two Women

1 John the Baptist is sent as a witness to testify "so that all might believe through him" (John 1:7). He is described as a witness whose testimony produces belief, but the text has little narrative in which his words actually have this direct effect. Just prior to the story of Mary and Martha and the raising of Lazarus, Jesus withdraws to the area across the Jordan that had been the setting for John the Baptist's activity. The text says: "Many came to [Jesus], and they were saying 'John performed no sign, but everything that John said about this man was true.' And many believed in him there" (10:41–42). This interweaving of Jesus' sign and John's remembered words captures the complexity of the relation of John and Jesus in the text. John was sent so that all might believe through him, but we do not see much evidence of such belief apart from Jesus.

  Jesus himself arrives, and he, too, speaks "so that they may believe" (11:42, 14:29).

2 In John, she, and not Peter, is primary. The two components essential to the apostolate are having seen the risen Jesus and being sent to proclaim him. Mary Magdalene not only satisfies both but is the first to do so (Sandra Schneiders, "Women in the Fourth Gospel and the Role of

Women in the Contemporary Church," in Stibbe, *Gospel of John as Literature*, 139–41; Brown, *Community of the Beloved Disciple*, 189–91). See also Gail O'Day, "John," in Newsom and Ringe, *Women's Bible Commentary*, 300–302.

3 See Brown, *John*, 29:lxxxvii–cii.

4 Commentators have noted the theatrical quality of the encounter, and Brown divides it into scenes (*John*, 29:166–68).

5 The Samaritan woman occupies chapter 4. John the Baptist fades out of the text in chapter 3. In his last words he describes himself as a friend of the bridegroom who must decrease as the bridegroom increases. As the awaited bridegroom appears, the groomsman recedes. The next story is that of Jesus and the Samaritan woman who has five husbands. They meet at a well. In the stories of the Hebrew Bible, such meetings of a man and a woman—Moses and Zipporah—lead to marriage. The conversation between Jesus and the Samaritan woman is scandalous to the disciples. The text gives no indication that they are shocked by sexual innuendo. But see Alan Watson, *Jesus and the Jews* (Athens: University of Georgia Press, 1995), 29–37.

Schneiders proposes that Samaritans were an integral part of the Johannine community and that the disciple's shock is aimed at those traditionalist male Christians who were shocked by the apostolic initiative of women ("Women in the Fourth Gospel," 133–34).

Gail O'Day points out that the Samaritan woman's reputation for immorality is not a necessary function of the text: "The text does not say, as most interpreters automatically assume, that the woman has been divorced five times but that she had five husbands. There are many possible reasons for the woman's marital history" ("John," 296).

6 Her audience ultimately comes to believe not from the words she bears but from the words Jesus himself addresses to them. This circumstance does not diminish her office or the power of her words. It follows the Johannine formula according to which, prior to the resurrection and for a short period afterward, "the witness of a believing disciple brings a person to Jesus but then the disciple fades away and the prospective believer encounters Jesus himself" (Schneiders, "Women in the Fourth Gospel," 133).

22. The Power of the Word: Moses and the Spirit

1 I take this point and the following one about Moses' last discourse from Brown, *John*, 29:491–93.

2 Deuteronomy 29:2–33:29 includes a variety of material placed at the end of Moses' life. Chapters 29–30 are an address to Israel in Moab.

Chapter 31 contains words of Moses to Israel, the commissioning of Joshua, the institution of a covenant ceremony, and Moses writing the words of the law in a book. Chapter 32 is a song of Moses (32:1–43) followed by concluding comments of his (32:44–47) and then words addressed to Moses by God (32:48–52). Chapter 33 is a blessing of the tribes of Israel by Moses. For present purposes, I include in Moses' final discourse those portions of 29:2–32:47 that the text identifies as spoken to Israel gathered in Moab near his death.

3 See Ashton, *Understanding the Fourth Gospel*, 456–59.

4 Compare my discussion of the writing of the decalogue in chapter 1.

The accessibility and life-giving power of the law when it soaks through a person is emphasized when Moses says that the law "is not too hard for you, nor . . . too far away" and that "the word is very near to you; it is in your mouth and in your heart for you to observe" (Deut. 30:11, 14).

The connection between writing and the heart is made earlier. After Moses' injunction "Keep these words that I am commanding you today in your heart," he adds: "Recite them when you are at home and when you are away. . . . Bind them as a sign on your hand, fix them as an emblem on your forehead, and write them on the doorposts of your house and on your gates" (Deut. 6:6–9; see also 11:18, 32:46).

5 Ashton, *Understanding the Fourth Gospel*, 420.

6 See also 14:18–26, 15:26–27, 16:12–15, 6:63. It may be that the Spirit and the commandments/words of Jesus in the heart help explain the meaning of 7:37–39.

7 Jeremiah's vision of the restoration and a new covenant includes a related image: "I will put my law within them, and I will write it on their hearts" (Jer. 31:33).

The chapter 12 poem makes no mention of the Spirit. I have assumed that it is properly read together in this regard with the cited portions of the last discourse in chapter 14. The omission of the Spirit from chapter 12 can be explained as a matter of its function and placement in the text. It looks back to the public ministry when "as yet there was no Spirit, because Jesus was not yet glorified" (7:39). The last discourse looks ahead to the trial and glorification.

8 Moses writes his words to serve as a witness against the people. There is no difference in function between the words of the law serving as a witness and, as the poem in John puts it, the word of Jesus serving as judge (12:48). On an overlap between witness and judge, see Harvey, *Jesus on Trial*, 46–47.

9 The only other writing is that ordered by Pilate: "Jesus of Nazareth, the King of the Jews" (19:19).

10 Ashton notes that to keep Jesus' words, the disciples "must literally keep

a record of his *words,* which means in practice keeping a copy of the Gospel. The actual composition of the Gospel is part, and an essential part at that, of the carrying out of Jesus' last commission" (*Understanding the Fourth Gospel,* 459).

11 Biblical scholars speculate about the origins of chapter 21, its author, and how it fits in the text. I believe that the text has to be taken seriously as it is. The question for me is what its sense is, not how it got there and by whose hand.

12 On the "author" and the various "Johns," see chapter 18, note 3. See also Brown, *John,* 29:xcii–xcviii. The beloved disciple is the first to believe in the scene at the tomb and the first to identify the risen Jesus in the concluding scene on the beach at daybreak (21:7).

13 Ashton, *Understanding the Fourth Gospel,* 522, emphasis omitted. Words and works are parallel terms in 14:10–12. "The words that I say to you I do not speak on my own; but the Father who dwells in me does his works" (14:10). Then verse 12 adds: "The one who believes in me will also do the works that I do and, in fact, will do greater works than these, because I am going to the Father." See Ashton, *Understanding the Fourth Gospel,* 521–22; Brown, *John,* 29A:633–34.

14 The authority lies with the words, not the author. See Ashton, *Understanding the Fourth Gospel,* 459.

15 A major theme in modern academic discussion of the gospel has been the situation in which it was written. The construction of that situation as one of bitter conflict between synagogue and church extends the textual conflict between "the Jews" and Jesus into extratextual history. This move can — but does not necessarily — give the conflict an unwarranted, exaggerated character, an unwarranted reality as a conflict between Jews and Christians, and an unwarranted textual location to supposed, subsequent, extratextual events. It can — but does not necessarily — thereby lead to pernicious interpretations that are basically unsupported by the text and that divert attention from other interpretations that the text does support.

Severino Pancaro's well-regarded *The Law in the Fourth Gospel* says about an issue absolutely essential to his thesis: "It is the controversy between the Church and the Synagogue which is at the root of the meaning John gives the term nomos [law]" (514). The "controversy" in issue he confidently identifies as "the battle 'normative' Judaism waged against Jewish-Christians towards the end of the first century" (ibid., 511). That conflict is then read as the subject of the gospel: "John has reduced the opposition between the Church and the Synagogue (Christianity and Judaism) to a confrontation between the Law and Jesus" (ibid., 8). And in that confrontation, the Law condemns the Jews rather than Jesus. It condemns the Jews because they pervert justice and procure the condemnation of Jesus on grounds that have nothing to do with the law (ibid., 363).

One textual difficulty with this notion is that Jesus dies *"kata ton nomon"* (according to the law). See *Law in the Fourth Gospel*, 363. Pancaro resolves this difficulty with the extratextual maneuver of reading subsequent developments into the text. He says that there must be two different understandings of law in John: "The Jews" in the text must hold the understanding of later Judaism, and John must mean by *nomos* what the later Church meant. The two are not coincident. Jesus died according to "law" as later Christianity but not Judaism understood the term. See *Law in the Fourth Gospel*, 510.

This maneuver requires maneuvering the text. For example, it entails reading Pilate out of the story. He becomes "extraneous to the whole religious drama" (ibid., 315). He is merely "a bystander" who "acts as a dramatic foil to the Jews" (ibid., 324). To the degree that he is present, he is "less guilty than" they (ibid., 323). To the contrary, as I have already noted in the text, the Apostle's Creed holds that Jesus "suffered under Pontius Pilate" and does not charge the Jews. And it enters into no judgment about comparative guilt.

And then Pancaro engages in a scandalous wrenching of the text. In his reckoning, the lawsuit against the world becomes a lawsuit against "the Jews" and, potentially, a lawsuit against the Jews: "We have mentioned that some authors see the end of the Jewish nation as the 'people of God' in the outcry: 'We have no king but Caesar'. By rejecting Jesus, they abdicate their rights as the 'chosen people'. This is no doubt what John wished to show, but we must go further. It was the Law which made of the Jews the people of God. The condemnation of Jesus is contrary to the Law since it was meant to lead to him. The rejection of Jesus coincides with the 'perversion', abuse and rejection of the Law and, since the Law is the '*Existenz-grundlage*' of Irael, the Jews cease thereby to be the 'people of God' " (ibid., 318).

As should be evident from the account I have given, the text of the gospel does not permit me to interpret John as Pancaro does. Pancaro's book is an abridgement of his doctoral dissertation accepted by the University of Münster in 1972. It troubles me that a theological faculty, especially a German one, in the late '60s–early '70s, would not have guided a graduate student away from such an extravagant, inflammatory interpretation. After the Holocaust, why wouldn't any Christian theologians anywhere regard such a use of the text as requiring extraordinary examination of conscience, extraordinary substantiation in the text, and extraordinary grounds for rejecting conflicting interpretations better or equally grounded in the text?

Robert Jenson notes "that the present existence of Judaism is a vital *theological* topic" for the theology he is developing (*Systematic Theology*, 82 n. 57). It is a vital theological topic for the modern Church as a whole. If scholars of John are to have a positive role in developing this topic, they would do well to take note of Moody Smith's reading of the Gospel: "Jesus Christ belongs, and is intelligible, only in his Jewish and biblical context, while at the same time an adequate assessment of who he is sheds a radically new light on that context, causes it to be viewed differently, but does not destroy or negate it. It is in the interest of the evangelist not to destroy or negate Judaism, but to remain in dialogue with it. . . . John holds traditional Jewish messianism and his own distinctive christology in creative tension" ("John," in Barclay and Sweet, *Early Christian Thought in Its Jewish Context*, 109).

23. The Power of the Word: Disbelief

1 On the "impossible possibility" of disbelief, see Karl Barth, *Doctrine of Reconciliation*, vol. 4 of *Church Dogmatics*, pt. 1, 408–10.

2 My point is drawn from the texts and not from extratextual reference to a Johannine community and its historical situation. If extratextual, historical evidence of disbelief is needed, plenty of it has accumulated in the Church in the centuries since the gospel was written. Also the texts themselves bear abundant witness to the possibility of the impossible.

Brown is among the scholars who have devoted attention to construction of the situation in which the gospel was written. I noted in part 1 that I have been helpfully influenced by the useful mode of modern biblical scholarship that attempts to look through the texts to what can be constructed of their original contexts. I have also observed that this approach can be diversionary.

In scholarship on John, J. Louis Martyn is famous for his *History and Theology in the Fourth Gospel*, 2d ed. (Nashville, Tenn.: Abingdon, 1978), in which he reads the gospel as dramatizing events that took place in its immediate historical circumstance. Such a reading depends upon distinguishing bits of the text of John that can be said to be traditional (material the author received) from what can be said to have been added by the author (material from events in the author's present). The gospel is then to be seen as a play whose actors mount "a two-level stage so that each is actually a pair of actors playing two parts simultaneously," a part in the life of Jesus and a part from the author's community (ibid., 37).

Martyn's book displays great learning and ingenuity and has had a profound impact among scholars of John. I have two reservations about the book's approach or, really, about the general approach that it exemplifies and that has dominated the discipline of biblical studies in my lifetime. First, Martyn says his endeavor enables us to take up temporary residence in the Johannine community and therefore enables John to speak in his own terms (ibid., 18; see also 29–30, 38, 135–37). This is to claim far too little for the obvious role of his own wonderful imagination and far too much for what it can deliver of the past as it really was and of John's own terms. Second, although Martyn fruitfully considers the text of the gospel as a whole, the text he considers is one he has reengineered in conformity to his construction of what lies behind it.

D. Moody Smith has been a primary player in Johannine studies in the academy and has made many inside contributions to the field. See, e.g., the collection of essays in his honor titled *Exploring the Gospel of John*. The advantage of his scholarship for an outsider like me is that he employs work such as Martyn's, and his own of that genre, to serve the reader's confrontation with the text and not what lies behind the text. See, e.g., *The Theology of the Gospel of John*.

3 On the Isaiah text and a related one in Mark, see Ball, *Word and the Law*, 106–17. See also Brown, *John*, 29:484–86.

4 Ashton provides an analysis of its chiastic structure (*Understanding the Fourth Gospel*, 542 n. 40).

5 Ibid., 543.

6 See Brown, *John*, 29:490; Ashton, *Understanding the Fourth Gospel*, 541–45. The familiar words of 3:16–18 are an example: "In this way God loved the world, that he gave his only Son, that everyone who believes in him may not perish but may have eternal life. For God did not send the Son into the world to condemn the world but that the world might be saved through him. Those who believe in him are not condemned, but those who do not believe are condemned already, for they do not believe in the name of the only Son of God."

7 In fact, the poem is the conclusion to a section that follows the pattern. At the end of his public ministry Jesus speaks of light, darkness, and belief, and then he hides (12:35–37). Next, the editorial intervention raises the question of disbelief in the starkest terms by quoting the harsh text from Isaiah about God hardening hearts. The narrative then moves quickly to the poetic performance of Jesus speaking.

8 In a review of work by Cormac McCarthy, Robert Hass says that McCarthy "parts company with post-modern practice in thinking, not that everything . . . refers to nothing, but that in human life certain ancient stories are acted out again and again. A writer's moral relation to these stories is like nothing so much as a craftsman's relation to his tools, and nothingness is not to be counted for the pleasure of merely circulating, but built against, sentence by sentence . . . if hopelessly, in the knowledge of the doom of all human intention, then indefatigably, in the knowledge of the skills of a trade that has been passed down to one

and that will be passed in turn to other hands." Hass describes this as "a male ethic. It may be *the* American male ethic, but it descends to us from sources as old as the 'Odyssey' and the 'Aeneid.' . . . [It is an] old ethic of work, a male ethic undertaken in pity and desperation" (*New York Times Book Review,* June 12, 1994, sec. 7, p. 1, col. 3). This is not the ethic of John.

24. John's Freedom from and for Law

1 Harvey, *Jesus on Trial,* 58. If a Jewish court "found Jesus guilty on a capital charge, either Jesus must have been properly condemned in the sight of God . . . or else, in some way, the system itself must have been at fault" (ibid., 6).

2 Ibid., 81.

3 Watson, *Jesus and the Jews,* 46–47.

4 See Harvey, *Jesus on Trial,* 103.

5 Watson, *Jesus and the Jews,* 76.

6 Harvey, *Jesus on Trial,* 45.

7 See Bultmann, *Gospel of John,* 633.

8 Such an assumption would require elaborate justification. It would have to be shown that law does evolve from worse to better according to a shared standard of goodness. Whether law is good or bad is not John's concern. Law falls under judgment either way.

9 How this is so and what consequences it has for law has been the subject of much of my writing. For example, in *The Word and the Law* I employed the figure of Dilsey from Faulkner's *Sound and the Fury* to explore the characteristics of postresurrection life, and I devoted the last chapter of that book to death in law and the making it alive in practice, that is, the embodying of new life in law (*Word and the Law,* 87–90, 136–64). In *Lying Down Together,* I took up what it might mean to take responsibility for law (15–17) and explored the subject in the extended example of environmental law and the law of the sea (21–118). I concluded by employing the metaphor of law in a peaceable kingdom to describe law in the wholly different context suggested by the biblical stories (119–36). "New beginning" was the metaphor I followed in *The Promise of American Law* to propose how constitutional law, and to a lesser extent property law, might be read in light of the biblical stories of creation, reconciliation, and redemption.

10 He could have employed other languages, including that of apocalyptic poetry as is done in the Book of Revelation, identified as The Revelation to John.

11 Macrae, *Theology and Irony in the Fourth Gospel,* 105.

12 Umberto Eco describes the Book of Kells as "the product of cold-

blooded hallucination" (*Kells Commentary* [1990], 14, cited in Bernard Meehan, *The Book of Kells* [London: Thames and Hudson, 1994], 9). At the top of the page containing the opening of John in the Book of Kells perches a figure holding a book or tablet. Presumably this is the writer of the gospel. I have kept a copy of that page at hand as I have written. My wife is uncertain of the attitude the face displays. I am sure that John is smiling. There is laughter in him.

In the second Cana sign, a father leaves his dying son to beg Jesus' help and returns to find the child made well. In between the two, Jesus has spoken of destroying the temple and rebuilding it in three days, a saying the disciples are later made to remember and understand as a reference to the resurrection. These events reveal the core action in the story: illness is turned to health; death is turned to life.

Jesus' saying about rebuilding the temple is uttered just after he has raged through the temple in an extraordinary scene in which he drives out animals and people with a whip, overturns tables, and pours money on the floor. Commentators suggest that, based on the location of the event in other gospels, the scene is out of place and belongs later in the story. Such a displacement would only emphasize the fact that the author's account is juxtaposed to the Cana miracle for a purpose. One purpose may be to express a sense of the action of the *krisis*. The delightfully drunken exuberance of the wedding celebration is matched at the other extreme by excessive rage.

13 The same could be said of the Church's appropriation of the cross. To torture a person to death by crucifixion was an authorized form of capital punishment in the legal system. To seize upon the cross as a symbol for the story of resurrection is a form of transfiguration. Perhaps centuries of abuse of the symbol—including its use as a magic wand and as a triumphal sign of conquest, typically in colonizing wars of aggression—may have severely compromised its significance. Ongoing translation of the Bible has not been accompanied by an equivalent translation of symbols. I am uncertain that the translation of the cross into an electric chair would restore the startling integrity of the symbol.

14 The biblical tradition has been thought to supply a ground for an obligation to obey the law. I think that it does not. The texts usually cited in support of such an obligation are Romans 13:1–7, Luke 20:25, 1 Peter 2:17, 1 Timothy 2:1–2, and Titus 3:1–2. I think that these texts lead in a very different direction. I think that they and the biblical tradition as a whole support an obligation to the neighbor but not to the law. I set out my arguments in *Obligation: Not to the Law But to the Neighbor*, 18 Ga. L. Rev. 911, 919–27 (1984). My chief focus there was upon the central Romans text. At the time I did not see the relevance of John as support for my argument.

15 My understanding of the relationship of the penultimate to the ultimate is drawn from Dietrich Bonhoeffer. I elaborated my understanding of the subject in Ball, *Lying Down Together*, 126–38.

25. Lawyers' Independence

1 Robert Gordon notes that lawyers talk about professional independence in the sense of corporate self-regulation and control over conditions of work, but he is chiefly interested, as am I, in the political, social independence of lawyers (*The Independence of Lawyers*, 68 Boston U. L. Rev. 1 [1988]). His article is a thorough, well-taken assessment of the subject.

2 ABA, *Model Code*, Canon 5; ABA, *Model Rules*, Rule 2.1.

3 See, e.g., ABA, *Model Code*, EC 5-1, Canon 7, EC 7-1, EC 7-19; ABA, *Model Rules*, Rule 1.2; ALI, "Restatement," sec. 34, 115, 117A.

4 The issue has been most recently and publicly ventilated in conjunction with the question of attorney-client privilege between counsel to the president and the president and in the circumstance of the independent counsel's investigation of President and Mrs. Clinton's involvement in the bundle of matters known as Whitewater.

5 ABA, *Model Code*, EC 7-13.

6 Gordon, *Independence of Lawyers*, 17. Because corporate lawyers, for whatever reason, find little or nothing to challenge in their clients' interests, they may need particular encouragement to maintain their independence. See ibid., 56–58.

7 "Lawyers are sometimes in the best position to know when some of the strategic tools of law—formalism, proceduralism, and adversarial attitude—will defeat their clients' overall goals by poisoning the cultural environment in which their clients operate" (Gordon, *Independence of Lawyers*, 18).

This kind of hoped-for moral limitation on clients' power does not explain another example of mandated distance between the attorney and her client known as the rule against vouching for clients: An attorney may not publicly assert her personal belief in a client's innocence or in the justness of a client's cause (ABA, *Model Code*, DR 7-106.C.4 [1981]; ABA, *Model Rules*, Rule 3.4 [e] [1983]). (The voucher at the end of John would be off-limits: "We know that his testimony is true.") This rule does share with the others the belief that an attorney should never become fully the servant of her client, but the arguments in favor of it are not strong and neither the letter nor the spirit of it appear to be often observed.

Thomas Shaffer points out that the ethical injunction against vouching for clients is routinely avoided by the use of indicative statements and the avoidance of first-person pronouns. Instead of, "I believe the defendant is innocent," an attorney says: "I believe the evidence shows the defendant is innocent," or better: "The evidence shows the defendant is innocent." This is a side point to the real business of his article, which is to make an appeal to lawyering as friendship: "The way to avoid pretense in advocacy is to say what you mean and to mean both what you say and what you seem to mean in what you say and do. We come to mean what we say about the subjects and the objects of our advocacy — the people involved, rather than the words — by approaching them with benevolence. We are then, in the ordinary meaning of the word, *friendly*" (Shaffer, *The Legal Profession's Rule against Vouching for Clients: Advocacy and "The Manner That Is the Man Himself,"* 7 Notre Dame J. of L. & Pub. Policy 145, 169 [1993]).

8 Much of Thomas Shaffer's extensive, affecting writing and personal-professional example have been devoted to the kind of friendship that appropriately characterizes a lawyer's relation to clients.

Shaffer holds a robust Aristotelian view of friendship and does not mean by it that lawyers should be running dogs for clients. See, e.g., Shaffer, *A Lesson from Trollope,* 35 Wash. & Lee L. Rev. 727 (1978). His views are therefore very different from those of Charles Fried. See Fried, *The Lawyer as Friend,* 85 Yale L. J. 1060 (1976). See also Edward Dauer and Arthur Leff, *Correspondence: The Lawyer as Friend,* 86 Yale L. J. 573, 578–79 (1977). And Clyde Spillenger states the obvious in noting that it is irrelevant to advise corporate counsel for RJR Nabisco to develop greater empathy toward her client and bizarre to suggest that the legal services lawyer practice steely independence from the embattled person she represents (*Elusive Advocate,* 1522–23).

It is also unclear to me that distance is always, everywhere correct for judges. See, e.g., the examples of judges Margaret Taylor and David Harding in Ball, *Word and the Law,* 24–49. See also below on the International People's Tribunal in Hawai'i.

9 Part of the difficulty may lie in confusing the sought-for independence with personal distance or lack of empathy. The independence that arises from commitment to the larger responsibilities of law and lawyering may well require a lawyer to identify with her clients. It was the Hebrew midwives' regard for the transcendent ("they feared God") that led them to close alignment with their clients. Because he is committed to justice, John Rosenberg is thoroughly committed to the legal services clients among whom he lives in eastern Kentucky: "They are asking for justice, and what they ask for is usually right" (Ball, *Word and the Law,* 24). See also Michael Winerip, "What's a Nice Jewish Lawyer Like You Doing in Appalachia," *New York Times Magazine,* June 29, 1997, p. 24. And lawyers who serve business people may equally realize a commit-

ment to justice in close relationships with their clients. In contrast, those lawyers with no commitment to public good may be the most professionally and personally distant from their clients. The independence of judges should be reexamined with respect to the same issue.

10 Conceiving and practicing independence in terms of interests may constitute another difficulty: a lawyer withholds something from serving clients' interests in order to serve the public interest.

Hannah Arendt pointed out that, in a governmental system like ours as it has come to be, interests are represented, but a citizen's opinion and action cannot be represented because they are nondelegable (*On Revolution*, 228–32, 272–73). (I explored the general issue throughout *The Promise of American Law*, and this specific point of Arendt's at pp. 89–90 of that book.)

A citizen is left to bring various forms of pressure on her representative to execute her interest. ("If you don't vote for my interest in Congress, I won't vote for you in the next election." "I have lots of money for candidates. Vote my way.") This residue of political power held by the citizen resembles the coercive power of the blackmailer and is not "the power that arises out of joint action and joint deliberation" (Arendt, *On Revolution*, at 273).

Similarly, if a lawyer represents clients' interests rather than clients, and clients' opinions and actions are excluded, the same dynamic takes hold. Clients pressure hesitant lawyers to execute their wishes, and lawyers can only express independence by either declining or terminating the representation. They cannot express independence as freedom to participate in joint action and joint deliberation as they can if they represent people.

Thomas Shaffer points out that " 'client interest' is a prominent notion in codified American legal ethics, where it seems to mean either the purposes stated by a lawyer's client when he comes to a lawyer, or (more often and more dismally) the purposes a lawyer supposes, without asking, that his client has or should have in view. 'Client interest' is not a given, in either of these ways, when your client is your friend. It is then, at first, not so much a purpose as it is a project. Friends collaborate in the good; if the interest one of them claims is not consistent with the collaboration in the good, friends who have a stake in one another's character collaborate in what Karl Barth called conditional advice" (Shaffer, *Legal Profession's Rule against Vouching for Clients*, 175).

On the question of political representation, see Hanna Pitkin, *Representation* (New York: Atlantic, 1966); and especially her *Concept of Representation* (209–40). See also her discussion in the latter book of political representation of people who have interests (ibid., 190–208). She remarks that an attorney is "a specialist who acts for others" (ibid., 138).

David Luban develops the idea of representativeness as a way to analyze and think about the public interest lawyer's representation of a client class (*Lawyers and Justice,* 344–55 passim).

The notion of public as well as private interest may also color an attorney's understanding and performance of her role. A commonweal expressed and experienced as an interest is unstable. If public interest is a pool of differing private interests, then, as Augustine said, "what is longed for either suffices for none, or not for all" (*The City of God,* trans. Marcus Dods [New York: Random House, 1950], bk. 18, chap. 2, 610). Because citizens and nations compete with each other for what not all can have, the "earthly city" is necessarily "divided against itself by litigations, wars, quarrels, and such victories as are either life-destroying or shortlived" (ibid., bk. 14, chap. 4, 481).

I explored these matters generally in *The Promise of American Law,* and Augustine's point specifically at pp. 37–38, 92. I returned to the issue of representation in the processes of government in *Lying Down Together,* especially at pp. 65–118, and to Augustine's point in particular at p. 101.

If public interest is some higher interest above others, it must nonetheless compete with them. Perhaps this is why public interest law has become a specialty that must compete with and often against other types of practice for money, personnel, attention, power, and victory. In a world composed of interests—common or higher—the lawyer must maintain the vigilant independence of the heroic but mercenary warrior.

11 The third difficulty in sorting out the independence of the lawyer is the assumption, or temptation, that a lawyer has privileged knowledge of what clients want, what is good for them, and how to get it.

The assumption is rarely if ever valid and generally always works harm to both clients and attorneys. Clark Cunningham successfully undertakes an extraordinarily sensitive, instructive examination of the presence and negative effect of the assumption in *The Lawyer as Translator, Representation as Text: Towards an Ethnography of Legal Discourse* and *A Tale of Two Clients: Thinking about Law as Language.*

The dangers of the temptation are also explored in a thoughtful and challenging way in Clyde Spillenger's study of Louis Brandeis's lack of concern for both solutions other than his own and dialogue with clients that might prove morally improving for him (Spillenger, *Elusive Advocate,* 1527–35).

The assumption also denies the opposite possibility, that law is invitation and that lawyers bring their vulnerability to clients and to dialogue with them, a possibility wonderfully realized in Emily Hartigan, *The Power of Language beyond Words: Law as Invitation,* 26 Harv. Civ. Rts.–Civ. Lib. L. Rev. 67 (1991).

David Luban has pointed out that it may be "the lawyer rather than the client who will eventually modify her moral stance. If it is a mistake to take the client's ends as preset and inflexible, it is also a mistake to assume that the lawyer is incapable of learning from the client what justice really requires" (*Lawyers and Justice*, 174).

Independence granted to lawyers on the ground that they possess superior as well as expert knowledge subverts the profession.

12 Gordon, *Independence of Lawyers*, 13. See also David Luban's notion of "moral activism" (*Lawyers and Justice*) and William Simon's idea of "ethical autonomy" (*Ethical Discretion in Lawyering*, 101 Harv. L. Rev. 1083 [1988]).

13 See, e.g., Mary Ann Glendon, *A Nation under Lawyers* (New York: Farrar, Straus and Giroux, 1994); Anthony Kronman, *The Lost Lawyer* (Cambridge, Mass.: Harvard University Press, 1993). For a recent collection of assessments, including a wonderful evaluation of lawyer jokes, see Galanter (from the inside), Goldstein (from a journalist's perspective), Tyler (from the psychologist's perspective), collected in 66 U. Cinn. L. Rev. 877 (1998).

14 Marc Galanter and Thomas Palay, *Tournament of Lawyers: The Transformation of the Big Law Firm* (Chicago: University of Chicago Press, 1991), 2–3.

15 Commission on Professionalism (Stanley Commission Report), ". . . *In the Spirit of Public Service": A Blueprint for the Rekindling of Lawyer Professionalism*, 112 FRD 243, 248 (1987) (quoting Roscoe Pound).

16 Ibid., 261.

17 Thomas Shaffer and Mary Shaffer, *American Lawyers and Their Communities* (Notre Dame, Ind.: Notre Dame University, 1991), 66.

Since the chief justice's call and the commission's response, Shaffer notes, "professionalism has become the A.B.A. party line; lawyer professionalism has a national office, a logo, a motto, its own journal . . . , and a budget" (ibid., 65). The bar has not been discouraged from thinking that the lawyer has "license to lie, to cheat, and to abuse, if only we are *professional* when we do it" (ibid., 72).

The commission noted that law schools and their faculties have the first cut at a student's professionalism. The Association of American Law Schools took the hint and shortly adopted a "Statement of Good Practices." It serves less as a statement of guidance than as a sad commentary on the realities we settle for. It contains such admonishments as teachers should prepare for and meet classes, treat students with respect, be impartial, and refrain from muscling colleagues on governance votes. The statement does tack on to the conclusion two aspirations that are welcome even if they are non sequiturs: teachers of law should engage in pro bono work, and, because they do not live off client fees, they are specially obligated to pursue justice (AALS, *1994 Handbook*, 89 [adopted by the executive committee, Nov. 17, 1989]). The bland, widely and deservedly unnoted statement did not forestall an ABA move on the law schools in the form of the MacCrate Report. See below.

18 This was the ABA Section of Legal Education and Admissions to the Bar's Task Force on Law Schools and the Profession: Narrowing the Gap. "The gap" refers to a gap between law schools and the practice of law.

The Association of American Law Schools was established in 1900 at the urging of the ABA. The two met regularly until 1915. The elite law schools, seeking to engage the bar's help in raising law school standards, successfully promoted the ABA's Section of Legal Education and Admissions to the Bar founded in 1920. It became the law school accrediting agency.

19 The task force report is titled *Legal Education and Professional Development — An Educational Continuum, Report of the Task Force on Law Schools and the Profession: Narrowing the Gap* (1992) (hereafter MacCrate Report).

20 According to the report, the practice of law is composed of solving clients' problems (skill no. 1) (141–42); organizing rules and principles to apply to the problems (skill no. 2) (151); having a "working knowledge" of the rules and institutions that apply (skill no. 3) (157); investigating the facts of the problem (skill no. 4) (163); and applying "communicative skills" to the process (skill no. 5) (172).

21 Ibid., 203–4.

22 "Fundamental Values of the Profession," sec. 2, "Striving to Promote Justice, Fairness, and Morality" (MacCrate Report, 213). This section is also keyed into the prior skill of counseling (ibid., 177, 181–82, 184).

23 Ibid., 259 n. 38. See also 258 n. 37.

24 The profession does have worthy characteristics, and one that is both wonderful and dangerous is the capacity for just subversion, elegantly accomplished, as though it were an endorsement of the thing subverted. So was it with the group who wrote this installment.

25 *Teaching and Learning Professionalism*, Report of the Professionalism Committee, ABA Section of Legal Education and Admission to the Bar (1996) (hereafter *Teaching and Learning*).

26 Ibid., 6.

27 Roger Cramton is sharply critical of the report. He views the bar's old moral tradition as one in which, if client interests conflicted with the rule of law, the lawyer would respect the rule of law. He believes that the bar has abandoned the old morality for the new heresy of making client interests the first and only consideration. He also believes that the report instead of addressing the problems affirms abstractions as lying at

the heart of professionalism (Cramton, "On Giving Meaning to 'Professionalism,' " in ABA Section of Legal Education and Admissions to the
Bar Professionalism Committee on Professionalism and Lawyer Competence of the ABA Center for Professional Responsibility, Symposium
Proceedings, October 2–4, 1996 [1997], 7, 9).

28 *Teaching and Learning,* 6 n. 22.
29 Robert Cover, *The Folktales of Justice: Tales of Jurisdiction,* 14 Cap. U. L.
    Rev. 179, 190 (1985).
30 See Ball, *Word and the Law.*
31 Gordon, *Independence of Lawyers,* 63.
32 The committee that commended "dedication to certain ideals as a way
    of life as part of a specialized group" presumably meant that the group
    was the bar and that the ideals are those of the rule of law.

     Carol Weisbrod observes that "lawyers cannot be pure outsiders, after
    all. Their subject is intrinsically social and in America at least some de-
    gree of satisfaction with existing institutions is taken for granted . . . ,
    often under the heading 'the rule of law' " (*Building Community in
    Sarastro's Dungeon,* 9 Yale J. of L. & Human. 443, 449 [1997]).

     On the rule of law, John Rawls proposed "that the conception of
    formal justice, the regular and impartial administration of public rules,
    becomes the rule of law when applied to the legal system" (*A Theory of
    Justice* [Cambridge, Mass.: Harvard University Press, 1971], 235). A legal
    system fitly requires: (1) only what can be reasonably done; (2) that simi-
    lar cases be treated similarly; (3) that laws be known and general; (4) that
    due process be satisfied (ibid., 236–38). "The principle of legality has a
    firm foundation . . . in the agreement of rational persons to establish for
    themselves the greatest equal liberty. To be confident in the possession
    and exercise of these freedoms, the citizens of a well-ordered society
    will normally want the rule of law maintained" (ibid., 239–40).

     A very different view is held by Howard Zinn: "The 'rule of law'
    in modern society is no less authoritarian than the rule of men in pre-
    modern society; it enforces the maldistribution of wealth and power as
    of old, but it does this in such complicated and indirect ways as to leave
    the observer bewildered. . . . In slavery, the feudal order, the colonial
    system, deception and patronization are the minor modes of control;
    force is the major one. In the modern world of liberal capitalism (and
    also, we should note, of state socialism), force is held in reserve while . . .
    'a multitude of moral teachers, counselors, and bewilderers separate the
    exploited from those in power.' In this multitude, the books of law are
    among the most formidable bewilderers" ("The Conspiracy of Law,"
    in *The Rule of Law,* ed. Robert Wolff [New York: Simon and Schuster,
    1971], 1819).

     The shortest definition I have seen is "Rule of law means exercise of publicly justifiable power" (Michael Zuckert, "Hobbes, Locke, and the Problem of the Rule of Law," in *Nomos XXXVI: The Rule of Law,* ed. Ian Shapiro [New York: New York University Press, 1994], 64). It is short but neither simple nor uncontested, as witness the remainder of Zuckert's essay and the range of debate in the other essays contributed to that same, interesting volume.

33 ABA, *Model Code,* 1.

34 Quoted in Cover, *Folktales of Justice,* 201.

35 Richard Posner, *The Problems of Jurisprudence* (Cambridge, Mass.: Harvard University Press, 1990), 468.

36 See ibid., 442.

37 Ibid., 467.

38 In different ways, Thomas Shaffer and Aviam Soifer have developed this point well and persuasively, and I am indebted to them and their work. See Shaffer and Shaffer, *American Lawyers and Their Communities;* Soifer, *Law and the Company We Keep* (Cambridge, Mass.: Harvard University Press, 1995).

39 Robert Granfield, *Constructing Professional Boundaries in Law School: Reactions of Students and Implications for Teachers,* 4 S. Cal. Rev. of L. & Wom. St. 53, 63 (1994).

40 Ibid., 68.

41 Ibid.

42 Ibid., 69.

43 I cite the Granfield study, but I could have offered my own anecdotal evidence about some students and about the professionally competent lawyers they become and about how ten, twenty, or thirty years out, often in practices of great financial value, they have come to wonder what human worth their practices have. And they find very little.

   See generally, Walt Bachman, *Law v. Life* (Rhinebeck, N.Y.: Four Directions, 1995), an important and readable book.

44 Granfield, *Constructing Professional Boundaries in Law School,* 70–72.

45 Ibid., 71.

46 Ibid.

47 I am among the many who have been profoundly influenced by Stringfellow. I was and continue to be struck in particular by his *Private and Public Faith*; *My People Is the Enemy* (New York: Holt, Rhinehart and Winston, 1964); *An Ethic for Christians and Other Aliens in a Strange Land* (Waco, Tx.: Word, 1973); and *Conscience and Obedience* (Waco, Tx.: Word, 1977).

   Andrew W. McThenia of the Washington and Lee Law School has rendered exemplary service in continuing to confront the bar and the legal academy with Stringfellow's example. See, for one instance, *Radical Christian and Exemplary Lawyer* (Grand Rapids, Mich.: Eerdman's,

1995), a book he conceived, gathered, and edited. This is not his only labor of love. He is himself a keeper of the Word as a practitioner of law.

48 See, e.g., Stringfellow, *Ethic for Christians and Other Aliens in a Strange Land*, 84–86. Selections from Stringfellow's writings are available in *A Keeper of the Word*, ed. Bill Wylie Kellermann (Grand Rapids, Mich.: Eerdmans, 1994). The passage cited above can be found in this book at pp. 242–44. It is clearly best to read Stringfellow's works in their original form, but his books are presently out of print and can be difficult to locate. The Kellerman selection performs a useful service.

49 William Stringfellow, "A Lawyer's Work," *Christian Legal Society Quarterly* 3, no. 3 (1982): 17; Stringfellow, *A Simplicity of Faith* (Nashville, Tenn.: Abingdon, 1982), 125–33. The churning that kept bringing the question to the surface was a function of his ongoing, serious reading of the Bible. That was the source, too, of his understanding of the fallenness of institutions and the dispiriting hubris that leads people to think they can humanize institutions: "Americans particularly persevere in belaboring the illusion that at least some institutions are benign and viable and within human direction or can be rendered so by discipline or reform or revolution or displacement" (*Ethic for Christians and Other Aliens in a Strange Land*, 83).

50 Stringfellow, *Ethic for Christians and Other Aliens in a Strange Land*, 86, emphasis omitted.

51 See ibid., 133.

52 Andrew McThenia observes: "It is not, as some have argued, that Stringfellow thought that law was nothing but a tool of oppression or, as others have maintained, that he was unconcerned with justice. He saw law as necessary, even as a gift from God. And he spent his life in the struggle for justice. But law, like all other powers and principalities, is fallen. Law is one means, the primary one, that a modern liberal democracy has to safeguard itself and the promised freedom of its members. Stringfellow never denied the value or the necessity of law for those purposes. But many liberal academic lawyers insisted on going further. They asserted that not only is law necessary to preserve the peace treaty of a liberal democracy; it is in fact the source of our values. Law is that which gives expression to those 'objective' values in our culture. These lawyers saw a large role for law, linking the reality of the present with the world as we imagine it should be. Law had an almost transcendent quality" ("An Uneasy Relationship with the Law," in McThenia, *Radical Christian and Exemplary Lawyer*, 174).

53 William Stringfellow, *A Simplicity of Faith: My Experience in Mourning* (Nashville, Tenn.: Abingdon, 1982); *Keeper of the Word*, 31.

54 *Private and Public Faith*, 73.

55 See Stringfellow, *My People Is the Enemy*, 97–101; McThenia, *Radical Christian and Exemplary Lawyer*, 178–79.

56 *Simplicity of Faith*, quoted in *Keeper of the Word*, 33.

57 Ibid., 33–34.

58 Stringfellow, *Conscience and Obedience*, 95.

59 Stringfellow, *My People Is the Enemy*, 42.

60 Emily Hartigan, "Advocacy and Innocence," in McThenia, *Radical Christian and Exemplary Lawyer*, 122, 127.

61 Ibid., 124.

62 Ibid., 126.

63 Ibid., 127.

64 McThenia, "Uneasy Relationship with the Law," 178.

65 "The business of the Johannine style," Wayne Meeks says, "is subversion of reality as perceived in the common sense of a certain tradition" ("The Ethics of the Fourth Evangelist," in Culpepper and Black, *Exploring the Gospel of John*, 317, 319). Meeks notes that the gospel is no vehicle of moral formation: "First, its form is wrong: It offers no explicit moral instruction. . . . Second, the narrative does not provide a plausible and universalizable model for behavior. . . . Third, if we take the narrative as supplying neither rules for behavior nor models of character or action but simply as rendering a narrative world to which readers are invited and challenged to respond by imaginatively appropriate performance, this narrative is profoundly troubling to rational kinds of moral discourse. . . . Fourth, the decision that characteristically divides Jesus' audience between those who come to the light and those who remain in darkness, between those who 'abide' to eternal life and those who draw back and are condemned, is shrouded in mystery" (ibid., 318–19). Meeks quotes from David Rensberger the observation that the gospel's challenge lies in its sectarianism: "No religion that sees itself as the backbone of a society, as the glue that holds a society together, can easily lay down a challenge to that society's wrongs. A cultural religion is all too readily told to mind its own business, because it *has* a business, a well-known role in maintaining society's fabric unmolested. It is the sect, which has no business in the world, that is able to represent a fundamental challenge to the world's oppressive orders" (ibid., 325).

Epilogue

1 James Muilenburg, "Literary Form in the Fourth Gospel," in *The Gospel of John as Literature*, ed. Mark Stibbe (Leiden: Brill, 1993), 68.

2 "What we are up against is the self-referring quality of the whole gos-

pel . . . which confronts the reader in a fashion somewhat like the way a Semitist once explained to me how to learn Aramaic: 'Once you know *all* the Semitic languages,' he said, 'learning any one of them is easy.' The reader cannot understand any part of the Fourth Gospel until he understands the whole. Thus the reader has an experience rather like that of the dialogue partners of Jesus: either he will find the whole business so convoluted, obscure, and maddeningly arrogant that he will reject it in anger, or he will find it so fascinating that he will stick with it until the progressive reiteration of themes brings, on some level of consciousness at least, a degree of clarity. . . . The book functions for its readers in precisely the same way that the epiphany of its hero functions within its narratives and dialogues" (Wayne A. Meeks, "The Man from Heaven in Johannine Sectarianism," *Journal of Biblical Literature* 91 [1972]: 67–68).

3 Karl Barth, *Anselm: Fides Quaerens Intellectum*, trans. Ian Robertson (Richmond, Va.: John Knox Press, 1960), 69.

4 Ibid., 70.

5 Ibid., 71. This may be the explanation for the division among scholars over whether the verb in John 20:31 is aorist subjunctive or present subjunctive: the gospel is written "in order that you may come to believe" or "in order that you may keep on believing." Is the implied reader someone who does not believe or someone who is already a Christian believer? Anselm and Barth would write for the former no differently than they would for the latter.

6 "Since the [testimony] of the Revealer is identical with what it attests, and not complementary to it, it finds confirmation paradoxically not by appealing from the word which bears witness to the truth of that to which it bears witness, but in its acceptance by faith. It is only in faith in the word of witness that man can see what it is to which the word is bearing witness, and consequently can recognize the legitimacy of the witness himself. Thus according to 1 John 5:10, he who believes in the Son has 'the testimony in himself,' that is to say, he does not need to look any further for something to confirm the testimony, for he already possesses it in the testimony itself" (Bultmann, *Gospel of John*, 163).

7 See Brown, *John*, 29A:555–72.

8 "At the heart of Jesus' ministry is the creation of a new family of God. The creation of this family is symbolized here. . . . Jesus was rejected by 'his own,' but the beloved disciple's reception of Jesus' mother signals the possibility of a future marked by acceptance, not rejection" (O'Day, "John," in Newsom and Ringe, *Women's Bible Commentary*, 300).

Index

Hamline Law School, 187 n.2
Hand, Learned, 189 n.6
Hart, H. L. A., 88, 222 n.2
Hartigan, Emily Fowler, 70, 144–45, 151, 187 n.2, 223 n.10
Harvard Law School, 142
Harvey, A. E., 114, 134, 135, 240 n.11
Hass, Robert, 251 n.8
Hauerwas, Stanley, 151
Hawai'i, natives of. *See* Kanaka Maoli
Hazard, Geoffrey, 23–24, 26, 200 n.26
Hebrews. *See* Israelites
Heston, Charlton, 9
Hoffheimer, Michael, 152
Holiness, of Israelites, 34–35, 41, 104–5
Homesteaders, Kanaka Maoli, 94–96
Hosea (prophet), 116

Idolatry, of the golden calf, 14, 19–21, 29–30, 74
Idols, laws as, 14–16
Intercession: of Moses, 18–21, 27–30, 31–32, 45–46, 82; of Rachel, 78, 82 (*see also* Rachel poem)
International People's Tribunal, Hawai'i, 90, 93–97, 98, 153–86
International Tribunal on the Rights of Indigenous People, 93
Irony, in the Gospel of John, 120
Isaiah, Book of, 2, 117, 120–21, 129–30, 131
Isaiah (prophet), 116
Israelites: exile of, in Rachel poem, 78, 79, 81; identity and independence of, 34–35; and observance of the law, 11–12; in priesthood, 11, 38, 74

Jackson, Te Moana Nui A Kiwi, 98
Jacob, story of, 77, 78
Jacobsen, Thorkild, 201 n.6

Jacobson, Arthur, 14, 16, 21, 27, 193 nn.22, 23, 201 n.2, 202 n.10
Jenson, Robert, 31, 35, 232 n.10, 248 n.15
Jeremiah, Book of, 79, 101–2. *See also* Rachel poem
Jesus Christ: disciples of, in Gospel of John, 118–19, 127–28, 136; execution of, by the law, 134; Last Discourse of, in Gospel of John, 129–32; miracle of, at Cana, 134–36; resurrection of, 127, 135–36; trial of, in Gospel of John, 109–14
Jewish law, and Jesus' execution, 134
The Jews, in the Gospel of John, 118
John, Epistles of, 129, 132
John, Gospel of, 109–49; author of, 122, 123, 128, 133, 147–49; belief as the purpose of, 111–12, 123–24, 128, 147–49; disbelief and, 117–18, 129–33, 148–49; divine lawsuit in, 115–22; foot-washing at Last Supper, 149; irony in, 120; Isaiah quoted in, 120–21, 129–30, 131; the Jerusalem trial, 109–14, 113–14; Jesus' disciples in, 118–19, 127–28; Jesus' Last Discourse, 129–32; law in, 111, 113, 115–22, 134–36, 142–43; miracle at Cana, 134–36; and the Paraclete, 115–16, 121, 125, 126–28; prologue, 109–10, 117, 131; women in, 123–24
John the Baptist, 2, 110, 116, 117
Joshua, 13, 38
Judah, kingdom of, 79
Justice: and lawful use of force, 86–88; and professionalism of lawyers, 141; promise of, in Moses saga, 41; Socrates on, 63
Justice, figure of, 56–57
Juvenile court, 66–67

Kanaka Maoli, 90, 93–97, 98, 153–86

Kennedy, Duncan, 214 n.17
Kennedy, Robert, 144
Kermode, Frank, 113, 189 n.1, 232
　　n.1(ch. 18)
Kingsfield, Professor, 59, 60, 69
Kingsley, Ben, 9
Kozol, Jonathan, 226 n.11
Kuhn, Thomas, 112

Laban, 77, 78
Labor pains image, in Jeremiah,
　　101–2
Land rights, Kanaka Maoli, 94–96
Last Stone, Suzanne, 187 n.2
Law: Arendt on, 85, 87; and counsel
　　for the situation, 20–21, 22–26,
　　35–36; freedom from, 134–36,
　　141–44 (see also Professional-
　　ism); as God's gift, 15; in the
　　Gospel of John, 111, 113, 115–22,
　　134–36, 142–43; as idol, 14–16;
　　limits and discipline of, 85–88;
　　moral scrutiny of, 88–89; self-
　　transcendence of, 89–90
Law and tears, 83–98; Arendt on,
　　89; emotion, role of, 83–85;
　　International People's Tribunal,
　　Hawaii, 93–97, 153–86; and law-
　　ful use of force, 85, 86–88; and
　　moral scrutiny of law, 88–89; and
　　self-transcendence of law, 89–
　　90; and supplication, 89, 98; and
　　Tennessee plant closings, 90–93.
　　See also Rachel poem
Law of Moses, 11–17; as idol, 14–
　　15; observance of, as protection,
　　11–12; writing of, 13–17. See also
　　Moses: as mouth for God
Law practice, Socratic. See Public
　　Interest Practicum
Law school: cynicism in, 142; and
　　professional ethics, 141–42;
　　Socratic method in, 58, 64. See
　　also Public Interest Practicum
Lawyers: as advocates, 144–45; dis-
　　empowerment of clients by, 69;

independence of (see Profession-
　　alism); as midwives, 65, 72–73; as
　　scribes, 71–72; sense of morality
　　in, 139
Leah, 77, 78
Lehmann, Paul, 3, 6, 36, 189 n.1,
　　204 n.22
Lesnick, Howard, 222 nn.1, 3, 5
Levinson, Bernard, 152
Levites. See Priesthood, Israelite
Lewis, Ted, 151
Lili'uokalani (Queen of Hawaii),
　　94
Liturgical calendar, in Gospel of
　　John, 113
Luban, David, 256 n.10, 257 n.11

MacCrate Report, 139, 141
Macrae, George, 136, 245 n.3
Madison, James, 86
Magdalene, Rachel, 152
Maieutic method, 58, 59, 64, 72
Manna, 18
Mannheim, Karl, 112
Maquiladora zone workers, Mexico,
　　90–93
Marshall, John, 86
Martyn, J. Louis, 250 n.2
Mary Magdalene, 123
Masson, Charles, 235 n.6
Matamoros workers, 90–93
Matsuda, Mari, 187 n.2
Matthews, Victor, 210 n.2
McCarthy, Cormac, 251 n.8
McCleskey v. Kemp, 87
McCormack, Virginia, 151
McKelway, Alexander, 151
McThenia, Andrew, 145, 187 n.2,
　　222 n.3, 261 n.47, 262 n.52
Meeks, Wayne, 263 n.65
Melville, Herman, 84
Menkel-Meadow, Carrie, 215 n.18
Mettenburger, Tammy, 152
Mexico, workers' conditions in,
　　90–93
Meyaledethic method, 58, 64

Micah, Book of, 75
Micah (prophet), 116
Midwifery, Socratic, 58–64; in Plato's early dialogues, 61–64; in *Theaetetus,* 58–60. *See also* Public Interest Practicum
Midwives, 51–57; God as, 55–56; Hebrew (Shiphrah and Puah), 51–53, 56, 146; lawyers as, 65, 72–73; Moses as, 51, 53–54, 56, 63, 74; scribes as, 72
Miller, Patrick, 35, 188 n.7, 191 n.8, 192 n.12
Minow, Martha, 187 n.2
Miriam, 74–76, 104–5, 149
Model Code of Professional Responsibility (1969), 24, 141
Model Rules of Professional Conduct (1983), 24
Moral scrutiny, of law, 88–89
Morgan, Jenny, 215 n.18
Moses: authority of, 146–47; birth and adoption of, 52–54; and the burning bush, 10–11, 146; as counsel for the situation, 20–21, 27–28; death and burial of, 34, 38, 39, 76, 105; exclusion from Canaan, 33–34, 38; identification with God and Israel, 33; intercessions of, 18–21, 27–30, 31–32, 45–46, 82; as midwife, 51, 53–54, 56, 63, 74; as mouth for God, 10, 12, 15, 31; as mouth for Israelites, 13, 18–21, 27–30; name of, 53–54
Moses Saga: authors of, 39–40; entry into Canaan, 13, 33, 38, 42, 44–45; slavery in Egypt, 51–53; the Exodus story (*see* The Exodus story); and God's authority, 146–47; Hebrew midwives in, 51–53, 56, 146; idolatry of the golden calf, 14, 19–21, 29–30, 74; promise of justice, 41; giving of the law, 13–17; as a spoken world, 37; strange details of, 9–10; promise of succession, 38–40; summary

of, 9; wilderness sojourn, 18, 42, 45–46
Muffs, Yochanon, 196 nn.5, 8, 201 n.5
Muilenburg, James, 147
Mullis, Vicki, 152

Native Americans, 86, 88, 97–98. *See also* Kanaka Maoli
Neusner, Jacob, 225 n.5
North American Free Trade Agreement (NAFTA), 92, 93, 98
Nuremberg trials, 93
Nussbaum, Martha, 63, 220 n.28

O'Day, Gail, 246 n.5
Olympian gods, 31
Osmosis, learning by, 59
Our Daily Bread, 67–68
Outsiders, 2, 75, 78, 105

Pancaro, Severino, 248 n.15
The Paraclete, 115–16, 121, 125, 126–28
Parallelism, 43–45
Penultimacy of law, in the Gospel of John, 136, 142–43
Peter (disciple), 119, 127
Pharoah, 51–53
Pharoah's daughter, 52, 53
Pitkin, Hanna, 201 n.1
Plant relocations, Tennessee, 90–93
Plato's dialogues, 58–60, 61–64
Platter, Charles, 151
Poetry, biblical, 43–44, 46. *See also* Psalm 22; Psalm 114; Rachel poem
Polzin, Robert, 39, 205 n.3
Pontius Pilate, 134–35
Posner, Richard, 141, 142, 222 n.2
Power, abuse of, 88
Priesthood, Israelite, 11, 38, 74
Priestly, Joseph, 112
Professionalism, 137–45; ABA commissions on, 24–25, 138–40; counsel for the situation, 20–21,

Professionalism (*continued*)
22–26, 35–36; and justice, 141;
necessity for, 137–38; of Stringfellow, 143–45; taught in law
school, 141–42
Prophets, succession of, 39
Proslogion (Anselm), 148
Psalm 22, 55
Psalm 114, 42–48; chiasm in, 44–45;
the Exodus story in, 42–43, 46–
47; simultaneity in, 46; themes
of, 42
Puah and Shiphrah, 51–53, 56, 146
Public Interest Practicum, 65–73;
effects of, on students, 68–72;
as midwifery, 72–73; tasks of,
66–68

Rachel, 77–78, 149
Rachel poem: "female surrounds
man," 81, 82, 99, 101, 104; as
intercession and supplication,
79–82; and the Womb of God,
99–105. *See also* Law and tears
Radin, Margaret Jane, 215 n.18
Rawls, John, 260 n.32
Resnik, Judith, 56
Restatement of the Law Governing
Lawyers, 24
The resurrection, 127, 135–36
Returning of the Word. *See* Word
of God
Rhode, Deborah, 215 n.18, 220 n.28
Riv (divine lawsuit), 115–19
Roman law, and Jesus' execution,
134–35
Rosenberg, John, 255 n.9
Roth, Martha, 152
Rule 2.2, Model Rules of Profes-
sional Conduct (1983), 24, 25
Russell, Bertrand, 93

Sakenfeld, Katharine Doob, 75, 105,
224 n.6
Samaria, 79

Samaritan woman at the well, 123–
24
Schneiders, Sandra, 246 n.5
Schwarzschild, Henry, 189 n.4
Scribes: lawyers as, 71–72; of Moses
Saga, 15–16, 39–40
Setel, Drorah O'Donnell, 54
Sexual metaphors, and God's image,
55–56
Shaffer, Thomas, 24, 139, 151, 189
n.6, 199 n.20, 222 n.3; on lawyers'
independence, 254 n.7, 255 n.8,
256 n.10, 258 n.17, 261 n.38
Shiphrah and Puah, 51–53, 56, 146
Shipley, David, 151
Simon, William, 204 n.21
Simultaneity, 46
Singer, Joseph, 187 n.2
Slavery, 83, 86, 87
Smith, D. Moody, 151, 248 n.15, 250
n.2
Smith, Nicholas, 62, 217 n.10, 219
nn.26, 27
Smith, Reynolds, 151
Socrates, 58, 61–64, 83, 84
Socratic midwifery. *See* Midwifery,
Socratic
Soifer, Aviam, 151, 187 n.2, 197 n.12,
227 n.4, 261 n.38
Song of Miriam, 75
Soup kitchens, 67–68
Spillenger, Clyde, 25, 197 n.2, 200
n.31, 255 n.8
The Spirit, in the Gospel of John,
115–16, 121, 125–28
Spurgeon, Ned, 151
Stanley Commission, 138–39, 141
Steiner, George, 218 n.23
Sternberg, Meir, 189 n.1, 206 nn.7,
10
Stibbe, Mark, 243 n.21
Stone, I. F., 61, 216 n.7, 226 n.14
Stories, role of, in law, 3–4, 36
Strangers, care of, 35, 41
Stringfellow, William, 69, 86, 143–
44, 145

Milner S. Ball is the Harmon W. Caldwell Professor of

Constitutional Law, University of Georgia. He is the

author of *The Word and the Law* (1993), *Lying Down*

Together: Law, Metaphor, and Theology (1985), *The*

Promise of American Law: A Theological, Humanistic

View of the Legal Process (1981).

Library of Congress Cataloging-in-Publication Data

Ball, Milner S.
Called by stories : biblical sagas and their challenge for
law / Milner S. Ball.
p.   cm.
Includes index.
ISBN 0-8223-2501-2 (alk. paper) — ISBN 0-8223-2524-1
(pbk. : alk. paper)
1. Bible and law.   2. Practice of law — Biblical
teaching.   3. Legal ethics — Biblical teaching.
4. Bible. O.T. Pentateuch — Criticism, interpretation,
etc.   5. Bible. N.T. John — Criticism, interpretation,
etc.   I. Title.
BS680.L33 B35   2000
261.5 — dc21   99-056925